Philosophy of Cybersecurity

Technology and digitization are a great social good. But they also involve risks and threats. Cybersecurity is not just a matter of data or computer security; Cybersecurity is about the security of society.

Why "Philosophy"? To understand how to reason and think about threats and cybersecurity in today's and tomorrow's world, this book is necessary to equip readers with awareness. The Philosophy of Cybersecurity is about the user's perspective, but also about system issues.

This is a book for everyone – a wide audience. Experts, academic lecturers, as well as students of technical fields such as computer science and social sciences will find the content interesting. This includes areas like international relations, diplomacy, strategy, and security studies. Cybersecurity is also a matter of state strategy and policy.

The clarity and selection of the broad material may make this book the first book on cybersecurity you'll understand.

It considers such detailed basics as, for example, what a good password is and, more importantly, why it is considered so today. But the book is also about systemic issues, such as healthcare cybersecurity (challenges, why is it so difficult to secure, could people die as a result of cyberattacks?), critical infrastructure (can a cyberattack destroy elements of a power system?), and States (have they already been hacked?).

Cyberspace is not a "grey zone" without rules. This book logically explains what cyberwar is, whether it threatens us, and under what circumstances cyberattacks could lead to war. The chapter on cyberwar is relevant because of the war in Ukraine. The problem of cyberwar in the war in Ukraine is analytically and expertly explained. The rank and importance of these activities are explained, also against the background of broader military activities.

The approach we propose treats cybersecurity very broadly. This book discusses technology, but also ranges to international law, diplomacy, military, and security matters, as they pertain to conflicts, geopolitics, political science, and international relations.

Philosophy of Cybersecurity is an ambitious and innovative attempt to look at the vast scientific field from a completely new perspective. There are hundreds of books on the market today that focus on the technical aspects of attacks on computer systems, or analyze the social consequences of selected technologies. The work you hold in your hands offers the reader something more. It presents a coherent intellectual model covering risks across the entire industry – from defense against phishing to the realities of cyber conflicts between hostile states. Sprinkled with numerous anecdotes and references to current events, the book is accessible and valuable read for anyone working in the IT industry or interested in this subject as a hobby.

— Michal Zalewski, former VP/CISO (Snap), renowned hacker, Lifetime Achievement Pwnie Award recipient

Just as we must be well versed ourselves in the laws that govern society to act responsibly and wisely as citizens, so must we understand a fast-evolving digital world where software is not always especially trustworthy and peril abounds. Less a treatise than a deeply informed how-to guide, *Philosophy of Cybersecurity* offers important lessons for safely navigating and shaping policy in a world where compromised computer code is wreaking ever more havoc. The authors clearly walk readers through vital issues: How to fend off cyber-crooks; how to separate hype from serious impact in reported "cyberattacks"; how to understand when cyber operations by state-backed hackers are tolerated under international law and what actions make them crimes. Timely and current, with analysis of cyberactivity in the war for Ukraine.

— Frank Bajak, technology correspondent, *Associated Press*

Philosophy of Cybersecurity tackles the industry's broad landscape, from technology to policy to offensive and defensive operations. It gives the reader context to understand how the field has evolved in the past, and how to understand future developments. Its insights – particularly in the context of international law – are illuminating.

— Bruce Schneier, author of *A Hacker's Mind: How the Powerful Bend Society's Rules, and How to Bend them Back*

This rich and insightful book provides clear and practical guidance for everyone interested in digital transformation and security. It prefers reason to fearmongering and places the user – you and me – at the heart of its analysis. An engaging cybersecurity primer for a general audience.

— Tim Stevens, King's College London, author of *What is Cybersecurity For?*

What matters? And more importantly, what doesn't matter? These profound philosophical questions are directly relevant anyone grappling with cyber-security. This topical, well-researched, and insightful book provides a rigorous but accessible theoretical framework, illustrated with provocative and all-too-realistic scenarios, and provides important suggestions that will clarify our thoughts and improve our effectiveness. I recommend this book strongly to professionals and lay people alike.

— Edward Lucas, author of *Cyberphobia: Identity, Trust, Security and the Internet,* formerly senior editor, *The Economist*

Philosophy of Cybersecurity

Lukasz Olejnik
Artur Kurasiński

CRC Press
Taylor & Francis Group
Boca Raton London New York

CRC Press is an imprint of the
Taylor & Francis Group, an **informa** business

First edition published 2024
by CRC Press
6000 Broken Sound Parkway NW, Suite 300, Boca Raton, FL 33487-2742

and by CRC Press
4 Park Square, Milton Park, Abingdon, Oxon, OX14 4RN

CRC Press is an imprint of Taylor & Francis Group, LLC

ISBN: 978-1-032-52760-4 (hbk)
ISBN: 978-1-032-52761-1 (pbk)
ISBN: 978-1-003-40826-0 (ebk)

DOI: 10.1201/9781003408260

Typeset in Sabon
by SPi Technologies India Pvt Ltd (Straive)

Contents

Preface

The importance of cybersecurity in the modern world is constantly growing. But how did we get here?

The world has been undergoing progressive computerization since the 1960s. Its overall scale is also growing. The last decades have seen a steady increase in the number of transistors in integrated circuits, the number of cores in processors, network bandwidth, memory, and the global aggregate data capacity in general. This is how the law of exponential, extremely fast, growth is realized: once in a while, efficiency is doubled.[1]

This development is associated with the progressive dependence of societies, states, and civilizations on computers and, more broadly, on technology. This evolution is progressing gradually. We may often be unaware of the scale of the increase in this dependence. After all, what would users need this knowledge for? Things, the world, technologies – all they have to do is, to put it simply, just work.

Computers are present at home, at work, in offices, and at universities. Today, we have chips and technologies not only in our pockets (smartphones) but also in cars, refrigerators, washing machines, and other electronic devices. Sometimes on or inside our bodies. Transportation systems, energy production and distribution, water treatment, etc., are computer controlled. This also increasingly applies to food production – starting from the level of a farmer and a farm (computerized agricultural machinery is only one element of it). This also applies to weapons systems: weapons are computer controlled and operated; often these elements are crucial for the entire system. For example, radar or anti-missile systems must rely on sensors and the rapid analysis of data. And this is just the beginning.

Apart from being computerized, such systems are also networked. Thus, we are dealing not only with a gigantic increase in computerization, but also in networking. Communication between the connected computers and devices is possible, for example, through remote access, i.e., the possibility of connecting to them also in the situation of a significant physical distance (from another city, country, or even continent).

If only all of these systems and technologies simply worked – flawlessly, without any problems, glitches, and breakdowns! However, we do not live in a perfect model. In the real world, malfunctions or failures might occur that can be risky, problematic, or dangerous. The events or incidents may be both accidental (e.g., malfunction, breakdown, natural disaster, accident) but also deliberate. The latter can be caused by people who have various motivations and goals, who can act individually or in groups.

In situations where there is a possibility of an occurring risk, special attention needs to be paid to safety. In our case, it will consist off securing hardware, software, and systems. Our activities will in fact concern the entire infrastructure – today already in the very broad sense of that word. As the importance of computerization has increased significantly, cybersecurity has become a major problem, not only a technical problem, but also an economic, social, and even political and geopolitical problem.

This is how broadly we'll understand cybersecurity in this book.

CYBERSECURITY – WHAT IS IT ABOUT?

Today, cybersecurity concerns almost everyone, even those who do not directly use computers, smartphones, or social networks. In practice, most of us depend on computers anyway, because they are everywhere and the functioning of the world is based on them to an increasing extent.

In a typical company, we may have computers, workstations, servers, devices responsible for backups, network printers, smartphones and, of course, networks, i.e., something connecting it all, connecting the infrastructure in such a way that it works. This is to help employees work effectively. If they have such a need, they choose the "print" command on their computer and a properly configured infrastructure will lead to the printing of a document on one of the network printers. When we connect a computer to a projector during a conference, the assumption is that the presentation should immediately appear on the large display screen (in practice it can be a bit more complicated; the so-called *projector problem* turns out to be one of the most difficult to solve in practice!).

Similarly, when buying a (physical, printed) train or bus ticket, we interact with the (computerized) ticket machine. If there is no such machine, perhaps we may buy the ticket, e.g., with a smartphone. The ticket controller should be able to use an electronic ticket reader to determine its validity. We ourselves are happy to use real-time information about transport traffic, for example, checking when the bus will arrive. All these operations are possible thanks to computers and networks. When we get used to these solutions, their lack (e.g., caused by a failure) will be perceived as a loss.

Infrastructure and technological solutions should be safe. It is not that cybersecurity is only the domain of institutions, companies, or other specialized entities. Cybersecurity is important to everyone and it applies to everyone. Regardless whether it is an ordinary person, a small company, a factory, or a large industrial production plant in which industrial electronics systems or even computer-controlled components are installed, cybersecurity is important – sometimes even critical.

Of course, in some areas where there are very advanced and specialized risks, cybersecurity can have very specific requirements. Let us think, for example, of a healthcare system in which digitization is playing an increasingly important role. It is not about ordinary computers in the office where a medical doctor enters the observations and diagnoses or where he/she browses the patient's file. It also involves computerized diagnostic devices and systems, such as a tomograph or an ultrasound. Even implants and implantable pacemakers are computerized. We write about this in more detail in the following chapters.

WHO IS THIS BOOK FOR?

This book is intended for a broad spectrum of readers. This book offers an intelligible contemporary image of cybersecurity as a technical, social, and simply human problem. Professionals of various fields (technical, political, legal) may appreciate the outlined connections of their scope of specialization and interests with other areas and how they are formed. Students of science or technology fields may learn the details of cybersecurity strategy and of legal issues, and how it all connects holistically in such a broad field, how it fits together. Students of social, political, or security sciences will find here a compendium and a textbook on such a complex issue in relation to human activity, states, diplomacy, and security.

This book will be appreciated by specialists, academics, students, and officials at various institutions. It is devoted to a very complex subject that has significantly expanded in recent decades, and the process is rapidly progressing – understanding the problems, mitigating risks, and increasing cybersecurity.

Lukasz Olejnik
Artur Kurasiński

NOTE

1 P.J. Denning, T.G. Lewis, *Exponential laws of computing growth*, "Communications of the ACM" 2017, vol. 60, no. 1, pp. 54–65.

Authors

Lukasz Olejnik (LukaszOlejnik.com) is an independent cybersecurity and privacy researcher and consultant.

He holds a Computer Science PhD from INRIA (France). He worked at CERN (European Organisation for Nuclear Research), and was a research associate at University College London. He was associated with Princeton's Center for Information Technology Policy, with Oxford's Centre for Technology and Global Affairs, and was elected a Member of World Wide Web Consortium's (W3C) Technical Architecture Group. He is a Fellow of Geneva Academy of International Humanitarian Law and Human Rights. He is a former cyberwarfare advisor at the International Committee of the Red Cross in Geneva, where he worked on the humanitarian consequences of cyberwarfare. He has also advised on science and new technologies at the European Data Protection Supervisor.

He helps various companies and organizations, including with cybersecurity, privacy and data protection, and technology policy.

His comments appeared in places such as *Financial Times*, *Washington Post*, *New York Times*, *Wall Street Journal*, *Sueddeutsche Zeitung*, *El Pais*, or *Le Monde*. He authored scientific papers, reports, opinion articles in venues like *Wired* and *Foreign Policy*.

Artur Kurasiński is a tech-realist, a serial innovator, entrepreneur, public speaker, and a game and comic book author. Artur analyzes and comments on technology from economic, sociologic, and geopolitical perspectives. He is a co-creator of numerous Polish startups. He is a mentor in many contests and the author of one of Poland's most popular tech blogs: kurasinski.com. He is a speaker and participant in Poland's leading important tech conferences. He is a co-creator of Poland's oldest series of startup meet-ups (Aula Polska) and the Auler awards.

Chapter 1

Introduction to the philosophy of cybersecurity

1.1 A FEW WORDS ABOUT HISTORY

We need to think about how we got here. Today, cybersecurity is a state, political, and even military problem. However, this is an area where – thanks to individual skills and devoted time – to a certain extent, specialist knowledge, information, and experience can be acquired by people who do not belong to the "formal" expert circles. Many techniques and methods in cybersecurity were developed and used by various "interest groups". We will not use the word "amateurs", because how can you call someone who has a broad knowledge and is actually a specialist an "amateur"?

1.1.1 The history of viruses and malware

It is worth noting that computer security as such has been considered at least since the 1970s. An increase in the interest in the subject was evident in the 1980s, when the first important descriptions or guides were created – mainly at American universities or in military structures. In the 1980s in the USA, malware[1] started to be talked about publicly, though this type of programs had already existed in the 1970s.[2] In 1984 these tools or programs were identified as computer viruses, because, like biological viruses, they are harmful under certain conditions and can spread and propagate automatically.

American academia circles (like MIT) were also the place from where a very famous (or notorious) malicious program emerged. Today known as the Morris worm (named after its creator), it has been in operation since November 2, 1988.[3] It was the first computer worm – a software that cracked the security of Unix systems and then self-propagated to infect vulnerable (i.e., those that can be infected) computer systems. About 6,000 computers were affected at that time, which in the 1980s was an impressive number, as there were 60,000 computers in the ("internet") network at the time, which means that 10% of all computers were infected with the worm! Back then, the network was much smaller than it is today. Currently, we are talking about billions of computers, to which you have to add smartphones and other devices.

1.1.2 Interest groups and hacker groups

This is how we smoothly arrive at the 1990s of the last century, at the gradual development of security and questions over risks. That was the time when problems with such a phenomenon as computer viruses appeared and began to grow. Those viruses were often created in the bloc of Eastern European countries, for example in the USSR and Bulgaria,[4] where groups interested in creating such malicious software were active. Back then, of course, the distribution of such programs was completely different than today – it could, for example, take place via floppy disks. They were plastic portable elements with rectangular geometry, inserted into a computer. Inside there was a disk on which information was written in a magnetic form. The capacity of the floppy disk would not impress anyone today (it was about 1.44 MB; today, it is the size of one photo in a reasonable quality). Currently, malware is spread mainly via e-mail (i.e., the network), via portable pen drives, and much less often via CDs or DVDs (which will soon be something as archaic as floppy disks or perforated memory).

In the 1990s, the so-called hacker groups, or – put very simply – groups interested in what can be done with computers, were operating. These were groups often associating teenagers, pupils, and students. And often they were significantly developing and building the body of knowledge on computer security, including security methods and ways to bypass these boundaries (hacking, breaking systems, etc.). These were often truly pioneering works. Here, it is worth mentioning a few well-known groups, such as the German group TESO,[5] the Polish group operating under the name Lam3rZ[6] but also many others, earlier and later ones. It is impossible to list them all; they were numerous, varied, and interested in a really wide range of issues.

It should be noted, however, that these were not the so-called cybercriminal groups known from contemporary reports of cybersecurity companies. These earlier groups, of an "amateur" (or "independent"?) nature, were not (at least not always) *strictly* criminal. Let us remember that in the 1990s, and even in the first decade of the twenty-first century, this area looked completely different than today. The potential of which systems could be digitally "reached" was also smaller, because digitization was less advanced than it is today.

1.1.3 Why cybersecurity has become important

Although we have already dealt with cyberthreats in the 1990s, in the twenty-first century we have recorded their continuous, though gradual, growth. It didn't come out of nowhere. As we said before, this is directly related to the fact that the digital world is developing faster and faster. Computers today are not some niche thing like they could have been thought as in the 1990s. Because today, in principle, computers are everywhere where there is technology.

For example, imagine how a modern metro, bus, train, or tram works. There may be some chip, processor, computer, and network in many places, such as in the driver's control console. Control over such a tram is, therefore, computerized. Also ticket validators in city buses can be computerized and connected by a network, if only to update the tariffs or the current time on the device. Moreover, in such a tram, there may be, for example, panels displaying advertisements or announcements, which of course are also computer-supported, and this content can be updated using actions utilizing network connections. Hence, there must be some outside access. It is not an isolated system, on the contrary – it is a utility system (within a professional framework), although it should not necessarily be accessible from the outside to everyone. There must, however, be a way to access them to change the content and upload a new one. This means that there must be a systemic and consciously designed method of accessing the function that uploads new data and displays them in some way. Potentially, therefore, it might (inadvertently, but still) also enable some kind of abuse, some breaking of the system designed in such a way. Potentially, someone, perhaps from the outside, could gain control over such a system, change it, influence it, abuse it.

This is, of course, a matter of design, because well-constructed systems should be "tight", resistant to at least simple or basic attacks and methods of circumventing security. For example, in a well-designed system, in the event of an attack on the advertising panels, it should not be possible to move from them ("laterally") to the systems managing the ticket validation functions in order to somehow interfere with them, for example, changing the ticket validity period from 15 minutes to 100 years, to infinity, or to –1.

The importance of cybersecurity is growing and is slowly becoming not only a technical problem but also a social one. Because we are considering a situation where computers, in addition to being important for technology or telecommunications companies (this is their industry in a way), are becoming increasingly dominant in areas with a more social dimension. They control, as described above, transport but also trade, including shops, financial systems (e.g., banking), healthcare or, for example, the infrastructure that supplies us with electricity.

If we realize that computerization is so common, it becomes obvious that **cybersecurity is a social problem**. Possible abuses or risks or failures could, therefore, have a direct or indirect impact on social life and functioning, on people, and even on the political or international situation. This is a gradual evolution, and we are still in the process. This process is in progress constantly. This is, among others, where another cybersecurity problem comes from – complexity. There are more and more functions of systems or software functions or features. At the same time, software and hardware perform a role in an increasing number of areas of social life. Thus it's a matter of scale.

It is worth considering a certain balance. Is the process of increasing digitization and system complexity ever going faster? Is the level of cybersecurity keeping pace with this development? Do these charts "diverge"? If we had a situation in which the degree of computerization and complexity of hardware and software increases but the level of security does not, the result would be an increase in risk. This risk would apply to the entire social system. For example, in Figure 1.1, we have several options for the degree of development of the "complexity" of the systems compared to the level of security. Depending on such differences, this "divergence" may increase or decrease. Charts A and C show an increase in differences (security improves insufficiently, vulnerabilities and risks increase). In diagram B, these lines are roughly parallel – security is able to keep up with the development to some extent. Chart D is the desired situation: at some point the security problems are resolved. At present, the most realistic expectation seems to be Chart B. There are, however, many systemic changes happening.

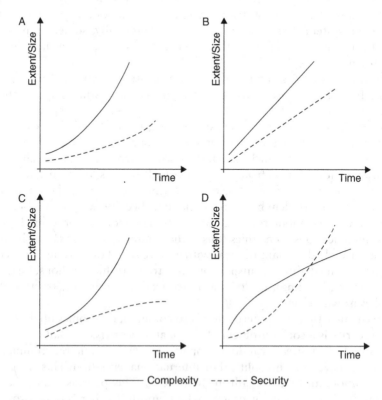

Figure 1.1 System complexity and the level of cybersecurity.

Source: Author-generated.

1.2 THE GRADUAL INCREASE IN THE ROLE AND IMPORTANCE OF CYBERSECURITY

In this book, we do not intend to scare anyone, to spread fear, to fearmonger. That's not the point. We prefer to present a balanced stance. It must be clearly stated that cybersecurity problems are real, but we are not dealing with a catastrophe. We are not in a situation where the world turns upside down. In fact, the sky, at least most of the time, is not falling. That is quite fortunate.

Let's not panic. Although it must be admitted that press reports can often refer to very serious and real problems. For example, if we are talking about the paralysis of an important industrial company, this is not a joke but a real problem. The extent of such a problem can be **measured**. For example, by taking into account financial losses, the number of users affected, types of downtime, and other such measurable factors. It could be tens or hundreds of millions of dollars depending on the company. This was the case, for example, with Norsk Hydro and the 2019 cyberattack,[7] where ransomware completely paralyzed the company's operations and at some point it was necessary to fallback to functioning in the *pen and paper* system. And we are talking about an industrial company that deals, among others, with aluminum production. Here, we can measure real losses in many ways, for example, by determining the percentage of loss of production capacity, total monetary loss, reputation loss, PR/reputation loss. Some manufacturing processes had to be significantly reduced to an efficiency of 50%. The losses were estimated at $70 million. In the case of this company, we were dealing with unprecedented transparency, public insight into decisions and actions. Such transparency was a very positive sign about the company, by the way. Very often we do not have such openness.

In general, for many companies, losses can also include losing control of personal information (of employees or customers) that may be stolen or leaked. It may also be associated with legal and regulatory liability (e.g., an administrative fine).

1.2.1 The problem of scale

Such problems on a national or economic scale can also be expressed systematically:

- There is a finite number of hacking or cybercriminal groups.
- There are many potential targets in the scale of the economy, country, or the world.
- Every day someone is unlucky to be the one affected, and sometimes, statistically speaking, the affected target or victim is actually important, a big, "loud" target, such as an industrial company, a pipeline operator, a hospital, or a ministry. It is "loud" because such a disruptive situation attracts interest, including that of the general public.

The action can be intentional (targeted attack) but also completely acciden-tal (attempts at wide-ranging attacks on targets: someone gets the payload, someone takes the bait, somewhere, at some point eventually there will be a success). And then such a situation is publicized by the media; it becomes important; it is analyzed and commented on. It is also (sometimes exagger-atedly) inscribed in a broader trend, attempted to be "put in a broader con-text", including that of other recent or opportunistic happenings, so a link is not always justified. Sometimes, it may also be interpreted by politicians as a "great attack on the state", which may not necessarily be true. Because in public when a cyberattack is called "sophisticated", very often it is in fact not very, or not at all, sophisticated.

So the point is that, given the scale of a typical country or economy, sooner or later an attack has to hit someone. Even pure statistics show that some-one will be attacked, hacked; even if from press reports, we can draw con-clusions about a certain trend in attacks, some connections between them (even if these may not actually exist), some specific targets.

So here we have one facet (or, side of the coin) of the cybersecurity risk phenomenon. Because there are always some systemic vulnerabilities that can potentially be exploited. We also have interest groups, i.e., those that have the will and motivation, which lead to actions being taken, as a result of which vulnerabilities in some entities are targeted, and that may lead to hacking, cracking – breaking of the security, compromising the target, or even paralyzing it.

The final conclusion from these considerations is that we will never run out of reports that there has been a cyberattack (and sometimes some "cata-clysm", factual or not). However, it must be taken into account that this is how it looks right now. That's the thing. We could say prosaically that such is life. And just as we have criminals outside of the computer world, we also have groups that are active in the digital realm. It will be difficult to com-pletely solve this problem as there are groups interested in dealing in this type of activity. There are also clear motivations, for example, monetary ones, that lead to the fact that such groups will be interested in taking action. So there will be no shortage of such attacks. Although we should remember that they are sometimes exaggerated in media reports, especially when they fit into current business and even political situations.

Therefore, the key problem for the recipient of the information is to know how to treat such reports. To be cautious and skeptical, to know the appro-priate, correct proportions. This is also one of the goals of this book: to make it easier to understand, after reading it, what is really important, what is maybe a little less important. What matters. And what doesn't matter much, or even at all. What could be real and what is exaggerated, when the problem does not exist at all. A lot of cyberattacks that we can read about don't really matter. But there are also some with grave consequences.

Such abilities – understanding this issue – seem necessary, even crucial today. This is due to the fact that, as we have already emphasized several times, we have a gradual development of digitization, and thus the role of cybersecurity is also growing. This applies to technology, business, finance, the education system, and even to state security. We refer that to internal security and, thus, the protection of companies, institutions, schools, and universities. External security is also important, i.e., counteracting foreign actors: foreign groups, states, even terrorists.

Cybersecurity is also important in diplomacy and international affairs, as well as in international security. There are known cases in which, for example, ministries of foreign affairs or embassies were targeted by cyberattacks. Important confidential information was stolen. For example, in 2022, the media published information about a series of cyberattacks against the Hungarian Ministry of Foreign Affairs. Also in 2022, Iranian actors apparently paralyzed some of the public institutions in Albania. As a consequence (one of them), Albania cut diplomatic relationships with Iran. There were also reports suggesting that Albania considered activating article 5 (collective defense) of the Washington Treaty, that famous NATO mechanism. To be fair, it sounded pretty ridiculous, as it would be something entirely inappropriate, what will become clear after reading Chapter 7 of this book. But such events cannot be ignored.

Cybersecurity is a constant topic of talks between state and military officials, diplomats of various countries, and politicians. It is an area of change, evolution, and negotiation. Many bodies are working on this problem, although the effects are not always immediately impressive. This is also because identifying issues, finding solutions, and implementing changes take time. You will appreciate this challenge when reading the subsequent chapters of the book.

1.3 THE INTERNATIONAL AND MILITARY DIMENSION

Both cyberattacks and cybersecurity can definitely have an international dimension, which we will talk about in the following chapters. Cybersecurity is a topic in international relations. It is the subject of debates, negotiations, and regulations of institutions such as the United Nations (UN), the European Union (EU), the G7 group, or the Shanghai Cooperation Group (SCO). It is considered in international relations, but also in blocs of states on all continents.

Finally, we arrive at purely military matters. As we may imagine, in the military, we have a lot of elements that are increasingly computerized: from ordinary office computers and networks to weapons systems. If we take a fighter jet as an example, there will be millions of lines of source code (which is compiled into a running program, the solution or "product" here). But the source code and computers are also relevant in the case of other weapons systems, such as rockets, bombers, and tanks, for example. And someone has to take care of the cybersecurity level of such a system. A possibility of unauthorized access (breach) of such systems is neither simple nor certain, but no one would want to lose control of the military's anti-aircraft defense system. This could undermine the security of the state. It could also lead to the accidental shooting down of an aircraft of other countries or the destruction of civilian objects. So to speak – it would have dramatic consequences. Cyber defense and cyberattack are a relatively new dimension of military cybersecurity and cyberthreats. Cyberspace is becoming the domain of military operations, which will also be discussed later.

We will not avoid a larger scale – the cosmic one. There are computers in the satellites (used to control them), and there are communication systems. Such satellites must communicate with the control system located on Earth. So there is a potential for such a system to be attacked. Security can be breached. Perhaps it is possible to take control of, disrupt, or destroy any or some of these subsystems, even paralyze the ground components.

Cybersecurity also applies to the area of biotechnology. As a curiosity, let's also note the research and demonstration in which a living organism was created containing a sequence that led to the breach of the security of the computerized DNA sequencing system.[8] It was the first such demonstration that designed a biological system in such a way that it was possible to hack or breach the technical security of computer systems; to make a cyberattack on a computer system, specifically one of a genome sequencing equipment.

On the other hand, there are also growing concerns about the cybersecurity of DNA sequencing systems. Whether, as a result of hacking the systems managing DNA synthesis in the future, there is a risk of implanting malicious sequences encoding malicious pathogens – harmful proteins, or toxins. Theoretically, this threat is imaginable, but such cyberattacks would be extremely complex, difficult, and the risk of their occurrence in the present decade is minimal. But what will happen in the future? Therefore, it is worth exploring such areas. Already today, standards and good practices are being created to pay attention to DNA sequences for synthesis. This risk of ordering malicious sequences is real and has already been demonstrated.[9] As areas such as space technologies or biotechnologies develop, the relationship with cybersecurity will grow, and with them – potential problems of domestic and international security, also in these dimensions.

1.4 WHAT IS THE PHILOSOPHY OF CYBERSECURITY – HOW DO WE UNDERSTAND IT?

The term "philosophy of cybersecurity" may sound cryptic. But it is worth considering what philosophy is. The *Oxford Dictionary of English* explains[10] that philosophy can be understood using several definitions, including (1) "Knowledge, learning, scholarship; a body of knowledge; spec. advanced knowledge or learning", (2) "Rational inquiry or argument", (3) "In extended use: a set of opinions or ideas held by an individual or group; a theory or attitude which acts as a guiding principle for behaviour", (4) "the study of the fundamental nature of knowledge, reality, and existence", (5) "The study of the general principles of a particular subject, phenomenon, or field of inquiry". Indeed!

Precisely these notions inspired the writing of this book, and describe it appropriately. These are exactly four definitions that guided the writing of this book, and they describe it well.

We are not concerned with drawing up a philosophical treatise on the world or on ethics. That is not the case. It is also not a purely philosophical approach that could be considered or inscribed in the philosophy of nature or the philosophy of science. Although personally I have nothing against these sciences, we steer clear and as far away as possible from such an approach to the subject. We really do not only think about such general considerations. By philosophy, we mean a way of thinking. How to understand things? How to reason? How to think about cybersecurity? How do we logically figure out how the systems work conceptually, what the potential threats may look like? How to talk about it?

The idea is to lay some solid grounds for how to think about threats, security, and cybersecurity. And how to think about the information or reports that reach us on a regular basis – from useful information to yet another "cyber cataclysm" that did not happen in the end. However, we are also concerned with activities and knowledge that are of the most practical importance.

Our hope is that the next time the reader of this book reads an article, for example, in the press, or hears reports of a threat or "attack", he/she should be able to critically interpret the given facts and assess how serious these reports are. Is it not an exaggeration by any chance? Did the writer of a given article really understand the topic, or did he/she just, for example, rewrite a one-sided message of a group, an announcement of some country, some company, and perhaps did so uncritically? Does the proverbial "minister" know what he/she is talking about, or perhaps not really (therefore, we recommend this reading also to ministers and candidates for these positions, who knows – perhaps it will help to avoid embarrassment)?

Such well-informed reader's skepticism will be a practical manifestation of the philosophy of cybersecurity.

1.5 IS CYBERSECURITY ACHIEVABLE?

Can we come to the point where we find ourselves immune to attacks, fully protected, and prepared for what might happen? Let's start with the fact that cybersecurity can be treated as a certain feature of the system. So the level of cybersecurity is the level of security of an IT system, device, or software.

In this context, cybersecurity may have a different weight and importance for different systems and actors (e.g., the common user). It is often said that cybersecurity is a process: something to be pursued, to be achieved – and which needs to be sustained.

1.5.1 Confidentiality, integrity, and availability

At its most basic level, cybersecurity can be understood as confidentiality, integrity, and availability:

- Confidentiality is the assurance that information will not be obtained by unauthorized parties.
- Integrity is the guarantee that information will not change its form in an unauthorized way, for example, no undesirable modification will occur.
- Availability is a guarantee that the ability to use systems, data, information, and resources will not be lost.

This is often seen by specialists as a high-level picture of cybersecurity. And this is also important for the philosophy of cybersecurity, because many threats can be included in this triad: confidentiality, integrity, and availability.

1.5.2 For an ordinary user

For an ordinary "just a user" (as in: not a developer, expert, and so on), cybersecurity may be important in relation to private devices, for example, a computer, smartphone, or home router. Such security qualities result from the configuration and are very often issues of the so-called cybersecurity hygiene (actually a term more philosophical than "medical"). Cybersecurity hygiene refers to good practices and principles worth sticking to. Taken and applied, it will mean that we will achieve a certain standard, a certain level of cybersecurity.

1.5.3 Business use

Cybersecurity is also important in the business context for companies. This applies to securing an organization's data and securing systems that are critical to the company's finances. It is also an operational issue, meaning that company systems must be available; that they can be used; that they will have an appropriate level of reliability and *resilience*, security, or confidentiality; that the risk of data leaks will be minimized; that the continuity of the company will not be affected in this way; and that there will be no reputational losses. Cybersecurity is becoming increasingly important and more and more is said about it: about mishaps, about violations. Probably no head of a company (CEO) would like to read about the scandal related to his/her organization on the front page of a newspaper. But it so happens that some of them do.

More technically, an example of an important component of business continuity is a working backup system. And there are a lot of specific things to consider here. It is useful to relate recommendations and best practices to certain specific applications. For example, in case of companies that have industrial automation systems – the considerations must be very specific. Or to the specific security features, such as those relevant in the case of healthcare systems or critical infrastructure. In such organizations, there is a need for a specialized and specific approach. More about this issue is explained at length in the subsequent chapters.

An example of reliability and resilience is shown by one of the events at the beginning of the Russian war in Ukraine in 2022. The satellite communication system used by the Ukrainian army was paralyzed, but because backup communication was in place, despite the fact that one system could have been disrupted, communication eventually was able to function.

1.5.4 State

With regard to the state, cybersecurity can be understood very broadly. Is the (collective) state's cybersecurity the same as the cybersecurity of all citizens (combined)? This would mean that the measure of a state's cybersecurity is the relative level of security of each citizen but also of key companies and infrastructures. This would be a very general metric, and, therefore, difficult to control. In a democratic environment, while it is possible to issue recommendations and set requirements for business, it may be a bit difficult (or tolerable) to issue strict orders to private citizens.

However, state cybersecurity can be understood as securing state systems, i.e., the national bank, digitized state registers, systems important for public life. Important could be, e.g., state personal registries (e.g., related to identity documents/cards, passports). The key systems for such domains as the management of pension systems, i.e., matters that basically directly affect citizens, are also very important. Here, business continuity is important, which is why, for example, important institutions have been using (and still use) mainframe computers, which are considered to be resilient.

It is also a matter of the stability of the political system, because cyberattacks can cause confusion within the state and interfere with its affairs. In countries that are unlucky because their electoral system is based on electronic systems (e.g., electronic voting), the security of this process is also an important element of the state's cybersecurity.

1.5.5 The global problem

Cybersecurity is also important to the world. Does that sound exalted? We have a large number of connections in cyberspace and very often data transfers occur naturally between countries. These data "cross many borders", which can raise problems of supervision, jurisdiction, surveillance, security, and protection of personal data.

Network data packets are often transferred over infrastructures in many countries. All such access and transmission points must be secured at every level. These systems must be reliable, for example, traffic should be routed in a predictable manner, while preventing censorship or surveillance (e.g., unless the particular country deems it necessary to be able to supervise and filter the content for some reason. But here also a practical, prosaic problem arises: in the case of abuse or cybercrime, there may be a need for cooperation between different jurisdictions, i.e., areas where the laws of specific countries apply. At this point, we want to emphasize that cybersecurity also means challenges of a legal nature.

1.5.5.1 The problem of international stability

We must also note that cybersecurity is important for stability, for security – not "computer" or "cyber", but the traditional one, and it can be equated with state security or national security.

More and more is being said about cyberattacks by one country on another. That is, about the activities of state services or groups supported or motivated by the state authorities. This can lead to various kinds of friction with international consequences.

1.6 IMPORTANT QUESTIONS AND A MYTH

There are some important questions that we should answer in this book. One of them is whether everything can be hacked. Well, it is often said that there are no systems that are perfectly secure and that everything is a matter of resources. Indeed, it is a question of how much time (and money) one will spend on breaching certain safeguards and how it will be done.

One popular myth is that cyberattacks are carried out within seconds (possibly minutes). Actions can be quick, as long as everything is ready in advance. Preparation takes time. In fact, cyberattacks on real systems, especially complex ones, require time and resources. It could be hours, days, or even months. Because carrying out such an action, i.e., a planned hack of an advanced system, can be a complicated process, possibly involving many people. And it doesn't have to be successful.

For example, Russians who hacked the energy distribution system in Ukraine in 2015 obtained the first access in spring, but did not take action until December. However, in 2022, during the war in Ukraine, similar attempts failed. Attempts were made to hack nine power substations, but the planned power outage failed because the operation was detected and foiled. Moreover, the operation happened under war conditions. It is hard not to notice that Ukraine's defense capacity has increased.

Therefore, we cannot provide an unambiguous answer to the question whether everything can be hacked. It would always have to start with the phrase "it depends" (by what means, in what time).

1.6.1 The question of physical destruction

Can cyberattacks lead to physical damage? This, in a way, has been an internet joke for a long time about the exaggerated report in one of the U.S. newspapers in July 2000 that it was possible to cause computers to explode with a cyberattack, which is not true. *Weekly World News* (titled "*Hackers Can Turn Your Home Computer into a BOMB!*", and adding "*...& blow your family into smithereens!*", well, not really) was, therefore, the source of many jokes among cybersecurity experts and enthusiasts.

But while we're in this strange area, for safety's sake, let's add that computer viruses cannot infect people, and *vice versa*, human viruses don't spread to computers. This should be obvious, but unfortunately apparently not to everyone and not always.

However, jokes aside, because there are known reports that as a result of a cyberattack, it was possible to break the security of printers, and subsequently – possibly lead to ignition (possibly also of 3D printers).[11] Moreover, there are also known examples of how cyberattacks have significantly disrupted the operation of industrial systems or also deliberately led to physical damage, which we will also talk about in the following chapters.

A very controversial issue is whether a cyberattack can kill a person. A cyberattack itself, a typical one that we might read about somewhere in the press or in the media, cannot kill. By the term "cyberattack", we usually refer to some kind of breach of information systems, digital systems, or data leakage. However, when we realize how far computerization has gone, this may change. For example, computers are responsible for systems that are important to life and health. Computers also control industrial automation systems. The question then arises, what will happen if one takes control of such a device, changes the configurations, forces a specific activity leading to instability. It is worth to consider it for a moment longer.

In this book, we will also answer the question of whether we are in danger of a cyberwar. Let us be clear here that we are. We are threatened with a cyberwar (as we write these words, cyberwarfare continues as part of the war in Ukraine). The only open question is how such a cyberwar should look like (and we provide an answer in Chapter 7). We can smoothly move on to the next question, which is whether a cyberattack can trigger a war. A thing that is being talked about more and more and what is being considered more and more. We believe it can. And we'll devote more time to that in Chapter 7. We'll do that too to the question what such cyberattacks during the war could look like.

1.7 IS CYBERSECURITY EVEN ACHIEVABLE?

Cybersecurity is achievable but under certain conditions and to some extent. We touch on the issue here of whether it is possible to secure systems (broadly understood: IT systems, computers, smartphones, etc.) in such a way that they cannot be hacked. It depends on the resources that will be employed to achieve the goal. The thing about the software is that it may contain vulnerabilities that can be used methodically, i.e., in such a way that control of the system can be taken over. On the other hand, cybersecurity is achievable insofar as it can lead to a situation in which a cyberattack will be very costly to conduct (too costly, so hopefully no activity would be initiated in light of the cost). And this is how we have to think about it when building security.

Thus, it is about increasing costs for a potential aggressor or a potential cybercriminal. It is about making cyberattacks difficult, challenging. To make the work of adversaries costly. This is the attitude we need to adopt. This attitude can be applied by a regular user, a small, medium, or large company, an institution, or even the military.

Increasing costs – it's such a general rule that it always works!

NOTES

1 F. Cohen, *Computer viruses: Theory and experiments*, in: *7th DoD/NBS Computer Security Conference Proceedings*, 1984, pp. 240–263.
2 P. Szor, *Fighting computer virus attacks*, in: *USENIX Security Symposium*, 2004.
3 J.K. Reynolds, *The helminthiasis of the Internet*, "Computer networks and ISDN systems" 1991, vol. 22, no. 5, pp. 347–361; T. Eisenberg, D. Gries, J. Hartmanis, D. Holcomb, MS Lynn, T. Santoro, *The Cornell commission: on Morris and the worm*, "Communications of the ACM" 1989, vol. 32, no. 6, pp. 706–709.
4 Vesselin Bontchev, The Bulgarian and Soviet Virus Factories, 1991, https://bontchev.nlcv.bas.bg/papers/factory.html
5 P. Baumard, *A brief history of hacking and cyberdefense*, in: *Cybersecurity in France*, Springer, Cham 2017, pp. 17–30.
6 Bulba, Kil3r, *Bypassing StackGuard and StackShield*, "Phrack Magazine" 2000, no. 56, http://phrack.org/issues/56/5.html.
7 Hydro, *Third quarter 2019 Report*, https://www.hydro.com/Document/Index?name=Report%20Q3%202019.pdf&id=252245
8 P. Ney, K. Koscher, L. Organick, L. Ceze, T. Kohno, *Computer security, privacy, and {DNA} sequencing: compromising computers with synthesized {DNA}, privacy leaks, and more*, in: *26th USENIX Security Symposium (USENIX Security 17)*, 2017, pp. 765–779.
9 R. Puzis, D. Farbiash, O. Brodt, Y. Elovici, D. Greenbaum, *Increased cyberbiosecurity for DNA synthesis*, "Nature Biotechnology" 2020, vol. 38, no. 12, pp. 1379–1381.

10 "philosophy, n.". OED Online. December 2022. Oxford University Press. https:// www.oed.com/view/Entry/142505?rskey=zcwcB3&result=1 (accessed December 14, 2022).

11 B. Sullivan, B. Sullivan, *Exclusive: Millions of printers open to devastating hack attack, researchers say*, November 29, 2011, https://www.nbcnews.com/technolog/ exclusive-millions-printers-open-devastating-hack-attack-researchers-say-118851

Chapter 2

Cyber threats and the necessary clarifications

2.1 RISK

A key consideration when thinking about cybersecurity is risk. It is often said that there is a risk involved in an action. In the case of cybersecurity, risk can relate to many areas and issues. It may be a risk of business continuity loss, data leakage or, more generally, of some unwanted events. Risk is a phenomenon that is related to the likelihood of an event which has consequences.

There are many methods of risk assessment and they are often used in a specialized manner. In a standard case, we can use a formula in which risk is a function of the impact and probability (likelihood):

risk = impact + likelihood of occurrence.

Risk is a function of the likelihood of an event happening and its impact. If the impact is serious and the probability is high, then this (in that case high) risk is better not to be ignored. But, for example, the probability that we will be hit by the proverbial bus tomorrow is low, although the impact would be quite serious. Therefore – due to the very low chance of occurrence – we assess this risk as low. Risk estimation does not necessarily have to be based on simply adding arbitrarily selected weights of an event (in the simplest situations, probability: low, medium, high; impact: low, medium, high – to which we can assign numerical values: 1, 2, 3). Because the point is that the risk depends on the function of the elements to the right of the equation sign in the formula above. It's a very simple formula, although we can build some very useful models (including thought models) on it, which can be very helpful. For example, in determining which threats should we spend more or less time (especially when not everything can be dealt with – and often that's the case) on. This is important when deciding how we manage time as well as financial resources.

For example, if the risk was to lose data, for example as a result of a cyber-attack, such as a malware (e.g., ransomware) infection, or as a result of any other event, then one of the possible safeguards might be to have a backup

DOI: 10.1201/9781003408260-2

copy of those data. There are other decisions and plans associated with this. How to implement a backup? If we are a regular user, is it enough to periodically copy data to an external drive? If we are a company, is a similar solution appropriate? In the end, maybe it's worth considering implementing an entire backup management system and to decide how to configure it (e.g., how often to make backups).

Of course, it is worth considering the risks we want to protect ourselves against. If it is, for example, accidental deletion of files or ransomware in fact, then the external hard drive may be physically next to our computer (but not connected to the network or permanently to the computer). However, if we take into account the risk of a data center burning down (accidents happen, for example, to recall the OVH data center fire in 2021) or even the threat of a full-scale war (to recall the war in Ukraine in 2022), then our solutions must be properly designed and calibrated. In such a situation, perhaps it is worth considering decentralized (geographically dispersed) backups located on remote servers, for example, on another continent. Then the risk of fire or war will also be included into the account.

If the considered threat is someone taking over control of the user's account, one of the security measures could be, for example, the introduction of multi-factor authentication,[1] i.e., using not only the password but also tokens – codes sent via SMS or generated by a one-time code generator.

Thinking about risks can also be largely intuitive. However, it requires a certain awareness of threats and knowledge of how to avoid them, because the analyses themselves should be precise, and strict. However, it is conceivable that some risks are less real than others. For example, the real risk may be data loss, and a less real risk may be a permanent change as a result of bit modification in the data (bus) line due to, say, cosmic rays, which theoretically could alter the logical[2] bits so that the data read are incorrect. This example is largely overcomplicated, although it was actually suspected at some point that this could have been responsible for the counting error in the Schaerbeck vote in Belgium (for which there is no evidence). We are deliberately giving this example to make the reader aware that not all risks are real and not all of them need to be taken seriously. Most people should definitely not be concerned with cosmic rays.

It is often said: "it cannot be ruled out that ..." or "there is a risk that ..." – but without taking into account the probability, it is only an eristic trick. Because the chances of certain events happening are simply very small, slim. They are so slight that the risk is ultimately extremely low, almost nonexistent, and irrelevant in practice. But an important note here! Events with a very high severity of repercussions (impacts, consequences) but low likelihood of happening should often still be seriously considered in some circumstances, by some organizations at least. For example, a truly global pandemic happening can be assessed as a low probability event. But because the effects (e.g., economic) could be catastrophic, we do not ignore such risks.

Returning to cybersecurity, for example, there is a small chance that the user will become the target of an attack by the Russian military intelligence, cyberintelligence (but: still can – as an offshoot or associated victim). This is due to very prosaic reasons – the so-called ordinary user is unlikely to be of interest to this type of structure. (Although it depends on who the user is, it is imaginable that some of our readers may actually become targets for this type of agency). We understand it intuitively. If we have these types of intelligence or military structures, they necessarily have **limited resources** and time. Thus, they must direct their actions to the specific targets. They cannot attack everything and everyone imaginable, "as they come". So if we have an ordinary user, we can ignore this type of (targeted) risk as improbable. However, if we have a so-called important user, say, a "very important person" (VIP), a "high-value target (HVT), let's say that our reader turns out to be a candidate in the presidential election, it would be good if he/she had access to appropriate competences, for example, to people who would take care of the appropriate level of security. Relevant to the way the potential target works. Nevertheless, we do not recommend being the target of intelligence organizations.

2.2 DIFFERENT TYPES OF RISK

"Risk" is a very broad concept and we can relate it to different areas of life and functioning. We can talk about risk in relation to cybersecurity, i.e., the risk of the occurrence and implementation of a threat (e.g., breach of security, theft, or data leakage). We can also talk about risk in the context of privacy protection or personal data protection. Here, the risk-based approach is the standard method required by the General Data Protection Regulation.[3] The risk is analyzed at different levels and in different situations. More generally, however, the idea is to select the appropriate methods to tackle specific threats, as mentioned before, so that the risk is minimized. However, we can imagine a specific risk, for example, financial data leakage as a result of an attacker breaching the security. These can also be more prosaic risks, such as losing a company laptop with data. Such incidents, when they occur, need to be detected and what happened should be established, possibly informing the relevant data protection authority (as GDPR mandates, when a risk exists) and even the affected users (when the risk is significant). Therefore, we consider the issues of compliance with legal requirements, with standards.

2.2.1 Artificial Intelligence and risk

We can also talk about the risk in relation to artificial intelligence (*AI*) systems. And here we can refer to the risk in relation to various threats. For example, we can consider the risk that an AI system will discriminate against the people whose data it processes. A concrete manifestation may be, for example, discrimination against job applicants as a result of the CV analysis system. As artificial intelligence systems are becoming increasingly complex, such risks will increase. The first regulation with regard to artificial intelligence, finalized by the European Union in 2022, will require companies to conduct a risk analysis in relation to artificial intelligence methods.[4] It will, therefore, be a formalized analysis. What if there could be an attempt to attack such an AI system? Such risks will also have to be considered, assessed, and analyzed. There may also be specific cybersecurity risks linked to AI use, on many levels of the deployed systems, including the risks of stealing data out of the trained AI model that is used to detect patterns in a specific AI application.

2.2.2 Human rights

Various technologies, standards, or technical proposals can be analyzed in the context of the risk to human rights. Here we go back to the basic formula in which we have the probability of an event and the severity of its impact (i.e., how serious the situation will be when the event does occur). Again, we can imagine the risk of discrimination in the case of a hypothetical system or standard, for example the QUIC network protocol, i.e., the protocol that will be used as standard for data transmission in networks. Its analysis concluded that "the QUIC protocol provides end-users with a significant improvement in terms of human rights".[5] Such an analysis of the impact of the QUIC protocol on human rights is another thing altogether. But it was created, and praise for this to the authors, because since recently, problems of this kind are finally being taken seriously, and as part of this analysis, the risk of discrimination was taken into account. So we can analyze technical systems in the context of human rights. Since technology has such a powerful impact, it is in fact necessary to analyze the consequences of the evolution of these technologies for people and societies. Both because of the technologies themselves and because of the risk of their use, abuse and, possibly, breach of their security.

2.3 BRIEFLY ABOUT CYBERATTACKS

Let's start with the fact that "cyberattack" is a colloquial term, a mental shortcut, a kind of journalistic-publicist term, a very general formulation. As we will discuss in detail in Chapter 7, a cyberattack is not really an attack under international law. Until then, we will not go into details. Let's agree that a cyberattack is an incident that may be experienced by individuals or information systems. So a cyberattack is associated with breaching security and gaining (i.e., unauthorized) access, leading to certain actions that would normally not take place in relation to a normally functioning system. They are deliberate, intentional, harmful actions taken by intelligent persons or automatons created by such persons (or automatons created by automatons, as at the end of 2022 the illuminating example of ChatGPT language model demonstrated capabilities of writing malware by an automaton).

It is, therefore, a non-standard action, a consequence of intentional actions taken by the attacker. Now an important note to keep in mind. When dealing with self-propagating software (network worms), it may be harder to talk about intention. Such a system selects targets and attacks them by itself. The intentional initial action was limited to releasing such a software, which may have largely become autonomous since then. Nevertheless, we should recognize that there is no such thing as a universal autonomy of an automaton and that the responsibility, eventually, always lies with the creator in some way, specifically the people deploying such tools into use. Someone made them. Someone used and deployed them. It did not happen by itself.

In the general situation, however, it is a consequence of the actions of some specific people, which lead to the breach of security and to unforeseen consequences. We can't hope to hold a binary or a code accountable. People are accountable.

2.4 KILL CHAIN – A USEFUL THOUGHT MODEL

Cyber kill chain is a model used in relation to cyber threats. It helps to understand how security breaches occur and how unwanted actions occur. This model is inspired by military thinking, has been processed by Lockheed Martin and adapted to the field of cybersecurity. In the cyber kill chain, we think about the target from the attacker's perspective, i.e., how to eventually breach the system's security (in stages). But also about how we can "frame" (or classify) a particular threat in the context of this model (and into its stages), which can help us understand the actions comprising an operation or malware activity, and even many methods used in a coordinated manner (i.e., constituting the stages).

We divide the cyber kill chain into seven phases (stages). We will discuss them in sequence.

2.4.1 Reconnaissance

The first phase is Reconnaissance, that is, identification and selection of the targets of a cyberattack, obtaining information about them. For example, it might consist of browsing different companies' websites from a certain industry. We can find information about them on the internet. We may collect email addresses, target phone numbers, and other such data.

2.4.2 Weaponization

The second phase is the so-called *weaponization*. It is the selection of means and methods for the goal that we want to achieve. This could be, for example, the selection of existing tools, their modification, or the creation of new tools to breach security or to perform cyberattacks. And doing it in such a way that the applied tools are adapted to the target of choice.

2.4.3 Delivery

It is about "delivering" tools to targets in some way. Again, we can imagine a lot of possibilities, as it could be, for example, delivery of the tools to the target recipient via an e-mail with an attachment or a link to an infected website configured to infect the targets (this is called phishing, which we'll talk more about in the following chapters). It may also be the leaving of a data storage device, for example, a USB flash drive or a USB key with infected software, in a specially selected place. For example, on the premises of a company, with the hope that someone will eventually connect such a USB device to company systems and run malware that will further take action automatically. That's not as silly as it sounds. In fact, it actually worked.

In 2008, on the initiative of one of the intelligence agencies, something like that happened in the US Department of Defense, when an infected USB flash drive was left in a parking lot in front of one of the department's buildings.[6] Once inserted into a computer, the malware spread throughout the network – both in its open and in its confidential parts. It was simple and effective at the same time. This tool was named Agent.BTZ, and it took several months to clean the network of it. Later, in order to prevent further attacks of this type, a special unit of the US Cyber Command, the command of cyber troops, was established. Since then, some organizations also prohibit employees from inserting unvetted devices into sensitive computers. Others may make it physically impossible altogether, by removing ports into which such a device could be inserted.

2.4.4 Exploitation

Exploitation is the execution of malicious code, launching malicious software on target systems.

2.4.5 Installation

Another point of the kill chain model is the embedding of this type of tool, malware, into the target's systems.

2.4.6 Command and control

The earlier steps lead us to point six, which is command and control (C&C). This includes the ability to communicate between the infected system, i.e., malware (operating tools) already installed on the target system, and the operator's infrastructure. An operator who will send orders, commands to such a system to make such malware do something, take selected actions that the operator intends. What are these actions? This could be, for example, data deletion or data download, i.e., stealing specific data. The type of operation (intelligence, or maybe military, disruptive, or destructive) might sometimes also be recognized from the types of performed actions.

2.4.7 Achieving goals

In the seventh phase, goals are achieved. So if there is already a constructed, compiled, built, and installed infrastructure for operations (gaining access to the system, maintaining this access, the ability to execute commands, i.e., control over the system), then we can use it to achieve certain goals. For example, if the target is user data, it means locating them on computers/systems and sending them to a remote server. Similarly, if we are talking about a cyber espionage operation and the goal is "installing oneself" in a company or institution, and the ultimate goal is to steal data, for example, e-mails, then with the commands executed, we will lead to a situation in which, inside such an infected system, we reach those data. We will obtain these data, prepare them for being sent outside, send them, and collect them elsewhere. Sounds easy right? But, naturally, the complexity is much greater in a cyber espionage operation. In an understandable way, such an operation may require many resources: time (days, weeks, months), people (from several to several dozen involved), and money (which depends on the requirements of time, people, and tools).

The risk calculation is also completely different. If we are a cybercriminal group or a state group, there is much less risk associated with hacking a random human compared to actions aimed at an institution, possibly at the military. But is it really? It is true that an individual criminal or a cybercriminal group must recon with criminal liability for their actions, if they are tracked and apprehended. However, if actions are taken against people located in other countries, i.e., jurisdictions (e.g., someone in Nigeria hacks targets in Germany), then first there must be a cooperation between the police services of these two countries. It is possible, but it will take time. However, if actions are taken, for example, by a Russian cyber espionage group targeting institutions of the European Union, Germany, Poland, or the USA, the responsibility may vary. In practice, not much happens. The worst that can happen is the disclosure of the operators involved in the activities, possibly the imposition of personal sanctions (or against employers of such operators in the framework of such organizations, that is, e.g., intelligence agencies), and some degree of ostracism against such States. In practice, however, such costs are rather low, unless we consider the inconvenience of travel difficulties of those involved in these activities as a serious limitation. Although this is only the beginning (from around the middle of the 2010 decade) of an attempt to enforce State liability for cyber operations, the approach is subject to change and evolve.

2.4.8 Kill chain – summary

Let's go back to our cyberattack model. We have discussed the seven phases into which we can divide it. This can help attackers to construct a cyberattack, defenders – in the understanding of cyberattack processes and protecting themselves against actions within each of these functional phases (stages). For example, by installing appropriate security measures, like – preventing malware from communicating with systems "outside". But also thanks to the prevention of malware delivery – for example, as a result of phishing (a method that uses social engineering to induce the target-victim to harm himself). Building resilience can be achieved through special awareness training for staff, i.e., for employees of a company or institution, installation of security software, or an appropriate method of system configuration. This is the simplified way in which you can prepare to repel cyberattacks.

Of course, you can always make your approach even more precise. Let's use the presented model to ensure that our activities are directed at solutions and defense against specific attack methods. We can be very careful in defending ourselves against very specific actions or operations. Knowing the so-called *indicators of compromise*,[7] specific signatures related to tools or used actions, we can detect unwanted actions against systems or networks. They can even help us discover the fact that, unfortunately, our systems have been hacked. These indicators can take the form of a "hash": 01b610e8ffcb8fd85f2d682b-8a364cad2033c8104014df83988bc3ddfac8e6ec, or for example IP addresses "template" such as 88[.]198.101[.]58[8] or other.

2.5 THE MITRE MODEL

Another method helpful in specifying the techniques and methods of cyber-operation is the MITRE ATT&CK.[9] It is a functional division, created by MITRE, a non-profit organization, within which we can divide the activities that make up a cyberattack – from the start (gaining access) to the end (perform actions). We can divide these phases, for example, by distinguishing the reconnaissance stage, within this model designated as TA0043 tactic, and within this tactic there is already a set of different techniques. For example, T1595 is an "active scan" that can be detected by the DS0029 "network traffic scan".

The next steps are resource development, initial system access, execution, and *persistence*, which is how an attacker can ensure that he remains successfully on the system, maintains access to it. In fact, the best groups are difficult to remove from systems, as was found, for example, in the hacking of the German Bundestag parliament in 2015 – attackers had access to systems for several months prior to the detection.

Another point in this model is the attempt to increase the privileges within the system. This means getting privileged permissions, for example, an administrator account (user accounts usually have restrictions). The next point is to bypass security using methods in which we gain access to authorization, e.g., we break passwords or obtain them from somewhere else (e.g., through phishing).

If interesting resources are still being sought in the system under consideration, it may involve the so-called *lateral movement*. Often, in the attacked companies or institutions, there may be many systems that are connected with each other. These can be computers, workstations, servers, printers, etc. Attackers of such complex systems may have specific targets or are simply looking for interesting things. The need to navigate between such different systems in search of something interesting, for example, is understandable (I remind you that at this point we are thinking like an attacker). Important is also the possible download of such data, and thus, for example, the installation of implants, i.e., programs that will collect data and send them outside – outside the target system, to the places over which the attacker has control (where he receives data). This could be data that are transferred within this network by its users. It could even be audio recording of system users. This can be the contents of the clipboard, familiar to all who use the ctrl+c, ctrl+v keyboard shortcuts (copy and paste functions). There are many possibilities when you gain control over the system.

An important stage, as in the cyber kill chain, is *command and control*, which consists in maintaining control and issuing commands from the outside.

The penultimate phase is exfiltration if we are preparing the data to be sent out.

And finally, there is the most important phase, that is, the impact, the effect – tactic TA0040. This is the phase of achieving the goals (cybercriminal, but also military or intelligence, depending on the attacker's motivation/goals). Such an effect can be, for example, data destruction (technique T1485), data deletion, system destruction. This could be data tampering, i.e., an integrity attack, such as data manipulation (technique T1565). This could be paralyzing the system. It all depends on the attacker's creativity – or rather, the goals – because if someone puts a lot of work and effort into such an operation, they must have something specific in mind. Especially if it is a way of life, such as in the case of a cybercriminal, cyberespionage, or cyber-military group. Such people do not waste time; they are effect-oriented in their actions. Therefore, poetic tales of the great exploits of lonely hacker-idealists should not be given credence, at least not uniquely. Of course, it is possible that someone is still in the school phase or a student and still has a lot of time and the need to put the skills and interests to some use. It can happen, and it has happened before; sure. Though it's unlikely that groups of this type would be able to achieve the ability to cause significant damage – i.e., physical damage, lethal effects.

MITRE ATT&CK is, therefore, another model that allows us to think and reason like an attacker and implement security at every layer of such a hypothetical attack. This is very helpful in security testing, as the model distinguishes between practical (technical) methods of operation within each phase. This is often used in the so-called exercises like *red teaming*, i.e., simulated cyberattacks on the system. Within this model, the methods and tactics of actions of specific groups, for example Russian intelligence, can also be classified, even divided into military and civilian counterparts.

We will not go into detail about other solutions here, for example, a very useful diamond model. It is worth noting, however, that both the cyber kill chain, MITRE ATT&CK, and other models are not very helpful for the end user, that is, for the ordinary user. Rather, they are models for professionals, for experts, or otherwise for people with deep interest in the subject.

2.6 SOCIAL ENGINEERING AND PHISHING

Social engineering is a combination of methods of exerting influence, persuasion, and technical orientation. Social engineering in relation to computer science are methods of persuading people, exerting influence, aimed at making people take certain actions. Such actions would usually be in accordance with the intentions of the person who initiated them, and against the interests of the person being persuaded.

We should immediately transition to speaking about phishing here. We've used this term before when discussing the cyber kill chain. The word "phishing" in pronunciation is similar to another word: "fishing". This is one of the primary ways to deliver "instructions" to potential targets – people. Phishing is a method of making contact with a target, which could be an end user, an employee of an institution, or a company. It may even be the boss of such a company or another decision maker. Phishing uses various communication channels. The contact can be made via e-mail or instant messaging, for example via WhatsApp. It can be a simple message that grabs attention or calls for action, possibly immediate. It may contain a link, maybe there will be something that will either directly infect the user's browser or allow the user to download a file, i.e., a program that, when launched, will infect such a system. As such, phishing can be a source of malware delivery. Generally speaking, it is making use of other people. Perhaps by means of deception.

If we consider, for example, an attack on a company or institution, and for the purposes of this example let us assume that it has about a thousand employees, then by sending all of them such a "bait" request, we have a good chance that at least one person may take such a "bait". That's why training is so important, but you need to do it wisely so as not to make matters worse – sometimes phishing training can actually even be harmful.[10] That is why proper communication monitoring is so important in identifying attack attempts early. If company employees help in immediately reporting suspicious communication, this form of proactive defense can be very effective.

Phishing can be directed, targeted. It's always about encountering users who can be persuaded to take certain actions. By this, they are supposed to harm themselves. They often do so because they have no knowledge or are unaware of the consequences of certain behaviors. Computers and systems are complicated things, after all. There are many options, configurable elements, various windows. Some users may not desire to be expert in being aware of everything, and perhaps choose to focus on their specific work needs. When a message appears prompting us to undertake an activity that is allegedly required and the consequences of which we do not understand – it is more difficult to imagine what its consequences and final effects will be. Such an activity can be, for example, installing software or executing some code, a system command.

Basically, phishing is about gaining the trust of users and getting them to take action that will have negative consequences for them. This could lead to financial or even reputational losses. It has been a very common form of cyberattack for years. This is how the system can become infected, for example, at first. This can even cause large financial losses for companies. Like in the so-called BEC variant (*business email compromise*), consisting in sending a communication that is convincing enough (e.g., the attacker claims to be a high-ranking person in the company) that it will induce a decision-making person to undertake unfavorable operations. What nature can these operations have? For example, they may be about financial matters like money transfers to a cybercriminal's account.

We don't want to go into the very advanced technical details of phishing here. Methods change, but the core remains the same: it is preying on people's trust and lack of knowledge, their lack of awareness, and perhaps rush. It is generating trust in some way, perhaps causing a sense of urgency, immediacy (that action must be taken quickly because "time is running out", allegedly). In such a situation of pressure, we may not be aware of the consequences of our actions. Unfortunately, with a deplorable effect.

2.6.1 Masquerade in France using the "minister" method

It is worth mentioning the events that took place in France. At one time, there was a group operating there that carried out phishing attacks on companies in a very specific way. A man disguised himself as France's defense minister and realistically imitated his behavior, expression, and voice.[11] He also had a proper mask on his face. He connected via videoconferencing with decision makers in companies, persuading such targets (victims), perhaps invoking their patriotism, to make a transfer. Allegedly, these funds were to be used for covert operations for France's national security. This was a very audacious operation. And although the success rate was relatively low, it was still sufficient to take over more than EUR 50 million. As has already been mentioned, such attempts are directed at many places with the hope that they will succeed somewhere. In France, it worked successfully, in some places eventually, and it didn't need an advanced deepfake technology, but just a mask, a "minister's office", and a computer equipped with a videoconferencing application.

2.7 THREAT GROUPS

With regard to groups, a useful functional model is used in which we name certain actors and classify them according to their skills, abilities, knowledge, and goals. This allows concluding in a simplified manner what are the possibilities of specific groups and, therefore, what are the threats. In this classification, hacktivists, cybercriminals, State groups, or other professionals are often mentioned.

2.7.1 Hacktivists

Hacktivists are informal groups associated with a purpose. It can be a social, political or any other goal. It is often recognized that these types of groups do not have significant resources or knowledge, and the disruptions they can cause are not significant. Of course, this may vary depending on who is within these groups, but on the whole, it is recognized that hacktivists generally do not pose a serious threat. However, you have to take them into account as there may be many of them. Examples of activities of such groups are, for example, the actions against Lufthansa in 2001,[12] but also some of the initiatives within the IT framework of the Ukrainian Army against Russian websites.[13]

2.7.2 Cybercriminals

Cybercriminals, in turn, are organized, mainly profit-oriented groups.[14] One of their core business models these days is the use of ransomware. In general, however, the point is that cybercriminals have a certain way of doing things. This makes them the easiest to recognize. However, it happened that cybercriminal groups were impersonated by state groups, for example, the Russian military intelligence launched the NotPetya worm, which was supposed to infect and encrypt systems, pretending to be ransomware, but in practice it destroyed them irreversibly.

Cybercriminal groups do not need to have significant resources or knowledge. However, sometimes, it is just the opposite: they have both the knowledge and the tools. So it all depends on the group. The situation can also change quickly, especially if the group has access to money so that they can afford advanced methods or tools. There are so many cybercriminal groups that we will not list them here.

2.7.3 State groups, APT

Worth mentioning are government groups, the so-called government hackers. While the latter term is sometimes used, it is not appropriate because, since these people work within government structures, they are unlikely to be hackers. A more appropriate name would be "cyber operators", implying a full-time job. We can introduce additional distinctions here, because these people can be employed, for example, by the civil service, the police, intelligence, or the army. Their activity will have a very specific dimension, depending on the purpose (we will return to the discussion of these specialized groups in Chapters 6 and 7).

Government groups usually have significant resources to achieve their goals. Of course, this involves access to advanced tools or the possibility of engaging external groups, sometimes cybercriminals, to carry out activities on behalf of the government groups. Government groups can constitute (and be known as) the so-called APT (*advanced persistent threat*), which take measures to gain and maintain access to systems. An action could be, for example, data theft, some kind of paralysis or disruption of the system, or perhaps even sending a political/military signal (also at a specific point in time chosen by the APT controller). Most often it is about obtaining data (espionage), because it can be both possible and profitable.

Why is it difficult to defend oneself against such groups? Because these groups have:

- knowledge,
- means (money, methods),
- a specific motivation and purpose.

Let's suppose the primary purpose of an exemplary company is to generate profit. Its core business is, obviously, therefore, not to repel cyberattacks. So there is an asymmetry here. Because on the one hand, we have an attacker whose main or only goal is to hack the victim. On the other hand, there is a victim for whom defense is not the sole purpose of existence. So who will win in such a situation?

2.7.4 Groups – synthesis

In summary, the actors can be well classified in terms of their abilities. Then, we can distinguish six ranks or classes[15]:

- Practitioners using someone else's tools,
- Experienced practitioners, able to build their own tools,
- Practitioners capable of finding and exploiting vulnerabilities,
- Highly specialized cybercriminal groups,

- Government actors with the ability to even embed vulnerabilities into products,
- Actors capable of performing the full spectrum of operational (defensive-offensive) activities to achieve political, military, or economic goals.

Although, to be fair, for practical reasons, different groups may also have abilities "in between" these classes. For example, when not very sophisticated cybercriminals could use simple tools, so would government actors if they were not of the "highest caliber". So much for the threat actors. Later in the book, we will speak about how to measure the impact of the cyberattack. But now let's promptly discuss the matter of tools.

2.8 CYBER TOOLS OR CYBERWEAPONS?

We have already talked about tools. But what are they? Let's start with security testing tools, though there are specialized tools for breaching the security, as well. Sometimes such tools can have multiple uses. That is to say: testing tools can also be used for hacking, breaching, breaking. Therefore, they are, in a way, dual-use tools. The same tools that in good hands can be used to secure the system, in the hands of others can be used for nefarious, including illegal, purposes. However, there are tools designed solely for attack that are not really useful specifically for security testing. Some of these are sometimes referred to as *cyberweapons*. Although it is better to avoid the use of this ("cyberweapons") term, as it compares digital tools to kinetic weapons, such as a gun, a missile, a bomb. There are, however, significant conceptual differences at very basic levels. This topic will be analyzed again, later in the book.

2.8.1 Types of tools – a question of aims

In short, several types of tools can be mentioned. Historically, these could be, for example, *distributed denial of service* (DDoS) attack tools, i.e., flooding information systems (computers, servers) with unwanted network traffic in such a way that, under the "pressure" of bogus network traffic, such a target would no longer be available (e.g., the website will stop loading) or the entire network (internet access) provider will go down (i.e., its users will lose access to the network, for some time, usually short, temporary intervals). This is because traffic flows in both directions. It's about sending and receiving data. But network bandwidth is limited. If too much bogus traffic enters our network, firstly, we may not (no longer) be able to establish connections with external systems (from our perspective, the connectivity will be lost), and secondly, actual users will not be able to connect to resources in our network (e.g., they will not be able to open a website).

There can also be tools installed on compromised servers or IoT devices in such a way that these servers or devices create a botnet. And someone who controls such a botnet (behaving like an automaton) feeds it commands to send packets. That is, attempts to establish a connection with some system, with some server, with a website. As a result of such flooding with traffic, such a target simply loses the ability to serve data, i.e., it loses the ability to provide services. It ceases to be available.

2.8.1.1 Estonia (2007)

This is exactly what happened in Estonia in 2007, when a significant part of the significantly digitized country was paralyzed, which then was a serious threat, or at least a great inconvenience. It was spoken of as the *first politically motivated cyberattack to paralyze the state*. Current and former Estonia's officials actually use(d) this line. Here, however, let us note that Estonia has paradoxically benefited from this cyberattack in the long run, at least in some specific contexts – as it could have built its reputation on digitization, on cybersecurity. Also perhaps even to some extent efficiently taking advantage of the fact that it has become a victim. It was thus turned into profit. Because, first of all, it was possible to show that security had been expanded, developed, improved. Secondly, thanks to this, the NATO cybersecurity expert center (NATO Cooperative Cyber Defence Centre of Excellence) was located in Estonia, and it routinely runs cybersecurity exercises. Third, it seems to be the first time that a state, a government, a particular state, presented itself as a victim and built a whole narrative around it. Such a political move was very skillful. Since then, it has been used extremely rarely, and almost never successfully on such a scale. In 2019, during negotiations on cybersecurity within the UN group of governmental experts, Iran tried to present itself as the site of the first major cyberattack, calling it a "cyber-Hiroshima" event (referring to the first city on which an atomic bomb was dropped), but without much success. Actually, it's very interesting that pulling off skillful cyber policy on this level is so extremely rare. We do not intend to accuse Estonia of instrumentalization of becoming a victim, but rather express admiration for the craftsmanship, statecraft, cybercraft.

2.8.2 Exploit

Exploit is a form of software that *exploits* (i.e., takes advantage of, uses) vulnerabilities (i.e., security weaknesses, vulnerabilities, bugs) of a program or a system. As a result of taking advantage of such a weakness, access is gained to certain *magical resources*, unusual opportunities. Why do we call them *magical*? Because in a way they are! By breaking security and using vulnerability, ability is obtained to force such an information system, for example, an operating system, to perform tasks that the attacker wants, and which have never been built into such a system by its creators – programmers, developers. So we can, for example, order the instant messenger we are attacking to take certain actions. For example, exploiting the vulnerability of WhatsApp messenger could then lead to certain actions on the target's (victim's) system via the WhatsApp software. These activities can be, for example, data preparation and exfiltration to the outside, i.e., data theft. It might just be taking control of the system and making it function as an active wiretap. One of the more famous systems that used such exploits on a large scale was Pegasus from NSO (and other vendors offering similar tools). This is a hacking-surveillance software, but it is a whole framework, a solution that has a set of exploits (here used as methods to gain access to the iOS or Android smartphone system), and which places a surveillance implant in the victim's system. It is when data can be downloaded from a smartphone, it can be turned into a wiretap tool, files can be placed on it, etc.

We (as in, the world) have been dealing with exploits for several decades. Sometimes, they were created as a hobby, they were shared on discussion forums or with software developers (to lead to patches). Nowadays, exploits, which are programs that take advantage of the vulnerabilities of other programs, can also simply be bought on the private market. Depending on what they are intended for, their price can vary significantly. It can amount to tens of thousands of euros for an exploit that uses a vulnerability in some Internet of Things system. But it can reach millions, for example if we want to break the security of a browser, operating system, or other popular software, like an instant messenger.

2.9 CVE AND SECURITY BUG BRANDING

Software bugs happen. This wisdom is well known in information technology. It is like that, always was, and always will be. Depending on the type, errors can have different consequences, ranging from inconvenience to users to the possibility of them being exploited as a security vulnerability. So you have to search for bugs, fix them, release patches, and install them regularly. When a security bug is identified, an identifier or a number can be assigned to it in order to catalog it. As an actual standard, it is done as part of the so-called CVE system (*common vulnerabilities and exposures*), managed by the MITRE company and co-financed by the U.S. Department of Homeland Security. For example, CVE-2014-0160 identifies a bug that allows attackers to intercept data through the flawed implementation of the once popular Transport Layer Security (TLS) protocol, OpenSSL.[16] Since this software was very common, it was a problem on a web-wide basis.

Logotypes are also created for certain vulnerabilities, bugs, and risks. This is called branding of security bugs or vulnerabilities. Such issues are given not only a logo, but also a name. An example of such a name was "heartbleed",[17] where the name came from the hermetic (or obscure) technical details of this vulnerability (the bug existed in the *heartbeat* procedure of the OpenSSL

Figure 2.1 Heartbleed Logo (CVE-2014-0160).

Source: https://heartbleed.com.

library). By naming them or even creating a logotype, such bugs may become commonly known. They are named, the information spreads. Perhaps this helps to build risk awareness, leading to the building and installing of patches rapidly. However, in most cases, serious bugs are still not named and do not have logos, while they obviously also need to be dealt with.

All in all, the phenomenon of branded bugs is an interesting and positive one. It also raises a stirr and adds a certain dose of humor to the hermetic world of security (Figure 2.1).

Other interesting branded bugs worth mentioning here were Shellshock (CVE-2014-6271; as it turned out, a very common and easy-to-use vulnerability in many systems; the logo in Figure 2.2)[18] or Spectre (CVE-2017-5753, CVE-2017-5715; a class of bug types targeting CPU microarchitecture, therefore, not a software bug; logo in Figure 2.3) or Hertzbleed (CVE-2022-23823, CVE-2022-24436; the logo of this CPU-level bug is in Figure 2.4).

This technique is a very interesting and helpful one. Especially in the case of such bugs – widespread issues, perhaps relatively easy to take advantage of or exploit (such as Heartbleed or Shellshock bugs were), and asking for a solution to the problem as soon as possible. In a way, it also is spectacular. In other contexts: the logotype is created because it is cool. However, not all vulnerabilities require a logo. These better remain exceptions and not be misused.

2.9.1 20-year-old security vulnerabilities?

As a curiosity, let's add that some security vulnerabilities existed in the software for up to 10^{19} or 20^{20} years. It took so long to find them, identify them,

Figure 2.2 Shellshock logo (CVE-2014-6271).

Source: https://openclipart.org/detail/202368/shellshock-bug.

Figure 2.3 Spectre logo (CVE-2017-5753, CVE-2017-5715).

Source: https://meltdownattack.com.

and then patch them. In view of such a long life span, some people may wonder about the hypothetical consequences. What if someone else found such a 20-year bug,[21] say, 10 years ago? Then they could have been using it – like, for hacking systems – for 10 years! But in practice it is not necessarily quite so, because it seems that thanks to the resources devoted to system monitoring, sooner or later the exploitation of some unknown vulnerabilities would be discovered and investigated eventually, anyway. Then these "unknown" vulnerabilities would perhaps be identified as indeed "very specific" vulnerabilities. Although, of course, it cannot be completely ruled out that someone or something has actually used vulnerabilities in the software

Figure 2.4 Hertzbleed logo (CVE-2022-23823, CVE-2022-24436).

Source: https://www.hertzbleed.com/.

for so many years. In the end, it must be admitted that 20 years ago security standards were much lower than today. The previous statement was also valid 10 and 20 years ago. The same statement will probably remain in force also in 10 and 20 years.

2.9.2 The economy of security bugs and exploits

It is worth mentioning the economy of exploits, although here we go far beyond what the tool itself is. Well, there exist companies that purchase information about vulnerabilities or methods of breaking security in order to exploit them. The rates vary depending on the type of software. It can be tens, hundreds of thousands, or even millions of euros. Companies that distribute these tools can earn good money. Is it expensive? Is a million euros for a tool a lot? Usability in practice has to be taken into account. For example, if we are a country's military intelligence and we want to build our own hacking tools, exploits may be useful to us (for breaking security). At the same time, the buyer who buys such a tool for, say, a million euros, gains access to some interesting economic effects. This obviously amortizes the costs, because the tools are purchased once, but they can be used several times, on several targets.

Consider a scenario when a million or even 50 million is paid, and such an actor will use the tool for several dozen or hundreds of targets within his interests, i.e., hundreds of systems. The actor has an access tool that they can potentially make extensive use of. So they can access the vulnerable systems, steal data from (potentially, all of) the systems of interest, monitor them, eavesdrop on them, perform some actions, and even destroy them if necessary or so desired. So, it is not at all that a million is allocated to one person, a purpose, or a target. Because when we divide this sum into, say, a thousand of targets (all of them valuable in themselves!), the average unit cost is no longer "a million" (or a figure of the kind), but much less, for example (arbitrary assumption) a thousand, even a hundred. Such action is, therefore, much more economical than it may seem at first glance due to the cost amortization. Remember: even if the public talks about "tools for a million" (it sounds so dramatic that it's asking to be put in a headline), it can be a confusing oversimplification. As is shown, the cost of using such a tool can in fact be much less than "a million".

2.9.3 Frameworks and other tools

Finally, it is also worth mentioning frameworks (cybersecurity tools "combine harvesters"?) for cyberattacks, such as, for example, Metasploit or Burp Suite. These are actually the systems for testing security, i.e., for securing systems. The idea is to streamline the process of selecting a method to break the system, constructing such a method and using it. We won't go into detail here, other than Metasploit having an exploit database, for example, and that it can be used for testing.

We could of course also talk about other types of malware and tools. These could be tools such as:

- auto-spreading malware, i.e., worms,
- surveillance software, such as Trojans,
- tools for remote access (and *control*) over an infected system
- tools for destroying and paralyzing systems (wipers). Such tools were widely used (e.g., the automatically spreading tool NotPetya, which paralyzed systems in 2017), also during armed conflicts (e.g., various tools of this type used before and during the war in Ukraine in 2022).

It doesn't really make much sense to divide these different "named" things these days. What matters is how they operate and what they do, but this may change at various stages. We will refer to them collectively as *malware*. Depending on the needs, appropriate tools are used or created, to attain specific goals.

2.10 RANSOMWARE

It is worth mentioning one type of tool separately. Ransomware is a type of malware that has gained special importance, notoriety. It infects the system and "freezes" it, disrupts it, puts it out of use. Ransomware has grown into one of the biggest cybersecurity problems. It is worth understanding what this threat is on a technical and conceptual level. Ransomware is a type of software that encrypts data on disk and, therefore, blocks access to them. So, it is an attack on data availability and integrity. It is a malicious software that can be delivered to computers of ordinary users, company employees (and company systems), or institutions – using various techniques. This could be, for example, phishing (getting the victim to infect the system, perhaps his/her own, e.g., by accidental clicking). Sometimes, it can be something triggered by someone who hacked the network security, got in, and just manually infected that network. These are, however, already operational issues.

The target can be one or more computers, even the entire network of a company or institution (then it is especially very painful as, as a result, employees may have to be forced to work in the "*pen and paper*" system). This can also impact backup systems. It is worth considering what makes ransomware so special.

2.10.1 Data loss and ransom

Ransomware encrypts the data on the disk in such a way that they can be decrypted quite easily. But the cybercriminal, that is, the ransomware operator, has to be involved, or it has to be done "through" the ransomware. In order to unblock access to data, the victim usually has to pay a ransom to such an operator. So, it's not like someone hacks some systems for fun or from boredom, breaks security, or puts a funny message on the home page of the institution. Here, this is a purely for-profit thinking. A company or institution is paralyzed. Often practically prevented from functioning. Money is demanded for restoring operation, to maintain business continuity. In this way, cybercriminals can "earn" from tens of thousands to even tens of millions of euros (depending on who the victim is).

Specialized ransomware groups choose specific targets. These can be hospitals, critical infrastructure, and other sensitive companies. If an enterprise loses access to all data, that may even lead to its destruction or bankruptcy.[22] Ransomware has grown into the most serious cybersecurity problem as it affects many important companies and institutions. Due to the fact that cybercriminals are becoming more determined and ruthless, this problem has gained the rank of a significant social and even political issue. The media write about it. The politicians (including heads of State) talk about it, and diplomats negotiate about it. Putin's meeting with Biden in Geneva in June 2021, during which cybersecurity was one of the key topics, will go down in the annals of history. It was then that Biden threatened Putin with retaliatory cyberattacks if cyberattacks against U.S. critical infrastructure systems happened. We will discuss the political consequences and the political dimension of cybersecurity in more detail in Chapter 6.

2.10.2 Business model – money is the target

What distinguishes ransomware from other online threats is its very clear business model (cybercriminal activity). It is clear here that access to the data is lost and a ransom must be paid to regain this access again. Its size may depend on the selected target. It can be several hundreds of dollars when it comes to an ordinary user, but the amounts that are asked from companies or institutions can go into thousands or even millions. It's no secret that cybercriminal groups involved in ransomware are able to thrive. They may even function as enterprises, unambiguously focused on profit. The approximate profit for cybercriminals with ransomware is the ransom price multiplied by the number of successfully infected targets (who paid the ransom), minus some operating costs (operations, infections, possibly tool development, although sometimes such groups even function as enterprises with their own HR departments, so the salaries also count in as costs, just like in any "ordinary" business).

2.10.3 How to protect yourself – Rule 3-2-1

The pressing issue, of course, is how to protect yourself, or the system. The good standard we will talk about is to have current software versions, and common sense. Essential here is also having a working backup. One that is regularly performed, just in case. Stored in several places, both locally in the company, and perhaps also with the option of external places, i.e., somewhere in the cloud. The idea is to increase the chance that the data will be protected, that access to them will not be lost completely (and that it can be brought back relatively effortlessly). This is the standard way to "disperse" a backup. That is: to duplicate it and to store it in several places, possibly in different countries, on different continents.

The so-called 3-2-1 rule applies here. To have three copies of data, on two media types, with one copy outside your systems (e.g., in the cloud).[23] This can greatly help in the survival of the company or even the entire country. For example, Estonia had the idea to store important data in "remote embassies", i.e., in different countries (the so-called data embassies[24]). In the event of an aggression against Estonia, threats to its sovereignty, for example, loss of control over a territory, this would help to maintain the continuity of the State's operation, as such backups would allow it to be "restarted". It is, in a way, an extension of the idea of a "government-in-exile". Coping with an armed aggression in 2022, this is also what Ukraine did – quickly moved its government systems and data to the cloud. In less organizational settings, chances are that in the case of an ordinary user, an external disk placed next to the computer suffices, so do it.

But why the need to disperse the data to distribute them? Cybercriminals or attackers sometimes gain great capabilities and can even take control of an entire network of their targets. They can also access and delete the backup system under certain circumstances. If that happened, it would be as if there was no such backup at all in the first place. Because here it's not about backups protected against a natural disaster or technical malfunction. It's about protecting them against an adversary, an intelligent enemy. Cybercriminals want to attain their goals, by paralyzing the operation of the company, by persuading it to pay the ransom. This is a very big threat. Ransomware attacks can actually be paralyzing for institutions or companies. It can actually mean a complete paralysis. We can imagine blocking the operation or functioning of a hospital, or even more broadly, the entire health service, as it happened in Ireland in 2021.[25] This may also lead to the shutdown of critical infrastructure, for example a pipeline, as in the United States in 2021.

2.10.4 Geopolitical and legal problem – Corsairs of the twenty-first century?

Who are the ransomware operators? It is no secret that many of these groups operate from Eastern Europe, for example, in some countries of the former Union of Soviet Socialist Republics (USSR). They thrive and their achievements sometimes even become "legendary". There are stories of people from such a cybercriminal group driving a very distinctive sports car, a Lamborghini; someone was flying a helicopter. And they generally do not care that the practice is illegal and causes many problems in the West. Somehow they manage to remain unpunished (although let's add that the Russian FSB pursued the members of one such a group – REvil – in early 2022). Their activities constitute the center of the geopolitical dispute between the United States and Russia. The United States would prefer its critical infrastructure not to be paralyzed. The "suppliers" of ransomware services can also be used by their "clients" (ransomware as a service), which means that the ransomware creators are not always directly behind the paralysis. Although they are of course also responsible – after all they are supplying the tools. Joe Biden and the Russian President Vladimir Putin talked about that in a meeting, which took place in Geneva in June 2021. It is, therefore, a subject of a political nature.

It is worth considering how to classify ransomware operators. Well, perhaps it resembles other famous actors from the past? There are analogies with corsairs, pirates,[26] the so-called Barbary pirates or pirates from the Barbary states, the "fallen states" of North Africa in the seventeenth and nineteenth centuries. Piracy flourished there. It also caused many trade problems, especially for the newly formed United States of America. This is why the United States built a navy to defend their trade against pirates. For it is no secret that governments that were "skeptical" of the early United States directly urged or encouraged these pirates to attack U.S. merchant ships. If only in such a way that diplomats from these "skeptical" countries, for example, from Great Britain, simply instructed representatives of the countries involved in piracy. For example, they instructed something along the line of: *"the British Navy no longer protects the US trade"*.[27] As we remember, at that time in history, Great Britain was in dispute with the United States. The ransomware analogy is therefore compelling. We have actors; they are involved in a certain practice that harms companies or countries. It might even bleed the economy, when seen holistically. Former corsairs, or privateers, often acted on the inspiration or direct instruction of State actors; similarly today cybercriminals sometimes provide services to States.

We arrive at the conclusion that ransomware is not only one of the most serious cybersecurity problems, immediate and practical, but it also has a geopolitical dimension. This underlines the strategic dimension of cybersecurity.

NOTES

1 A. Ometov, S. Bezzateev, N. Mäkitalo, S. Andreev, T. Mikkonen, Y. Koucheryavy, *Multi-factor authentication: A survey*, "Cryptography" 2018, vol. 2, no. 1, p. 1.

2 L.L. Sivo, J.C. Peden, M. Brettschneider, W. Price, P. Pentecost, *Cosmic ray-induced soft errors in static MOS memory cells*, "IEEE Transactions on Nuclear Science" 1979, vol. 26, no. 6, pp. 5041–5047.

3 Art. 25, 32, 35 of Regulation (EU) 2016/679 of the European Parliament and of the Council of 27 April 2016 on the protection of natural persons with regard to the processing of personal data and on the free movement of such data, and repealing Directive 95/46/EC (General Data Protection Regulation) (OJ L 119 4.5.2016, pp. 1–88; consolidated version: https://eur-lex.europa.eu/legal-content/EN/TXT/HTML/?uri=CELEX:02016R0679-20160504) – hereinafter: GDPR.

4 Proposal for a – Regulation of the European Parliament and of the Council laying down harmonized rules on artificial intelligence (artificial intelligence act) and amending certain union legislative acts (COM/2021/206 final), chapter 1, https://eur-lex.europa.eu/legal-content/EN/TXT/HTML/?uri=CELEX:52021PC0206

5 B. Martini, N. ten Oever, QUIC Human Rights Review, IETF, 25.04.2019, https://tools.ietf.org/id/draft-martini-hrpc-quichr-00.html

6 W.F. Lynn III, *Defending a new domain: The Pentagon's cyberstrategy*, "Foreign Affairs (Council on Foreign Relations)" 2010, no. 5, p. 13.

7 K. Paine, O. Whitehouse, J. Sellwood, A. Shaw, *Indicators of Compromise (IoCs) and their role in attack defence*, 21.01.2022, https://www.ietf.org/id/draft-ietf-opsec-indicators-of-compromise-00.html

8 These are indicators connected with the Chinese group, Cicada, targeting government and NGO organizations; see. Threat Hunter Team, Cicada: Chinese APT group widens targeting in recent espionage activity, 5.04.2022, https://symantec-enterprise-blogs.security.com/blogs/threat-intelligence/cicada-apt10-china-ngo-government-attacks

9 See. https://attack.mitre.org/

10 D. Lain, K. Kostiainen, S. Capkun, *Phishing in organizations: Findings from a large-scale and long-term study*, 14.12.2021, https://arxiv.org/abs/2112.07498

11 A. Breeden, *Defense Minister was on the line, asking for millions to aid france. Or was he?*, 02/04/2020, https://www.nytimes.com/2020/02/04/world/europe/france-Jean-Yves-Le-Drian-fraud.html

12 R. Dominguez, *Electronic civil disobedience: Inventing the future of online agit-prop theater*, "PMLA" 2009, vol. 124, no. 5, pp. 1806–1812.

13 K. Conger, A. Satariano, *Volunteer hackers converge on Ukraine conflict with no one in charge*, 4.03.2022, https://www.nytimes.com/2022/03/04/technology/ukraine-russia-hackers.html

14 D.J. Neufeld, *Understanding cybercrime*, conference paper "2010 43rd Hawaii International Conference on System Sciences", IEEE, 2010; M. Edwards, E. Williams, C. Peersman, A. Rashid, *Characterizing cybercriminals: A review*, 2022, https://arxiv.org/pdf/2202.07419.pdf

15 Office of the Undersecretary of Defense for Acquisition, Technology and Logistics, Task Force Report: *Resilient military systems and the advanced cyber threat*, 2013, https://apps.dtic.mil/sti/pdfs/ADA569975.pdf – table 2.7, pp. 22–23.

16 See https://cve.mitre.org/cgi-bin/cvename.cgi?name=cve-2014-0160

17 See https://heartbleed.com/

18 As a result of processing specially crafted input data (e.g., containing "() {:;};/bin/cat /etc/passwd") the software "parser" eventually reached the Bash shell, which then executed the requested command. This could lead to data theft and system takeover.

19 CVE-2021-3156 (2021), https://cve.mitre.org/cgi-bin/cvename.cgi?name=CVE-2021-3156

20 CVE-2019-1162 (2019), https://cve.mitre.org/cgi-bin/cvename.cgi?name=CVE-2019-1162

21 European Commission, 20-year-old open source bug found and fixed under the EU-FOSSA 2 project, 11/12/2019, https://ec.europa.eu/info/news/20-year-old-open-source- bug-found-and-fixed-under-eu-fossa-2-project-2019-dec-11_en

22 K. Makortoff, *Travelex falls into administration, with loss of 1,300 jobs*, 6/08/2020, https://www.theguardian.com/business/2020/aug/06/travelex-falls-into-administration-shedding-1300-jobs

23 K. Soltow, *The 3-2-1 backup rule – why your data will always survive*, 2.04.2019, https://www.vmwareblog.org/3-2-1-backup-rule-data-will-always-survive/

24 N.F. Rice, *Estonia's digital embassies and the concept of sovereignty*, 10/10/2019, https://georgetownsecuritystudiesreview.org/2019/10/10/estonias-digital-embassies-and-the-concept-of-sovereignty/

25 PWC, *Conti cyber attack on the HSE*. Independent post incident review, 03/12/2021, https://www.hse.ie/eng/services/publications/conti-cyber-attack-on-the-hse-full-report.pdf

26 EF Horsley, *State-sponsored ransomware through the lens of maritime piracy*, "Georgia Journal of International & Comparative Law" 2019, vol. 47, no. 3, pp. 669–681.

27 US Department of State, Office of the Historian, *Barbary Wars, 1801–1805 and 1815–1816*, https://history.state.gov/milestones/1801-1829/barbary-wars

Chapter 3

Cybersecurity from the user's point of view

3.1 CYBERSECURITY AS A PROBLEM OF ORDINARY PEOPLE

In this chapter, we will talk about user's cybersecurity. We will ignore such "big topics" as a cyberattacks on critical infrastructure (we will come to that later). Cybersecurity for ordinary users is very important, and the key premise of this book after all is the conviction that cybersecurity is for everyone and it is important to everyone.

3.1.1 Digitization is progressing and what comes of it

Cybersecurity is important because, as we have already said, the process of computerization and digitization (also the buildup of technological societies, actually: our societies) is progressing, which of course brings new opportunities, such as improving the efficiency of the economy, work, and new forms of entertainment.

People use computers or devices that are computerized in one way or another. Perhaps sometimes they do not even realize it; for example, when a processor and a computer are in an appliance such as a sandwich maker. But we also all use smartphones (these are computers after all) and the Internet (based on connections between computers, also providing, e.g., data transfer between a smartphone and a toothbrush, or a scale). Some users may even be unaware that they are using the Internet. From their perspective, they just use the app and that's all they're interested in. They just want their systems to work, be safe, and free of risks during usage. It is natural and reasonable, although it also implies that cybersecurity is clearly a problem that affects ordinary people. Can there be any doubts as to this when computerization may increasingly include devices that are commonly used in everyday life, such as an oven, a refrigerator, or a washing machine?

When it happened that servers, on which such electronic elements were dependent, were crashing (i.e., "down", unavailable) in the USA, such products stopped working. For example, Roomba vacuum cleaners stopped working. Other devices did too, such as "smart" doorbells[1] (these products

DOI: 10.1201/9781003408260-3

suddenly stopped being intelligent, because they did not work at all). Even if it was not because of a cyberattack, such "ordinary" events also show how increasingly dependent on technology human existence becomes. From such catastrophes and failures, conclusions can and must be drawn for the future, also in the field of cybersecurity.

3.1.2 Do we build dependencies ourselves?

If we look at our reality, we must come to the conclusion that we ourselves are gradually expanding our dependence on technology. We install in our homes and carry with us more and more advanced devices. For example, we use pedometers that count steps, or devices that track our physical activity (the so-called *fitness tracking*), and even health (the so-called *health tech*). Whether we like it or not, we become, and are, increasingly dependent on technology. Also from its manifestations that we do not fully comprehend, and perhaps the society at large is not even aware of their existence.

For example, is there a widespread awareness of the fact of data about us being uploaded to cloud servers, i.e., remote servers in some data centers on the other side of the world, or in a place that is directly difficult for us to identify? Clouds are very useful because they are simply a concentration of servers, a concentration of data. They are effectively managed by specific companies that deal with them and devote resources to that. These are solutions that are meant to be available in a perfect, reliable manner. Always, or almost always available. If the user uploads data there, these data will always be available. At least this is the assumption. Because it is not necessarily always true. A good example would be the Facebook crash in 2021, which had a large impact, caused by a problem with routine maintenance activities that accidentally led to a wide network disconnection.[2] Accidents can happen, also ones that are hard to imagine.

3.1.3 Data center on fire – talking about hard luck!

Although it is believed that such systems – data centers – should be universally reliable, this is not necessarily quite the case in practice. A perfect, albeit extreme, example is a threat of a different kind – a fire in a data center. There is, of course, this risk of equipment burning and thus of data loss. We would want to believe that it is extreme and should be successfully mitigated by properly deployed precautions. But such an event occurred in the OVH data center, in 2021,[3] as a result of which the data center in Strasbourg was completely destroyed. It burned down. Basically, a fire in the server room is something rather extraordinarily rare. A fire as a result of which the entire server room will burn down and data will be lost is even less expected. Therefore, it is probably not a risk often considered by companies, and certainly not by end users (and their data could also be lost in such a situation). Or put it differently: the risk is expected but its mitigation is understood to be well known, and functioning. So, is it, really? Even very unlikely events can happen in practice. Just because the probability of something is very low (even if extremely low) it does not mean that something is impossible. The point of the probability metric is that it is possible, it is just rare. Similarly rare was an issue of a different nature: Google's data center in Europe experiencing a "water intrusion", as happened in 2023.

3.2 YOU HAVE TO PROTECT YOURSELF – IS IT POSSIBLE? HOW DO YOU DO IT?

We emphasize that technologies have not always been built in a safe manner, taking into account cybersecurity or user privacy. However, this has been changing for the better in recent years. Such changes occur at various levels: hardware, software, technological standards and their implementation. These are changes for the better, both quantitatively (there are many changes, they are common, on many levels) and qualitatively (good solutions are built in, better and better practices are applied). It is clearly visible that attention, means, and resources are being devoted to it.

Because the case here is that, unfortunately, there were significant delays created from the very emergence of particular technologies. This is the so-called *technological debt*[4] (here on a historical scale), when problems pile up over time and eventually as a result, a very big problem arises, because it is increasingly difficult to manage such a creation. But if a lot of talented people devote their time to something (here, to the improvement), the situation ameliorates. Certain technological changes can increase cybersecurity on a significant scale. It is similar with privacy or even with handling the risk of disinformation.

The simplest example is the communication encryption: if you build a secure cipher and technical methods of its use, and integrate this solution into, for example, a widely used messenger, information security is significantly improved, on a large scale, and immediately. That is why the implementation of end-to-end encryption was so important, i.e., the method according to which data are encrypted at the point of data transmission and decrypted only at the destination point – no one except the sender and recipient has access to the content; unless one of the parties will share such content or one communication point will be hacked – so end-point security and trust is implied here. This enables hundreds of millions of ordinary users, not necessarily experts, to communicate securely.

At the same time, we are aware that "unbreakable" communication might raise some social or political problems and every now and then various politicians express concerns about the existence of something that is beyond the control of state security services. It's a matter of give and take. Safe and private means of communication should be accessible to people. It can all be reconciled with each other.

3.2.1 Problems also for experts

We note at the very beginning that even experts can have mishaps. Certain solutions may lead to undesirable, unexpected effects.

A particular example is phishing. Even experts can fall victim to a very well-targeted attack, when someone, for example, by impersonating someone else and thus gaining the trust (even of an expert), infects the system.

The second example is systemic. Apple introduced in its Safari web browser an *Intelligent Tracking Prevention*, which was supposed to increase people's privacy by blocking the possibility of tracking them while they were browsing the web using a browser. However, this system was designed in such a way that under certain conditions it could potentially be used for undesirable purposes. Even potentially to track a user or to extract some private data.[5] Could Safari users have done something about it? Unfortunately not. The system, which was intended to improve privacy, in practice, as a result of a design issue, namely the way in which this system interacted with already existing web technologies and standards, introduced unexpected risks. As a result of such weaves of, or interrelations between, the different technologies, there was a risk to user privacy (of course, improvements were made eventually). This example shows that even professionals can make mistakes or omissions. And even technology designed by experts can have vulnerabilities.

3.2.2 Security is the increase in costs for attackers

In general, security (also for ordinary users) can also be thought of as increasing the "necessary" cost of actions of cybercriminals or other actors, introducing the necessity to undertake some additional outlays and resources as a result of taking simple actions by the user or system maintainers. This means that cybercriminals will have to put more work into their actions to breach the security. If we increase the cost of operating for the cybercriminals, it will automatically reduce the chances of falling victim to them. Perhaps they will prefer to choose a different target, perhaps more easily accessible. Because for them it is also a matter of calculation: the cheaper and easier they can achieve something, the better.

And now the question is how to easily increase (improve, grow) cybersecurity (to raise the costs for attackers)? Because it's always worth knowing what you are doing, knowing the basics of the technologies or configurations used, and the selection of settings. After all, it is about the user's data (private, financial, medical), perhaps even direct access to the finances, etc. It may also be about reputation or image (PR), which are very important issues.

3.2.3 Pay attention to what matters

Let's clear up some doubts here. Well, very often attention is paid to risks and threats that are niche, because the probability of their occurrence is low. For example, there is a very small chance that a common user will become a target of Russian Military Intelligence. Why? For practical reasons, for example. Of course, some cyberattacks can be scaled (i.e., prepared in such a way that it will "automatically" work against thousands, even millions of targets), i.e., we can perform a lot of infection attempts at once (as we already talked about in the discussion of phishing), for example, targeting all employees in the company and assuming that at least one will open an infected attachment. However, there is a fairly small chance that a "military"-type solution will be used on a typical user. Such attempts are more likely to be perpetrated by ordinary scammers or cybercriminals.

3.2.3.1 The question of resources and scale

Here we have to emphasize that even intelligence, whether civil or military, has, to some degree, limited resources. And that's apart from the fact that such institutions usually have very specific goals. This means that they have to think and decide where to direct these resources. Let's say directly here that there is a very small chance that the so-called ordinary user will be of interest to such institutions. We do not intend to say that the reader of this book is uninteresting, but rather that perhaps he/she is not of interest to such institutions. Although we do not rule out that there will be readers of this book for whom this risk is or will be real. And in this case, we hope they are aware of it. If not, the very fact of such a lack of knowledge is a problem for cybersecurity.

We have to focus on real threats. Fortunately, risks to cybersecurity can be reduced, although it is difficult to eliminate them completely. As we have already said, even experts can have a mishap or an unfortunate accident. Very unexpected but rare things can also happen in real life. Although here it is worth keeping in mind that an event requiring two extremely unlikely events to happen at the same time is even more unlikely. Considering the two example events so far, the intuitive insight is that the existence of a man wearing a Minister of Defence mask who successfully convinces companies to part with their money is unlikely. It is also unlikely that an entire data center is torched down. So the probability of the man in a minister mask setting such a fire is even smaller. I note the coincidence that the two are related to the same country (France), which probably increases the likelihood, even if just slightly. However, the combined risk of a "man with a minister mask sets up a fire in a data center and it completely burns down" is extremely low, or at least let's hope so. That was an unorthodox, albeit simple, example of red-teaming exercise where a risk was modeled.

3.2.4 Risk modeling

If we want to think about risk, we must mention risk modeling. It consists in identifying the real threats faced by the company, institution or, in the case of this chapter – the user. Risk modeling is just thinking about what could go wrong. What are the chances that something will happen? What are the possible repercussions and will these consequences be serious? Will they be acceptable? Thus, it is about thinking about the likelihood or *impact*.

However, of course, we must emphasize that risk models for ordinary users and certain special users, for example VIPs, the so-called HVT (*high value targets*), for example, some politicians or journalists, businessmen or other people at risk, are completely different issues. Other dangers, other risks. In these cases, of course, specialist risk modeling is needed, because since these are completely different types of threats, they may require or deserve completely different types of security measures.

3.2.5 What are the actual threats to us?

Fortunately, in most cases, maybe we're not "as important"? That would be an advantage, in a way, if only because we, as regular users, could "hide in the crowd" of similarly "less important" figures. That can be an asset.

Let's mention phishing again. It is, as we have already mentioned, a method of inducing the victims, the target, to take actions that are not in their interest, as a result of which they will harm themselves or their organizations. This is a social engineering attack and it can exploit, to some degree, a naiveté of some kind, or ignorance about how technology, such as web browsers, works. It can also take advantage of a specific phenomenon, which comes down to the fact that certain phishing attacks can be more effective in certain specific situations. Everyone should understand, appreciate, and apply this knowledge. Well, if we use a computer or technology, we do it for a purpose. Perhaps we are busy. Perhaps we are doing many things at once. We don't have time and we want to take some actions quickly. Perhaps, under certain circumstances, we will not spend enough (proper) time thinking about our actions and their possible consequences. And **it is in this situation that, as a result of such a rush, we can take an action that will have negative repercussions**. So these are the favorable circumstances for the attackers. Often they try to bring it about themselves, to induce them, implying time pressure, for example, that if we do not take action immediately, something unpleasant will happen.

Phishing can also be targeted. Let's suppose it is an employee of the company. We can figure such a company employee out. We can determine what he/she does, is interested in, who he/she works with, who is his/her supervisor, what his/her family is like. In this way, we can select messages addressed to such a person that might gain the trust of that person. And that person (the target) will then perhaps more easily carry out actions that will be detrimental to him/her. It is especially dangerous when the attack is aimed at directors or other decision makers in the company. In this case, it is worth recalling the BEC variant mentioned in Chapter 2. When the decision makers in the company are the target, it can lead to multimillion losses.[6]

3.3 THE IRON RULES

3.3.1 Technology is for people

Let's start with the fact that we should not be afraid of technology. It is for people. It is not that it is a threat to everything and everyone. Many of the technologies used today are well developed. After all, there are ecosystems within Android or iOS. They are various devices (hardware) connected to the software. These can be devices such as a smartphone, laptop, or a watch, a smartwatch. Their manufacturers have taken the time to ensure the product safety.

Here, therefore, we have a question of how to protect ourselves within such an ecosystem. First of all, it would be necessary to know if the default settings are correct and appropriate for us. Unless we assume this is so. Nowadays, such an assumption can fortunately often be made in relation to self-respecting ecosystems with high levels of security; chances are that if you use hardware or software from some big vendors, the security level is high, and it is being properly monitored. It used to be not so obvious and clear, but the systems have been significantly improved in this regard since then.

However, we must reemphasize that in this chapter, we focus on things over which users have control. And mainly they have control over their own actions. It is obvious that users have no influence on low-level vulnerabilities, their introduction or resolution, as a result of which the operating system could be hacked. They don't create the systems they use, and they don't usually modify them either. We will not expect users to edit (after "disassembly") low-level software components, rebuild the software, etc. Likewise, we do not expect anyone to physically remove a microphone or camera from a newly purchased smartphone. However, such things happen.

3.3.2 Vendors should take care of basic security – the importance of ecosystems

It is recognized that at least the level of cybersecurity is something that operators of respectable ecosystems (Apple, Google, etc.) are responsible for and take seriously. If only because cybersecurity is something that interests just about everyone today – from ordinary users to regulators. After all, new legal regulations are emerging that require the protection of personal data (like the General Data Protection Regulation, the GDPR) or a level of cybersecurity of various types of systems[7] and devices. These are also guarantees for users, but let's leave the legal issues aside here. Let's focus on high-level rules, steps that will increase our level of cybersecurity. Where it is worth it, we will mention technologies.

3.3.3 The risk surface

Let's start with the fact that the basis itself is not very technical, which is very good indeed, because technologies change faster than more general rules. It's about figuring out your own way of using the computer, the internet, or technology in general, to identify risk points. Such an analysis can also be performed for oneself, not only in professional environments. We are talking about the so-called *risk surface*. In short, the point here is that the more risk points we make available for a potential attack, the more the "risk surface", i.e., the "area of vulnerability" that can be attacked, grows. What to equate such a surface with, such risk points? These could be, for example, access points – something that could make a cyber threat come to exist, that a cybercriminal or anyone else would take advantage of. These can be points related to the types of software or systems that we use.

For example, browsing the web with an outdated, non-updated version of the software browser increases the risk. And updating is very simple. Often you can also turn on automatic update setting (if it's not turned on by default) and it is worth doing so, because it is a very simple and quick way to reduce the risk. So why not do it?

Another example follows. If we have a lot of programs installed on a computer or smartphone, it is enough for someone who cares about breaking security in our system to identify only one such entry point, e.g., in one of such programs. Therefore, having many programs/applications, perhaps not updated, can increase the danger. Thus, one way to reduce such risk is to reduce this available risk surface. We need to reduce our potential vulnerability, and this can be done by reducing the chances of using the vulnerability in whatever we use. In this case, this can be done, for example, very easily – by uninstalling programs that we do not use and ensuring that all others have the current version of the software with the latest security patches. Such an exemplary (model) risk surface is defined in Figure 3.1.

In Figure 3.1, we see some general outline of the idea – the surface – related to the hardware and software we use. We want to reduce such a risk surface (and this is what it is about, for such risk to be manageable). For example, we have area A, which will reduce the risk surface after adjusting the configuration, for example, enabling multi-factor authentication. Area B disappears from the risk map because we uninstall unnecessary programs. Area C will disappear after installing software patches. When areas A, B, C are removed from the picture – the risk surface is reduced, decreased. To illustrate the threat, we left area D where, unfortunately, a vulnerability was found in the system or software that we use, and someone wants to use it against us. But what we had control over, we did right. And that's what it's all about.

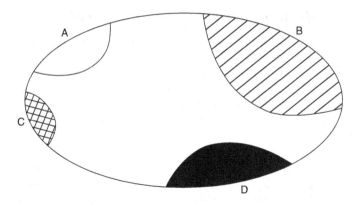

Figure 3.1 Sample risk surface – model.

Source: Author-generated.

3.3.3.1 Mapping the ways of use

The ways of using the computer, smartphone, hardware, and software in general by the user can also be written on a piece of paper or in some program, identifying the ways of using the technology.

We then check:

- the process of browsing the web, i.e., websites, as well as the methods in use, whether in a given case we use, for example, one or another web browser, this or that browser extension;
- what applications we use to watch movies, where do we get these movies from;
- what graphics programs we use, where do we get graphics from;
- do we use the computer on a mobile basis, on the go, and if so, do we have a lock screen that locks the screen after a certain period of inactivity (which would be one of the security methods);
- do we often leave the computer without the possibility of looking at it, or do we do it in a public place (e.g., when going to the toilet in a cafe);
- do we connect external storage devices (pendrive) or other peripherals, like a microphone, or USB-connected lava lamp – not a joke, as at one point demonstrated by a Google researcher as one way of taking over the control of a computer;
- do we install programs of unknown origin; do we even know what the unknown origin is (e.g., applications from outside the application store; for example, we used a "jailbreak" on our smartphone to install programs in a nonstandard way, which could significantly reduce the level of security).

When we understand how we use hardware and software and what we use them for, it will help to choose the appropriate security measures in an informed manner.

3.3.3.2 *Identification of risk points and a selection of solutions*

When identifying risk points, we select measures to prevent them (or: mitigate the risk).

For example, the way to secure the web browsing may be to keep the software up-to-date: operating system, browser, possibly installed extensions that increase privacy and reduce the risk that some malicious script will be delivered and executed (in 2009–2023, such extensions were, e.g., NoScript or Adblock Plus).

Another example would be the use of electronic banking. It is good to be aware of the risks associated with this form of banking in general. Some of them can be reduced by using a dedicated web browser to connect to the electronic banking system or only do this via an application installed on a trusted smartphone; and necessarily with the use of multi-factor authentication, i.e., not only with a password.

Luckily today, legal regulations help in applying authentication methods.

3.3.3.3 *Legal requirements to the rescue?*

An important point should be made here immediately. Current European regulations offer a good example by requiring multi-factor authentication in electronic banking, which is a very clear example of the fact that cybersecurity regulations increasingly keep pace with actual and real technical challenges. It is a requirement resulting from Art. 4 sec. 1 of Delegated Regulation 2018/389.[8] It reads as follows: "*Where payment service providers apply strong customer authentication in accordance with Article 97(1) of Directive (EU) 2015/2366, the authentication shall be based on two or more elements which are categorised as knowledge, possession and inherence*".

Sounds enigmatic? Perhaps, but this is an order for our bank to force us to use two-factor authentication, for example, a PIN and tokens – codes (e.g., sent via SMS).

What does the transfer of these technical standards into the area of legal requirements mean? This means that they will stay with us. It will only get safer in this area. In this case, the security philosophy has been inscribed in a hardcoded (but flexible) way in the legal requirements. Other legal systems will follow.

3.3.4 Up-to-date software

To reduce the risk, we must have an up-to-date operating system and software, especially the web browser (browsers are more and more such an "operating system"). If only because it often happens that a security vulnerability will be identified that can be exploited by various interest groups and groups interested in exploiting vulnerabilities, breaking security, hacking.

By updating the operating system when such a patch is released, we automatically patch the vulnerability. We remedy the attack. We generally reduce the risk. Of course, it will disrupt our work, some things will have to be temporarily suspended, ended, saved. But it's probably worth it, as it is a direct risk reduction. If an activity that takes seconds or minutes significantly improves real security issues, then, according to any (i.e., whatever) method of risk analysis, it makes no sense to think about it. Just do it.

3.3.5 The principle of limited trust in what appears on the screen

Another rule is to not always trust what appears on the screen. Or at least what we may conclude on the first appearance of things. Here I am referring to phishing again. Do we check where the SMS/text is coming from? Are we sure the sender really is our bank? We shouldn't always believe what is written in e-mails or messages on instant messaging. Even if the sender of the e-mail introduces himself/herself, because for years it was possible to impersonate someone quite easily and we can still freely select our first and last name, what others will see as the sender field of the message. Similarly, in social media, it's worth not to be naive. The fact that someone changes their description, name, and photo does not mean that it is actually an account of a given person, for example, a politician or a journalist. Many people fell for such seemingly simple fakes. In this case, probably also because people simply wanted to believe that it was true (which is why this method of disinformation is effective).

We emphasize once again that it is worthwhile to approach communication calmly. Often, there is no rush. Really. Again, anyone can introduce themselves with any first and last name. They can create an e-mail that is deceptively similar to a real e-mail, with appropriate signatures and logos. Sometimes they can even use the real one if they obtain unauthorized access to it, for example, after a break-in, a breach, a compromise. Although this happens in rather less common situations, when correspondingly more resources are devoted to hacking the target (or if someone provided login details, e.g., on a fake phishing site, which happens to politicians, analysts, and journalists).

And here again I must refer to the fact that the technologies being developed can also be used for evil purposes. Well, when browsing websites, certain windows sometimes do open. Some legitimate ones may ask for permission to display "notifications", but others could also display a message like: "A *virus has been identified on your computer. Click here to install something that will fix this problem*". Of course, if you think about it for a moment, it is almost impossible for such a website – without any other permissions that the user would have given directly and consciously – to scan files or programs installed locally on the computer. So such things should not be believed! However, according to the economies of scale, it can be assumed that someone will fall for it. If tens of thousands of people see this message, maybe one will take the bait. Maybe that is sufficient for the actors involved.

3.3.6 Verifying communication

Another point that relates to the previously discussed phishing and not to trust everything we see on the screen is the need to verify contacts. Especially when the stakes are high, when something important or potentially important is happening. For example, when we receive a message via messenger or e-mail, and in the message someone introduces himself/herself as our friend, a family member, but maybe also someone from outside of our close circle, for example, a public figure (a minister, a senator, a famous singer) and tries to convince us to make a financial decision, i.e., to transfer some funds to someone else's account. For example, he/she presents a story about how something happened that, of course, did not actually happen. That money is needed for some "legitimate" purpose. Perhaps he/she points out that it is important to act immediately (time pressure). It is worth trying to contact such a person through a different channel (excluding ministers or famous singers, which you might be unable to reach! But then it maybe worth to be careful anyway, how come they did contact you in the first place if you do not know each other?), for example, by calling them. It is important not to use a simple call back function at this point (if someone called us) – but to enter the number manually or select a contact from the address book.

3.3.7 Passwords

Passwords are still something crucial for security, despite the fact that we can increasingly, for example, unlock a smartphone using face recognition or fingerprint scanning, or we can log in using codes that we get on our devices. Passwords are still important, and we will use them for the foreseeable future.[9] This is for many reasons. Mainly because they are versatile and offer something other methods do not in proper ways – for example, that they are easy to implement (all other password replacement technologies are more difficult to implement in practice). Although the mass implementation of biometrics in smartphones, and perhaps even the smartphones themselves as "trusted devices" receiving codes, may change this situation. Nevertheless, passwords also mean very good usability (you know how to use them, how to implement them reliably, etc.), and when properly used, they also offer quite an acceptable level of security,[10] greatly enhanced by the use of password managers, which solves the problem of having multiple passwords for multiple websites.

3.3.7.1 Good passwords

Since passwords remain a very important method of securing systems, accounts, and devices, standards for their creation are important. It has long been said that a good password is one that has a certain number of characters and different types of characters (alphanumeric, special, and case-sensitive). So it should consist of letters, numbers, and special characters. It was also said that it is necessary to change it frequently. But today we know better. Some of this advice is inappropriate today, and other is downright harmful. Neither was it based on experience, nor certainly not on how password-protected accounts are used in practice in modern times. Such advice was very often spread by various kinds of experts and luminaries, also during training sessions. Nobody questioned them; nobody asked what they resulted from and why they should be good.

They seem to have their origin in some, from today's perspective, unclear sources, or at least by today's standards, pretty obscure ones. In military recommendations from the 1980s and even 1970s, contained in, for example, textbooks[11] of the U.S. Air Force. We find a similar indication, for example, in the 1984 publications. While it emphasizes the need to ensure that the entire process is user-friendly, it recommends routine, frequent password changes.[12] The 1977 US National Institute of Standards and Technology manual describes what the password should look like and that, of course, we need to change it frequently. If someone wants to read advice on what to do and what not to do, then the old U.S. Air Force recommendation from 1998 is such a classic textbook.[13]

Such recommendations perhaps somehow suited those times and realities, situations, environments. But was there any point in keeping them in force longer, even today? Unfortunately, as it usually happens, they became popular, and their military provenance helped with that (you know, intuitively, the military, they must know about security, right?). The public and experts have readily accepted at face value that if something is recommended by the military, it must be good advice on security issues (perhaps in those times and circumstances, we could have thought of it that way, but we live in the 2020s, not in the 1980s). So they were passed on and repeated automatically. Like a mantra. However, these principles do not necessarily have such an importance, validity, today. This is for many reasons.

First, we have different authentication methods, such as multi-factor authentication;[14] passwords remain valid, but without entering the second component (e.g., a token – a code received via SMS, a fingerprint, etc.), we will not be able to access the system.

Secondly, it is not necessarily easy to crack a password, because even if the database of hashed passwords is leaked, i.e., passwords processed with a one-way hash function (scrypt, Argon2id, PBKDF2, etc.) or a construct based on a hash function (e.g., SHA3), i.e., a function, which is easy to calculate but difficult to reverse, having the result of this function's calculation on the input data, it is very difficult to get its output – in our case the password. For example, for the password "cat" (very weak), the result of applying the Argon2id function is 2137bda0d2bd359d06ec817471f1b195.[15]

In the event of a password database leak, a *brute-force* attack could be made, which consists in checking all possible input possibilities to verify if any match the output data – the passwords, in this case. In the case of the *dictionary* attack, where we have a dictionary of words, as in the case of *brute-force* attack, we examine all these words (and their modifications, for example, combinations of words and numbers), hoping that one will match the result of the calculation. Then the corresponding input (what we are trying to compute, what leaked) would be the searched password. However, we can reduce the risk of such an attack, for example by using the password system design in such a way that we would have to compute the value of this one-way hash function for each password, say 500,000 times, or more, and using one-way hash functions, which are difficult to compute in parallel even on some of the specially designed hardware devices (ASIC, FPGA), because a certain amount of hardware memory is required to calculate the hash. This is one of the reasons and one of the methods of constructing passwords resistant to breaking in the case of leakage of the hash password database.

3.3.7.2 Breaking passwords is not that easy!

Remote password cracking, when using our local computer, we try to crack the password to the e-mail box by entering passwords on the login page one by one, is practically impossible today (unless the password is a simple word, really easy to guess). Hundreds of thousands or millions of tested password attempts are often needed. But in practice, it is not possible to make hundreds of thousands or millions of login attempts to a system such as an e-mail account, because such a remote system will detect these unauthorized access attempts, i.e., hundreds or thousands of login attempts ended with a wrong password, unsuccessful authentication attempts in a short timeframe. And it will take some actions, for example, block the possibility of logging in, and if the attempts are persistent, it may even inform the law enforcement authorities (i.e., police). So breaking passwords in this way is extremely difficult, if not impossible, in practice.

Now imagine that in a short period of time (e.g., one minute) you can only make 10 password attempts, and you need to test a million passwords for the attempts to be successful. Such an attempt would then take about 70 days. It is much more likely that access will be blocked or that such an attacker will get bored sooner (because it's a rather poor investment of time). It is better to try to take over accounts in a different way, if someone really cares.

3.3.7.3 We don't change good passwords (unless there are good reasons for it)

It is not worth trying to force frequent password changes. Why? There are plenty of reasons for this. This causes users to pick weak passwords, in the first place. If, as a user, I know that I will have to change my password in a month, or in several months, why bother investing in creating a good password and memorizing it? The following passwords are the stuff of legend: <word><year>. For example, "Cafe2023", and the password ending (trailing number) implicitly should change over the years, right? Meanwhile, you can often find passwords in which this year is already quite distant, such as "Cafe2017". I'm not kidding. Honestly, this is not a big problem for a cafe – it makes this password available to all visitors anyway, and the password is often displayed somewhere.

We may assume that users, knowing that they will have to change their password, will not want to spend much (or any) mental effort to remember something difficult, a difficult phrase, understood as a "good" password. Reasoning along these lines, it might be seen as much better to come up with some password, and change its ending, for example, in some ways. For example, to have the password "figohz8Zee", which after some time can be changed to "figohz8Zee_1", "figohz8Zee_2", etc. If there is no reason to believe that our password could have been taken over by an unauthorized person, it is worth doing so.

The idea behind the requirement for a frequent password change is, for example, to curb the potential unauthorized access to the systems, should the password be intercepted in any way, potentially, hypothetically. It's a "just in case". However, this means that we have here an assumption that an unauthorized person may already have someone else's password. Even for several months, which is unreasonable nowadays. This, along with the aficionados of frequent-password-change logic would imply that we may have even allowed such unauthorized access to the systems for several months. Is it reasonable? This is unacceptable today – unauthorized access has to be detected faster. At the same time, according to the Mandiant report from 2022, in 2021 the average time of detecting being hacked (i.e., from the moment of unauthorized access to the organization's system to detection) was about 21 days. This time is shortening. But this is still less than the typical "useful life" of a password, after which time a sad message pops up that you need to change it. As we said, just add another number to the end of a well-chosen password and forget about it. Unless there is really a good reason to believe that the password has actually been compromised – then it needs to be changed. Or unless in these specific settings password changes are really justified. I mean – really justified by something reasonable.

The final argument is the new recommendation of the American NIST, based on knowledge and research. It instructs as follows: *"[Password] Verifiers SHOULD NOT require memorized secrets to be changed arbitrarily (e.g., periodically). However, verifiers SHALL force a change if there is evidence of compromise of the authenticator"*.[16] So the requirement to change passwords is phased out. It's out. Unless there are indications that the security of the system has been compromised.

These recommendations are slowly being implemented by various vendors, such as Microsoft:

> Recent scientific research calls into question the value of many long-standing password-security practices such as password expiration policies [...], If a password is never stolen, there's no need to expire it.

And if you have evidence that a password has been stolen, you would presumably act immediately rather than wait for expiration to fix the problem. [...] Further, if your users are the kind who are willing to answer surveys in the parking lot that exchange a candy bar for their passwords, no password expiration policy will help you.[17]

It will certainly take some time to adapt and comply with the new recommendations (the previous ones were in force for over 30 years) before those earlier years of antiquated practices are uprooted and wiped out. Eventually, however, it will happen. The new recommendations will simply be repeated, implemented gradually. Perhaps as automatically and thoughtlessly as the previous ones, perhaps by the same people, even. Although some will probably have to bend over backward, giving advice that's quite the opposite of what they preached before.

It is also worth noting that since 2022, the European Personal Data Protection Authorities have started to strictly enforce recommendations for strong passwords. The French data protection authority imposed GDPR financial penalties (fines) in France on a couple of companies for the breach of good practice regarding password systems. In one case, a technical inadequacy has been identified in the design that accepted weak passwords (of length of six characters; in 2022, inadequate by any standard).[18] In another, a data protection infringement was found in the use of an obsolete hashing function MD5,[19] and that the password hashes were not "salted".[20] Such enforcement of the law significantly speeds up the migration in the companies to good, safe standards. Of course, this is not performed by the user but it definitely improves their safety.

3.3.7.4 *Good passwords are long passwords*

Even a password consisting of many different characters (e.g., an eight-character password, today) will unfortunately be cracked rather very easily and quickly. To solve this problem, the systems must include detection capabilities (to detect cracking attempts, or password breach). But you also have to create passwords in a certain way. First of all, one such good approach is adhering to the principle that it is better to have a long password than one consisting of many random numbers, digits, characters, symbols. In this case, length matters. But how do you remember such a long password?

3.3.7.5 *Passphrases – Diceware*

This is where passphrases, and the Diceware method, comes into play.[21] It's a way of creating passwords consisting of different words. It's easy! To create a "*passphrase*", simply combine the selected words into one string of characters, perhaps without spaces. To further strengthen such a password, each word included in the sequence of characters created in this way will start with, for example, a capital letter (so both lowercase and uppercase letters will be used). Perhaps we'll also put in a number (so the checkbox for the need of alphanumeric characters is ticked in the case of overzealous password strength meters) in there somewhere. This way of creating passwords makes the password very strong and, additionally, easy to remember. This is precisely because there are a few words here. At some point, it is very easy to remember these words one by one, i.e., the entire combination. We will simply memorize them. The key here is how to properly choose these words. They should be chosen randomly and not in a pseudo-random or machine manner.

How to choose such a good password (passphrase)? It's best to have a long list of words and roll the dice. For example, if we have 10,000 words, each of them will start with a certain number (you can create a dictionary yourself or use ready-made ones[22]). Roll the dice several times, each roll corresponds to a digit in such a number, uniquely identifying a given word. Do this several times and choose five or six words, for example. Therefore, such a password can have a dozen or even several dozen characters and will be very difficult to break, and after a relatively short time – it will be really easy to remember.

For example, by throwing the dice several times, I drew six words: attest, bubble, jogger, devil, breeze, officer. By combining these words into one string, I obtained "AttestBubbleJoggerDevilBreezeOfficer" (note the capitalizations of each word component). Certainly, this sequence of words is much more random than words chosen "by hand" by a person. And that's the point.

The main rules for creating passwords are:

- They should be easy to remember.
- They should be difficult to guess.
- They should be long.

Diceware meets both of these points optimally. What's with the breaking speed? Assuming the ability to test 10 billion passwords per second,

- a simple password in the form of "*aaaaaa*" (six identical characters) will be cracked in less than a second,
- cracking the much better password "peiNu6pa" takes... also less than a second,
- a good 12-character password "Aebaik0lah9O" takes less than a minute,
- it will take two hours to break "AttestBubbleJogger".

But breaking "AttestBubbleJoggerDevilBreezeOfficer" will take ages (which can be shortened a bit if it is known that Diceware was the generation method used). So we have an easy to remember and secure password. Could it be even better? Sure thing. Let's replace the letters "o" with zeros to get "AttestBubbleJ0ggerDevilBreeze0fficer".

But, why does it work? Why is it easy to remember a long password that consists of many words? It is a psychological *chunking* effect, where several pieces of information are combined into one whole.[23] Thanks to this effect, a person is able to remember a good and long password.[24] So in summary, the password strength is guaranteed by theory and practice; the memorization is guaranteed by psychology. This means that the scheme is very solid when it comes to scientific rationale.

3.3.8 Storing passwords

If we already have a good password, how do we store it, how to use it? The sad truth is that we may have to have several, even several dozen accounts, and many passwords for them (in the extreme case: a different password in each case, if we do not use federated authentication systems, i.e., we do not use passwords for Google, Facebook, etc., to log into different systems with these accounts). The same password must not be used on different websites; it would be similar to passing the password to service X to someone else, i.e., service Y. It is strongly advised against sharing your passwords with others! Reusing passwords means exactly this: sharing your password with another party.

So it is important how to manage such a password list. Password managers are used for this purpose. These are password management systems, very helpful solutions that identify logins and passwords and tie them to the systems (e.g., websites) where we log in. When we enter the website, the login/username and password are automatically filled in. This is very helpful as it means we don't have to remember passwords, so they can be good and strong (remembering dozens of strong passwords would be a big challenge).

It's also helpful if someone tries to approach us using phishing and e-mail prompts: "*click here, this is your typical system where you usually log in*" (e.g., for e-banking), says the message. When we click, the mechanical system, the password manager machine, will not recognize such a page (which to a human may appear confusingly similar/identical to the real one, in appearance and its address may also be almost identical). The machine will not be fooled. It will consider such a bogus site as unknown and will not automatically fill in the user/password field. For us, this will be a warning that something is abnormal: it is worth taking a moment to understand what is happening. Since we do not know our password by heart (or by mind), we will not enter it manually and we may be saved in this way. So for security, it's better not to remember passwords. If we do not have them memorized, the risk that we will give them to the phishing site without reflection – this risk decreases.

Of course, instead of using a password manager, we can jot them down in a physical notebook. It cannot be hacked remotely as it is in a paper format. However, there is a local risk here, i.e., whether we trust the people from our immediate vicinity or people who may come to visit us, for various reasons. If an unknown person gains physical access to our equipment or documents, this could possibly be a bigger problem than losing our forum login password. So as always, the methods must be adapted to the way we use the computer and to our own lives in general.

We talked about the fact that the level of system and software security is gradually increasing. The progress is that when logging into web systems (e.g., with the Safari web browser), browsers may suggest a randomly generated password. This password can also be remembered in our keychain/browser/system/password manager, making it easy to use in the future. It is, therefore, the integration of password generation with the password manager in a systemic way. This is another way in which the technology is moving forward while increasing the level of cybersecurity. This improvement happens before our eyes. Such systems did not function in such ways, say, in 2012. Now we take them for granted.

3.3.9 Two- or multi-factor authentication

Multi-factor authentication (MFA)[25] takes place when after we enter a password, we need to enter some code. This code may be generated by a device, for example a hardware token generator, by a program. This code can be sent to us via SMS. There is a controversy over how much this actually increases cybersecurity, and attacks on the latter are indeed possible; phishing techniques can also target this element.[26] However, it is recognized that multi-factor authentication increases cybersecurity, if only because today it is difficult to adapt certain types of phishing to two-factor authentication. Using it reduces the effectiveness of conventional phishing to zero. However, not everyone is convinced, and some experts even admit that multi-factor authentication (e.g., two-factor authentication with SMS tokens) does not increase security,[27] and it is only a "trick" that does not fundamentally change security parameters.

However, it is worth noting that accessibility is also one of the important parameters of cybersecurity. It so happens that if we lose (or forget) our password, it is easier to regain access to our account using the "password reset" function. That's not much? And yet, it's not nice to lose access to our account. Occasionally, threat monitoring and prediction functions are also in use. That is, the systems automatically learn how we use the accounts: where we log in from, at what times, etc. If, for example, we traveled to a country from which we usually do not log in, such an anomaly detection system could block the access. How to unlock it? For example, with a code received via SMS (or an installed application). Alternatively, we can rely on a friend who happens to work at the right place in such a company, and on that that this friend will be kind enough to ping someone internally about the issue. But this is not a universal solution we should rely on. We could, of course, also be a very famous person, for example the president of the USA or other high-ranking official. Again, this is not a universal solution. For the typical user, the MFA for the password reset might work much better.

3.3.9.1 Toward passwordless systems

Many researchers, experts, specialists, and companies have been working for many years to increase account security. In practice, this work is devoted to verification (authentication, login process, etc.) and vulnerability identification. However, since it is known that the login and password process is a problematic and risky area, solutions and improvements are sought. Technical web standards have been developed for a long time to support this process,[28] with support for various types of login components (passwords, PIN codes, biometrics, etc.). This is also why companies responsible for digital ecosystems (Apple/iOS, Google/Android, Microsoft/Windows) are working on system solutions, and this is why in 2022 they established cooperation for this purpose.[29] To some extent, "passwordless" authentication solutions are already available on devices (laptops, smartphones, etc.). There will be more of this and to a greater extent. The result will be greater security for users. This is the way toward technology with a limited use of passwords, and therefore less chances for users to make mistakes, and a reduced risk that something will go wrong and someone steals the password or takes over the login method. As such systems are supported by technological standards (W3C), and there is an agreement as to their implementation by large digital ecosystems, the expected effect will be universal availability for users. This is the best way to systematically increase the level of security for everyone and at once. Moreover, there is no requirement for complicated actions to be taken by the user. There is technical support for a certain solution built in and we can simply use it. This is the best way to increase security on a large scale. After all, a lot also depends on how users behave.

A certain culmination of this work at the end of 2022 was the implementation of the Passkeys solution. They work on many devices; they are supported, for example, by Apple[30] or Google,[31] on computers and mobile systems. The process of using this password replacement is related to unlocking the device we have (e.g., smartphone), which allows logging in to the service or website. This provides a high level of "ease" and convenience for the user, and is also safe and secure. And it is impossible to steal such a "way" of logging in, which is possible, for example, in the case of a password. It's a transformational, evolutionary solution. It will lead to increased security and reduced misuse. In 2022, a kind of big, qualitative change took place. By 2032, the improvement will be huge, and difficult to comprehend in 2023.

3.3.10 Paranoia

Some people in the cybersecurity industry have a mindset called a *professional paranoia*.[32] It consists in, approximately, seeing or finding threats everywhere, perhaps also always. This may come in handy sometimes, as it increases the chance that we will see a risk point, but in the long run it is not necessarily always good and advisable for us to have it always on. Paranoia makes us see or search for a problem everywhere; it takes away the joy of life, and can even be personally harmful. It is associated with a certain mental overhead, due to the fact that, after all, we are always, constantly, everywhere thinking about threats, risks, i.e., about work. It is tiring. Paranoia may be useful for some people working professionally in this area (especially if they can turn this approach on and off), but it may not be of much use to users.

3.3.11 Up-to-date knowledge

Returning to the technical issues, it should be emphasized how important the software configuration is. First of all, it is important to know the software we are using. We have already talked about the importance of software updates and that if we do not use and do not need some programs, it is worth simply removing them. Furthermore, it is worth knowing the security or privacy settings of programs or systems that we use on a daily basis, including their capabilities and limitations, and adapt them to our own needs. We will not list the possible settings of individual programs or systems here, because it does not make sense. There are many of them. They often change. They differ among the various ecosystems. Everyone has to do it on their own; there are no shortcuts here, although of course we can read specialist descriptions, documentation, guidebooks of the ecosystems used, if only they are up to date. Reading documents older than a few years may make little sense. This is good advice precisely because technologies and programs change, and so the scope of your cybersecurity and privacy settings will also change.

Can we trust something we don't understand? Here it is also worth paying attention to legal or organizational issues. For example, privacy policies and regulations that often have to be accepted. To work, an activity tracker must of course send data via the internet, to remote analytical servers. This may happen through communication with a specialized smartphone application. The question then arises, what are the security and privacy standards offered when processing such data? These are important issues because it is about user guarantees. Due to the application of the GDPR, especially users in Europe may have high expectations here. These are issues, for example, relating to the regulation and protection of personal data, to privacy.

Once I wanted to test a system that I received as a gift. It was a fitness tracking armband. While looking for the privacy rules of such a smartphone application, I clicked on the privacy policy on the provider's website. I wanted to read it. However, it turned out that the privacy policy was only available in Chinese, a language which I don't know. Perhaps more users found themselves in this situation. What did they do? Since I do not know Chinese, I cannot read what are the security or privacy guarantees for the processed data. In this case, it would be better not to use such a system. If the guarantees are enigmatic, unclear, vague – this is a signal to avoid those systems or products. If nowadays you cannot read an understandable privacy policy, it is worth turning on the distrust mode toward such a solution, such an application or such a device. Sometimes similar gems could be found on the occasion of various types of "instant messengers" that wanted to position themselves as trustworthy. Here, a large dose of skepticism is necessary, especially if such companies engage in aggressive marketing without justification and without any grounds. Ultimately, for the armband, I returned it to the person who gave it to me as a gift. It would be a shame to have even more electro-junk at my house. So it turned out not to be a good gift in the end, but the person giving it could not be aware of the complexity of the situation.

3.3.12 Web browser

The Web browser is basically a key program today. You can use it every day, not only on a computer, but also on a smartphone. There are different web browsers. Let us use it, but let us apply the principle of limited trust.

3.3.12.1 Use different browsers

It is worth using different browsers for different things. This is *assigning* programs to certain specific functions and generally sharing the risk between different browsers. You can imagine that different programs have different vulnerabilities, security bugs, but the problem here is something else. It is more about minimizing the risk of mistakes. Let's say, while logged in to some sensitive system, we enter another website. Meanwhile, someone used a security vulnerability in the browser, as a result of which the browser will load another page on which we are logged in, for example, in another tab of the same browser, in an embedded frame (iframe, HTML element), and it will try to read the content from that completely different page opened in a different browser tab. Such attacks, leading to all sorts of data leaks, have happened in the past. Therefore, bugs in web browsers are constantly being patched.

As a curiosity, I am going to mention the case I was examining, as a result of which it was possible to detect the content of external websites by abusing the light sensor.[33] As part of the possible methods of use, it was also possible to display the content of the outer frame pixel by pixel on the screen of a smartphone or computer.[34] This was related to the emission of light of different intensity. This light was read by the device's light sensor, and thus any attacking party could potentially gain access to the data of a completely different party. This broke the basic principle of web security that such communication between different websites must be impossible (otherwise there will be chaos and the possibility of abuse), the so-called same-origin policy.[35] This particular bug has been fixed, but there are bound to be others of a similar nature with similar effects. This is the experience of the last 20 years and it is worth bearing in mind.

Such risks can be minimized. For example, by following the rule that in a specific and only this particular web browser we will log into certain accounts, for example bank accounts. And in others – "for everyday use" – we won't do it. Never. But then remember: do not use this browser selected for "sensitive applications" for anything else.

3.3.13 Different risks to different "drawers" (or "pigeon holes")

This is related to the concept of risk compartmentalization,[36] which in this case can be done manually. The idea is to divide and assign information access and risk into different zones. We can imagine that we put some of our interests and goals into all kinds of boxes. There is a proverb not to put all our eggs in one basket. Here we have a similar and analogous problem in a way. Such a digital basket of eggs. If we lose security control over a "basket", we lose all this valuable content: data, information, etc.

This is about risk division that can be done as explained before, for example with regard to browsers and how to use them. Likewise, we can have multiple e-mail addresses for different things. For example, one e-mail, with which we will always log into various websites that for some reason require us to register, but we do not want to provide our real data there. This will reduce the number of unsolicited e-mails we will receive. If, as a result of future actions, we lose access to our mailbox or someone takes over this access, we will potentially lose the ability to use various websites and systems in which we logged in using it (but then only some of them). Although if we have multi-factor authentication enabled, it is possible that we will not lose access to any. This too is spreading the risk with regard to authentication across multiple "channels" (passwords, tokens, biometrics, etc.). So it's a general rule to have "a few different things" that will be applied to something.

3.3.14 Safe e-mail

Let's start with the basics, i.e., how we use e-mail. Historically, this has been done in such a way that an e-mail client was installed on the computer. It was configurable and the program allowed access to the e-mail box. In such a situation, it is obvious that we need to learn about the configuration options and adapt them to our own needs. For example, this might be installing an extension that will allow us to send and receive encrypted messages. A long time ago, it was also necessary to mark that the communication itself was encrypted (using SSL/TLS), but today we have to consider it as a standard. And here, too, it is obvious that it is always worth updating such a program. There may be security and even privacy bugs in such programs, too.

3.3.14.1 Webmail

Nowadays, however, we often use e-mail from within the web browser by connecting to a webmail website, such as Gmail or another provider. It is a good and safe solution. It is certainly convenient and probably even safer than using the program (developer focus is constantly being carried out on web browsers, perhaps less time is spent on e-mail client programs, which allow the content to be displayed using the "engine" of the web browser, anyway – and thus exposes a risk surface of own program, and web browser).

We are often logged in to this e-mail all the time, even to several at once. However, it is a good idea to make a decision never to log into such an e-mail on computers that we do not control, or to avoid it. Because who knows, maybe there is some program there that logs everything we write and in this case it would log our password. Or maybe there would even be a program that directly monitors everything that is happening on the computer? Subsequently, later on it can be reviewed – what actions were taken, what content was read. How we use the computer should depend on whether it is ours, or our friend's or even enemy's, whether it is in a publicly accessible place (e.g., a library, shop) or we received it from our employer. If it is not our hardware, we cannot be sure what happens to the information typed on it. It must be recognized that anything entered in such a device could have been taken over by someone. And it is certainly better not to log into sensitive accounts from equipment that we do not control. We log into such accounts only from our own equipment, even from a smartphone, which is basically a standard today. But the point is that it should be *our own equipment*! Of course, we don't share passwords, even potentially, with anyone else. Even assistants, employers, bosses (unless it's some professional application). It's just the repetition of the rule not to share passwords with others. This also applies to equipment that does not belong to us.

3.3.14.2 Is big safer?

With regard to Gmail, it is also worth realizing what happens when a cybercriminal or cyber-intelligence group attacks people who have e-mail accounts, or the e-mail operator itself, i.e., servers (not individual users, but servers, the service provider). Here, Gmail and other similar large-scale email service providers have a distinct advantage over smaller providers. This is because they devote a lot of resources to ensuring a high standard of security. Such a large supplier, say Google, has a lot of resources to hire good cybersecurity and information security people, to have resources, solutions, and technologies. Having large funds for software, hardware, and people, it devotes them to keep track of threats, actively search for them, fight them, and disclose them. An ordinary user or a small or medium-sized supplier (and even some state or government structures) do not have such means and capabilities. So automatically the security level is higher when using the e-mail service from such providers.

Nowadays, it happens that the "exemplary" Russian military intelligence or intelligence services of other countries, or other cybercriminals, attack e-mail users, starting with phishing attempts. Since Google has a specialized team that tracks such threats, it can work with the Gmail team to inform such users, who become the targets. This can be very helpful, because the user will receive information that a very serious group is interested in breaking their security and threatening the security of such a person. This can and should give someone a lot to think about. In 2022, Apple started doing something similar: inform users about the possibility of being targeted by resourceful attackers. Teams of large companies also publish cyclical reports on threats. It is an invaluable resource for researchers and cybersecurity specialists.

3.3.15 Instant messaging

We should move from safe e-mail to instant messaging. Because nowadays, its use is a standard and is often a safer form of communication than e-mail.

We use various messengers: WhatsApp, Signal, Facebook Messenger, Instagram, Snap, Telegram, Skype. The question is: which one is the safest? The answer is that it depends on what this messenger is used for, how it is used, who uses it, and with whom they communicate.

The basic rule is that you use the safest and best messenger that the other party you talk to also uses. Because that is the basic assumption here: the other party must be able to communicate with us. This is the common denominator, and yet it is often difficult to convince the other person to switch to a better, safer communicator. Because maybe they do not see the point, because they do not want to, etc. In this respect, some people are limited, for example, by their own needs and interests. There is no point in arguing with it, because ultimately it is about being able to communicate. That's the goal, isn't it? So keep it real.

3.3.15.1 Encryption

End-to-end encryption is a good standard of a communication protocol today,[37] i.e., a model in which communication is encrypted locally on the system, on a smartphone or on a user's computer, and decrypted at the end point, at the recipient. Thus, there is no decryption in any middleware system. In such a system designed in this way, there is basically no technical possibility of eavesdropping on someone (unless someone devotes time and resources to somehow build it in, for example, by implementing the so-called ghost protocol). It wasn't always like that. In the past, systems operated in such a way that it was possible to decrypt data at some transmission point. It was, therefore, possible to turn on eavesdropping, for example in a mobile phone. Today, it is no longer possible, which is not to the liking of some security and counterintelligence services – these would like to retain the possibility of eavesdropping.[38]

In order to break the security of such a system, we need to attack the point of such a conversation, i.e., hack the device of one of the interlocutors. It is possible, but the risk of eavesdropping is significantly reduced due to the fact that such attacks do not scale, because we have to target specific users.

The privacy of communication is, therefore, much better, as it is not possible to perform extensive and common surveillance, supervision, or monitoring. As I mentioned, some secret services do not necessarily like that, and very often indicate that there should be some insight, some "view" into such communication. In countries where we have the rule of law and judicial supervision, consent to such surveillance is issued by the court on the basis of certain conditions. It can be about fighting against a serious crime, for example, child safety is often emphasized. The protection of state security may also be at a stake.

So, do we build in a deliberate backdoor that allows undermining security guarantees and view communications? This is a sensitive and very controversial issue. The argument is often raised that if such a secure end-to-end encryption system is deliberately weakened, there will be a risk of introducing security bugs that could be used in other situations, not only in those where for various reasons enabling access to communication would be considered.

The arguments vary. The basic one is that although we have been devoting time, attention, and resources to building systems and building cybersecurity for several decades, we still do not know how to build a 100% safe system. Moreover, if a software provider with a global reach introduces such a "weakening" in, for example, Europe, the United Kingdom or the USA, arguments are raised about the existence of independent judicial systems in these places, the rule of law, etc. But what if the same system will be used like this in less democratic, slightly more authoritarian, perhaps totalitarian places? These are very difficult decisions. It seems that cybersecurity and privacy should be prioritized. If only because law enforcement has always had to deal with tracking and evidence issues. The fact that smartphones and instant messengers have become, in a way, the center of our lives (we have very sensitive data there) is a kind of novelty. It is unclear whether access to all this information would be proportionate, i.e., that the interference with privacy would be limited and proportionate with respect to the possible offense.

3.3.16 Social media

As the name suggests, social media allows for contacting and interacting with many different people. They are very useful tools and helpful in maintaining contact and, more broadly, in communication. However, it is worth bearing in mind that it is not always a good idea to post very private, sensitive, ill-considered content there. If we really have to or have reasons to post it there, we should target it to specific groups – it is possible to define certain groups of recipients, for example on Facebook. For example, if we want to inform our family that we will not be at home on certain days, we can do it in this way. We don't have to inform everyone about it, including potential thieves and burglars. After all, we never know who will view the communication we direct *urbi et orbi*. Certain information can also be used against the user, for example in phishing attacks.

With regard to account security, we apply basically the same rules as for all other services, i.e., a good password, the use of multi-factor authentication.

It's not a good idea to lose access to our social media account where we have lots of followers or private data, for example. It is also a matter of accountability to people who follow such an account. Some basic responsibility. This should be remembered especially by public figures, because it may end very badly for them. When such a social account with a huge number of followers is hijacked, we can even talk about the possibility of an information operation aimed at many recipients, which we will also talk about in Chapter 6.

3.3.17 Do we need a VPN? Probably not

Very often it is said that we need something called a VPN (*virtual private networks*). This is a useful solution because it enables, for example, a secure way to connect to a corporate network. Therefore, it is possible to define safe rules for the use of equipment, strengthening information security in companies or institutions. However, it is often said that a VPN gives us something more – even privacy or additional security. This is not necessarily true. Nowadays, most website connections are already encrypted because TLS (*transport layer security*)[39] solution is being in use, and with Let's Encrypt, over a billion TLS certificates were issued in 2020.[40] Due to these infrastructural changes, encryption is almost always used today when communicating with a website. Otherwise, the web browser will inform us that such a connection is unsafe (by marking it, e.g., in red). So we do not need a VPN to ensure the security of the link layer, communication security, because the data encryption guarantee is already in place. On the other hand, a VPN can be useful if we want to mask our internet address, especially if we use some websites that have an access block, i.e., access to certain internet addresses or content is assigned to certain countries. However, this is not a security or privacy problem, but rather a usability problem. A separate issue is the situation when the user lives in a country where access to certain internet resources is blocked.

At the same time, when it comes to the encryption itself, it should be added that properly used modern ciphers are also practically unbreakable, so it's not the ciphers that fail as much as the methods of their incorporation into systems or selection of weak encryption keys. Of course, there are extremely rare and exceptional situations. Cosmic rays are able to disturb data processing, for example, by causing a "0" bit to jump to "1" in electronic components of computers, causing problems with the encoding/decoding of the information. We encounter such problems on the surface of the Earth rather rarely, and the equipment we use is good at error correction. Sometimes it can be more difficult, for example, with a spacecraft in outer space, which is not protected by the Earth's atmosphere. There, to protect against cosmic rays, special equipment and shielding are used. Even so, sometimes there can be "bit swapping" events. Why are we talking about this? The point is that in the ciphers used today, even changing one bit of the key completely changes the encryption output (the ciphertext), making the data completely incomprehensible. Something like this happened to American satellites in the 1990s,[41] and probably also to Voyager 2 in 2010, an object already outside the Solar System.[42] Such a satellite with a modified (due to cosmic rays) encryption key sent data in a completely incomprehensible format. To solve this, it was necessary to break such a (functionally) "new encryption key". And at least once this has been done (NASA, with the involvement of the NSA), which of course took a lot of time and resources. But what would you not do for science?

3.3.17.1 Tor

Coming back to more down-to-earth problems, it is also worth mentioning the Tor network (*the onion routing*),[43] an anonymizing network, using a network of distributed servers that mask where we connect from. It is not a good idea to always use this network, if only because the speed in this system is much lower than that provided by our standard internet service provider. Occasionally, however, an anonymizer can be utilized if it is deemed to be useful. If we think it is necessary for us, it probably is. However, it always depends on what the needs of a particular user are.

Such masking of the source IP address is also made available in the Apple (i.e. in Private Relay service) ecosystem, and, to some extent, Google's web browser Chrome.

3.3.18 Remember that the threat model depends on who you are and what you do

We must now move on to the issue on a higher level of abstraction, which refers to remembering the key principle for cybersecurity and security: *the threat model always depends on who we are and what we do*. So, whether we are a person who is exposed to a specific risk, and whether the activities we take on the internet are risky. For example, if we are a politician, a journalist, a businessman, then perhaps there will be groups interested in breaking our security and gaining access to data that we process, create, receive, send – that is, to the communication systems we use. If, for example, we are a cybersecurity researcher and we study malware, it is very important to protect ourselves and, for example, research malware on dedicated devices or in virtual machines. That is, it is all about compartmentalization and risk minimization. If we are a farmer, a member of the election campaign staff, a baker, or a programmer – then our way of using the software will also be specific, special, and there will also be specific risks.

So what is important here? The fact that these threat models are completely different! We need to understand the use modes of systems, software, etc., and choose the right methods. We repeat ourselves here because it is really important.

3.4 ARE WE ALWAYS IN DANGER AND DOES SOMEONE ALWAYS WANT TO HACK US?

The risk really depends on who we are. But it's not like we're always going to get hacked. It is not that the dangers and risks are everywhere and always present. That everything and everyone can be hacked, and at any time. A lot depends on who the group or people interested in breaking security are, and what kind of security we have. Because not everything and not everyone is able to be broken immediately – not always can it be done easily and quickly. And sometimes it's just not worth it. So let's not go crazy and attribute all the strange things that happen on our computers to "bad hackers".

Of course, common sense and caution are important, which means not clicking on all clickable links. Because today, it is still the case that not always when entering a website, we are guaranteed to be safe. It is worth mentioning such risks as malvertising.[44] When entering websites, we often see advertisements. These ads are delivered by ad infrastructures. It is a system of scripts that run in our web browser. At times, cybercriminals have used these advertising infrastructures to deliver malware. Sometimes by directly exploiting security bugs in web browsers or web browser extensions. However, this is not always the case.

It may also happen that we will talk to someone on the internet who will perhaps claim that they can do something bad to us, hack into our system, etc. This is probably not the case. Because if he could do it, he would probably have done it a long time ago and would not have had to communicate it.

3.4.1 Not all threats are technical

As we said before, it is also not that all threats are purely technical. Of course, exploits appear that can be used, tools are made that can be used against the user's system and against the user automatically. For example, there were security vulnerabilities, bugs in instant messaging applications – including those considered "safe", in WhatsApp or in Signal – as a result of which it was possible to automatically breach security and directly and immediately hack, take control of the user's system. Very often, however, it is the users who have to somehow help in harming themselves, for example by participating in a phishing conversation. This can happen, for example, out of ignorance or in a hurry: the user enters the account password on some phishing website, and from then on, it only gets worse.

3.4.2 We may not have any influence on some problems

Speaking of user cybersecurity, it is also worth emphasizing that – a prosaic matter – cyberattacks do not always have to be directed against a specific user, because they can also be cyberattacks on companies, the state, or service providers. If a company is hacked and our data are there, someone can obtain, steal, or use them. And that will very much be a cybersecurity or security problem for us. But we will have little to no control over it. For example, if someone hacks a medical doctor's office or a hospital and our medical data are stolen, then this is also a problem for us. Obviously, it is. Of course, as regular users, customers, and patients, there is little we can do about it. It is very important that not everything is up to us when it comes to cybersecurity. For example, it happened that the data of clients of a psychotherapeutic clinic were leaked,[45] as well as data from other healthcare places (e.g., the Irish health service HSE in 2021), hospitals. This is not a situation the patient wants to be in. These are negative consequences of the digitization of medicine, medical care, and healthcare. It is, therefore, worth remembering that the data that we provide to companies or service providers, unfortunately, may be leaked sometimes. And here it is worth mentioning that the GDPR, i.e., the general regulation on the protection of personal data, requires companies to inform users about such detected leaks if there is a risk that such data may be used in some way to the detriment of the user. That's at least something: the affected users may become aware of it, and perhaps take some action. We cannot take any action when we are not aware of the problem.

3.5 ANTIVIRUS SOFTWARE

An important issue is also antivirus or firewall software. Is it worth considering if these programs are needed? They used to be useful in the past. Times change and so do threats. It is worth realizing that the level of cybersecurity has increased. And it is not necessarily crucial to have an antivirus installed. This has been talked about especially when operating systems other than Windows were used.

An antivirus is a kind of prosthesis. It is especially useful when users are doing something automatically, or in a hurry. This prosthesis can increase safety as users are by no means experts. So it can reduce the risk of something going wrong by sometimes blocking certain suspicious activities and giving the user the time and opportunity to reconsider what they are doing. However, it is worth remembering that modern operating systems, such as Windows, have a built-in system for detecting or combating malware. We are talking about Windows Defender (it is an antivirus and a built-in firewall). Perhaps they are not as advanced as other specialist solutions. However, they are good enough and should be turned on. It is also useful to have firewalls enabled to filter network traffic or scan software on the MacOS operating system – here to some extent the standard Gatekeeper, XProtect, or MRT[46] system protects against malware – or on Linux (there is no standard solution here and it is still said that such solutions are not even needed,[47] but it's still probably best to have some network packet filtering in place).

However, antiviruses are sometimes necessary in business environments, if only because they are legal or organizational requirements. Because it is, for example, a question of risk reduction and the insurer requires it. In such a situation, we have to install them, because there is such an obligation. Whether they are useful is then a completely different problem.

We also do not believe that clicking on an innocent website which automatically results in the user's system being hacked is the user's fault. This is the system's fault. Of course, if the user directly takes action against himself/herself, for example, clicks on a program that will execute a code that steals his/her data, then it is the user who did it. So let's be careful about what we do.

3.6 USER PRIVACY – A BROAD TOPIC

We must also at least briefly mention the important issue of privacy. Although this is not a book devoted to this subject, today it is difficult to talk about the cybersecurity of users without discussing the topic of privacy or not mentioning it to some extent. It is almost impossible. Privacy is very important, although it is a complex topic that may fill a book (or even several) on its own.

In short, privacy is control over information relating to a user. It's the management of information flows. This is knowing how these data are (or can be) used. It is also deciding how these data will be used. In practice and technically, this applies to our activity on the Internet, which is what we consent to. For example, if we enter a website and are asked there by our web browser for consent/permission to access the webcam, we grant or refuse to grant it. This does not necessarily mean that we give legal consent (there are separate pop-ups for that, at least in Europe) for the processing of such data for any purpose, but here we emphasize that nowadays the requirement for a website to have access to a webcam is if the user has given such consent (e.g., he clicks in the right place) in his/her own web browser. In this way, he/she gives *permission*, at the level of the web browser, locally on the user's computer. Another matter is the legal basis of such a website for the possible subsequent use of such data. However, this is a separate issue.

3.6.1 Settings

For privacy, software settings are also important, i.e., how we enable access to components, sensors, and various data that we have on the computer. However, the software settings on our device (computer, smartphone, refrigerator, etc.) are something else, and the settings in various web systems to which we log in are completely different. For example, these are decisions about whether we agree to tracking, or whether we consent to the processing of data for advertising profiling purposes.

Privacy is a very important thing because digital information describes us nowadays. And it is neither desirable nor normal for everyone to be able to access all of our data. It is also not true that if we have nothing to hide, we do not need to fear anything (e.g., eavesdropping),[48] and that only bad people, criminals, terrorists, etc. should be afraid of sharing data.

If someone claims they have nothing to hide, it is worth considering whether they would agree to give access to their private e-mail inbox or to the history of all pages viewed in the past month, to record communication with other people.

In this sense, a very legitimate question also arises: Can a person who claims that they have nothing to hide at all be trusted? How do we talk to someone who has nothing to hide? What can we tell such a person and what can't we? And these are not technical problems!

3.6.2 Not only bad people have something to hide

It is not true that only bad people should be *afraid*, because a lot depends on who determines that someone else is a bad person (by the way, historically, this notion of what/who is "bad" sometimes changed in particular countries, sometimes the changes were quite abrupt, but that is another issue). Often this argument refers to the fact that we should not be afraid of sharing our data with, for example, various institutions, the police, the state, services, companies, anyone.

However, we must consider the construction of this argument. Because it doesn't really make sense. It also makes no sense to allow such direct access. If the use of these data is legal (e.g., by law) and legitimate, then that is one thing. However, if there may be some abuse, it is a completely different problem. Then the user cannot be sure what will happen with his/her private information, and he/she should be able to have confidence in the legal system, supervision over companies, services, etc.

3.6.3 Smartphone – the center of life

Nowadays, a device such as a smartphone is actually our center of life. We have a lot of private data there. This is the first time in history that there is so much information about everything that concerns us in such a small device. About the activities we have taken in the past. About things we will do in the future. About our contacts. About our communication with family and friends. About the state of our health. This is the first time such a data center has been established, formed, created, put in use. We agreed to it. We do it voluntarily. We trust that it is safe. It is hard to imagine that we would like to provide access to it to unauthorized persons, for example – to practically everyone. It is hard to imagine that even the police could have reasons or even unlimited right to access all data about our entire lives. It would be hard to accept, even ridiculous. These are not things that the user can easily control (apart from encrypting, securing their devices, deleting old data, setting passwords, PINs, etc.). Therefore, it is also a matter of political and legal culture, principles, and the rule of law – when and on what terms such content would be viewed by, for example, state services.

3.6.4 What do they know about us?

If we are talking about modern technologies and the smartphone life center, it is worth realizing that various websites to which we log in, social networks or even banks can learn a lot about us based on our activity. We share quite a lot of data about ourselves. There are entire systems and ecosystems that track our online behavior by analyzing it in real time. These are very advanced algorithms. They can process the data to which they have access in such a way as to extract additional knowledge from them.

For example, by analyzing our browsing history, it is possible to determine our approximate age, gender, psychometric profile. Find out if we are extroverts or introverts. It is also possible to determine our views, religion, perhaps sexual orientation, our culinary preferences. This is a lot of private data that can be used in the future for various things, for example, to target advertising, including political ones. It's easy to imagine the potential here, including the abuse potential.

What can the user do? For example, install web browser extensions and configure it in such a way that these data do not flow out, do not leak. There are many indications that such analytics will also be "civilized", and such information will not be intercepted, at some point. Technological changes are also expected to affect analytics and tracking for advertising purposes – this is about creating systems that would work without tracking.

3.6.5 Privacy as a product feature and business advantage

Nowadays, privacy is also a phenomenon in a sense. It is something that can even make products or services stand out. Different companies may prioritize privacy. They can even emphasize it. They can make it a distinguishing feature of their technology. It can be a marketing value. Here, for example, we have companies like Apple, and even Google that have started to emphasize the importance of privacy for some time now because they have identified that it is something that is becoming important to people. If it is important, they are working on it.

3.6.6 Privacy versus technologies and standards

As we have already mentioned, the basic technologies of the Internet were not built with cybersecurity in mind. Same with privacy. With regard to privacy, the situation began to change in the second decade of the twenty-first century. Basic technology standards are evolving. They are changing for the better, they are being reinvented. For example, in the present decade, we have a very broad debate on the Web architecture. How to fix some vulnerabilities, how to make changes to improve privacy? It will take a long time, maybe years. However, these will undoubtedly be changes for the better. The level of privacy in our technologies will continue to increase. From there it's a short path to designing technology with privacy in mind. This is becoming the standard. It is also legally supported. For example, the GDPR in article 25 requires designing technology with data protection in mind, it's the Data Protection by Design (or Privacy by Design) approach.

NOTES

1 BBC, *AWS: Amazon web outage breaks vacuums and doorbells*, 26.11.2020, https://www.bbc.com/news/technology-55087054
2 Meta/Facebook, *Update on the October 4th outage*, 18.10.2021, https://www.facebook.com/business/news/update-about-the-october-4th-outage
3 OVH, *Fire at our Strasbourg Site*, 6.04.2021, https://us.ovhcloud.com/press/press-releases/2021/fire-our-strasbourg-site; M. Rosemain, R. Satter, *Millions of websites offline after fire at French cloud services firm*, 10.03.2021, https://www.reuters.com/article/us-france-ovh-fire-idUSKBN2B20NU; Bureau d'enquêtes et d'analyses sur les risques industriels (BEA-RI), *Rapport d'enquête. Sur l'incendie au sein du centre de stockage de données OVH situé à Strasbourg (67) le 10 mars 2021*, 24.05.2022, https://lafibre.info/images/ovh/202205_bea-ri_rapport_enquete_incendie_datacenter_ovh_strasbourg.pdf
4 C. Izurieta, M. Prouty, *Leveraging SecDevOps to tackle the technical debt associated with cybersecurity attack tactics*, 2019 IEEE/ACM International Conference on Technical Debt (TechDebt), IEEE, 2019, pp. 33–37; NA Ernst, S. Bellomo, I. Ozkaya, RL Nord, I. Gorton, *Measure it? Manage it? Ignore it? software practitioners and technical debt*, in: *Proceedings of the 2015 10th Joint Meeting on Foundations of Software Engineering*, ESEC/FSE, 2015, pp. 50–60.
5 A. Janc, K. Kotowicz, L. Weichselbaum, R. Clapis, *Information leaks via Safari's Intelligent Tracking Prevention*, 21.01.2020, https://arxiv.org/abs/2001.07421
6 L.H. Newman, *The decade big-money email scams took over*, 26.12.2019, https://www.wired.com/story/business-email-compromise-scams/

7 Proposal for a Directive of the European Parliament and of the Council on measures for a high common level of cybersecurity across the Union, repealing Directive (EU) 2016/1148 – hereinafter: proposal NIS 2.

8 Commission delegated regulation (EU) 2018/389 of 27 November supplementing Directive (EU) 2015/2366 of the European Parliament and of the Council with regard to regulatory technical standards for strong customer authentication and common and secure open standards of communication (OJ L 69 of 13.3.2018, pp. 23–43). See also Directive (EU) 2015/2366 of the European Parliament and of the Council of 25 November 2015 on payment services in the internal market, amending Directives 2002/65/EC, 2009/110/EC and 2013/36/EU and Regulation (EU) No 1093/2010, and repealing Directive 2002/65/WE, (OJ UE L 337 of 23.12.2015, pp. 35–127; consolidated version: https://eur-lex.europa.eu/legal-content/EN/TXT/HTML/?uri=CELEX:32018R0389&from=EN)

9 J. Bonneau, C. Herley, P.C. van Oorschot, F. Stajano, *Passwords and the evolution of imperfect authentication*, "Communications of the ACM" 2015, vol. 58, no. 7, pp. 78–87.

10 J. Bonneau, C. Herley, P.C. van Oorschot, F. Stajano, *The quest to replace passwords: A framework for comparative evaluation of web authentication schemes*, *2012 IEEE Symposium on Security and Privacy*, IEEE, 2012, pp. 553–567.

11 M. Zviran, W.J. Haga, *Password security: an empirical study*, "Journal of Management Information Systems" 1999, vol. 15, no. 4, pp. 161–185.

12 B.F. Barton, M.S. Barton, *User-friendly password methods for computer-mediated information systems*, "Computers & Security" 1984, vol. 3, no. 3, pp. 186–195.

13 Air Force Manual 33-223. *Communications and information. Identification and authentication*, 1998, https://apps.dtic.mil/sti/pdfs/ADA404983.pdf

14 A. Ometov, S. Bezzateev, N. Mäkitalo, S. Andreev, T. Mikkonen, Y. Koucheryavy, *Multi-factor authentication: A survey*, "Cryptography" 2018, vol. 2, no. 1.

15 With "salt": "dogdogdog" parameter set, and the configuration for Argon2id: memory cost of 16, 2 iterations, and hash length 16. If this is incomprehensible – don't worry, we don't need this knowledge except to be precise.

16 NIST Special Publication 800-63B, *Digital Identity Guidelines. Authentications and lifecycle management*, 2017, https://pages.nist.gov/800-63-3/sp800-63b.html - section 5.1.1.2.

17 Microsoft, *Security baseline (FINAL) for Windows 10 v1903 and Windows Server v1903*, 5/23/2019, https://docs.microsoft.com/en-gb/archive/blogs/secguide/security-baseline-final-for-windows- 10-v1903-and-windows-server-v1903

18 CNIL. Délibération SAN-2022-020 du 10 novembre 2022, point 66, available at: https://www.legifrance.gouv.fr/cnil/id/CNILTEXT000046562676?init=true& page=1 [accessed at 7.12.22].

19 Melnikov, A. (2011). Moving DIGEST-MD5 to historic (No. rfc6331).

20 CNIL. Deliberation SAN-2022-021 of November 24, 2022, available at: https://www.legifrance.gouv.fr/cnil/id/CNILTEXT000046650733?isSuggest=true [accessed at 7.12.22].

21 Diceware Password Generator (n/a), https://dykware.dmuth.org/. See also MD Leonhard, VN Venkatakrishnan, *A comparative study of three random password generators*, in: *IEEE International Conference on Electro / Information Technology*, IEEE, 2007, pp. 227–232.

22 See. https://www.diceware.net/?dicelist

23 M. Thalmann, A.S. Souza, K. Oberauer, *How does chunking help working memory?*, "Journal of Experimental Psychology: Learning, Memory, and Cognition" 2019, vol. 45, no. 1, p. 37.

24 J. Bonneau, S. Schechter, *Towards reliable storage of 56-bit secrets in human memory*, in: *23rd USENIX Security Symposium (USENIX Security 14)*, 2014, pp. 607–623.

25 CISA, *Multi-factor authentication (MFA)*, 2022, https://www.cisa.gov/sites/default/files/publications/MFA-Fact-Sheet-Jan22-508.pdf

26 B. Kondracki, B.A. Azad, O. Starov, N. Nikiforakis, *Catching transparent phish: Analyzing and detecting MITM phishing toolkits*, Proceedings of the 2021 ACM SIGSAC Conference on Computer and Communications Security, 2021, pp. 36–50.

27 T. Ormandy, *You don't need SMS-2FA*, 2020, https://blog.cmpxchg8b.com/2020/07/you-dont-need-sms-2fa.html

28 M.B. Jones, A. Kumar, E. Lundberg, *Web authentication: An API for accessing Public Key Credentials Level 3*, 2.06.2022, https://w3c.github.io/webauthn/

29 FIDO Alliance, *Apple, Google and Microsoft commit to expanded support for FIDO standard to accelerate availability of passwordless sign-ins*, 5.05.2022, https://fidoalliance.org/apple-google-and-microsoft-commit-to-expanded-support-for-fido-standard-to-accelerate-availability-of-passwordless-sign-ins/

30 Apple. Passkeys, 2022, https://developer.apple.com/passkeys/

31 Google Chrome Blog, Introducing passkeys in Chrome, https://blog.chromium.org/2022/12/introducing-passkeys-in-chrome.html

32 M. Dark, *Thinking about cybersecurity*, "IEEE Security & Privacy" 2015, vol. 13, no. 1, pp. 61–65.

33 L. Olejnik, A. Janc, *Stealing sensitive browser data with the W3C Ambient Light Sensor API*, 2017, blog.lukaszolejnik.com/stealing-sensitive-browser-data-with-the-w3c-ambient-light-sensor-api/; L. Olejnik, *Shedding light on web privacy impact assessment: A case study of the Ambient Light Sensor API*, w: 2020 IEEE European Symposium on Security and Privacy Workshops (EuroS&PW), IEEE, 2020, pp. 310–313.

34 Artur Janc of Google made a cool demonstration of such an attack.

35 J. Schwenk, M. Niemietz, C. Mainka, *Same-Origin Policy: Evaluation in Modern Browsers*, in: *26th USENIX Security Symposium (USENIX Security 17)*, 2017, pp. 713–727.

36 R. Anderson, *Security engineering: a guide to building dependable distributed systems*, John Wiley & Sons, 2020.

37 K. Ermoshina, F. Musiani, H. Halpin, *End-to-end encrypted messaging protocols: An overview*, in: *International Conference on Internet Science*, Springer, Cham 2016, pp. 244–254; A. Herzberg, H. Leibowitz, *Can Johnny finally encrypt? Evaluating E2E-encryption in popular IM applications*, in: *Proceedings of the 6th Workshop on Socio-Technical Aspects in Security and Trust*, 2016, pp. 17–28.

38 Internet Society, *Ghost Proposals: What are they, what is their impact, and can they achieve their goals?*, 2020, https://www.internetsociety.org/wp-content/uploads/2020/03/Ghost-Protocol-Fact-Sheet.pdf

39 E. Rescorla, *The Transport Layer Security (TLS) Protocol Version 1.3*, 2018, https://www.rfc-editor.org/info/rfc8446

40 Let's Encrypt, *Let's Encrypt has issued a billion certificates*, 2020, https://letsencrypt.org/2020/02/27/one-billion-certs.html

41 AstroEngineer's Blog, *Voyager 2 has flipped its bit*, 2020, https://astroengineer. wordpress.com/2010/05/12/voyager-2-has-flipped-its-bit/

42 Jet Propulsion Laboratory, *Engineers Diagnosing Voyager 2 Data System -- Update*, 24.05.2010, https://www.jpl.nasa.gov/news/engineers-diagnosing-voyager-2-data-system-update

43 D. Goldschlag, M. Reed, P. Syverson, *Onion routing*, "Communications of the ACM" 1999, vol. 42, no. 2, pp. 39–41.

44 A.K. Sood, R.J. Enbody, *Malvertising – exploiting web advertising*, "Computer Fraud & Security" 2011, no. 4, pp. 11–16.

45 W. Ralston, *They told their therapists everything. Hackers leaked it all*, 2021, https://www.wired.com/story/vastaamo-psychotherapy-patients-hack-data-breach/

46 Apple, *Protecting against malware in macOS*, 2021, https://support.apple.com/guide/security/protecting-against-malware-sec469d47bd8/web

47 Ubuntu 21.10 (n. d.), *Do I need anti-virus software?*, https://help.ubuntu.com/stable/ubuntu-help/net-antivirus.html.en

48 D.J. Solove, *I've got nothing to hide and other misunderstandings of privacy*, "San Diego Law Review" 2007, no. 44, p. 745.

Chapter 4

Cybersecurity of healthcare infrastructure

4.1 THE DIGITALIZATION OF HEALTHCARE IS PROGRESSING

What is infrastructure? Infrastructure is, in simple terms, resources operating within a broader system. According to the dictionary definition, those are "the basic systems and services that are necessary for a country or an organization to run smoothly, for example buildings, transport and water and power supplies".[1] For the considerations in this chapter, such a basic definition is sufficient. Such an infrastructure could, therefore, be the equipment. Or it could be software. It could be people. It is simply a system consisting of various components.

Healthcare infrastructure refers to the healthcare system, i.e., hospitals (buildings), diagnostic equipment (e.g., CT scan, ultrasound, X-ray equipment, and others), communication systems, information management (e.g., patient records such as electronic health records), and other elements of this type. As we said in the earlier chapters, computerization and digitization are progressing. This also applies to healthcare, medical care, places such as hospitals or doctors' offices. Today, every doctor has access to a computer, smartphone, or tablet. And we do not limit ourselves here to the private devices of doctors, nurses, and other staff. Because this also concerns devices normally used in medical work.

Digitalization touches also patient information. Once upon a time (although in some places – also today), the creation and storage of medical data involved large collections of paper files – with test results, with diagnoses, with prescriptions. This is being digitized to an increasing extent and electronic health records are in use. They contain a full record of the patient's state of health and medical condition. These are private data such as first and last name, gender, address, but this includes also information about specific diseases, conditions, and elements from the medical history (health record) of such a patient. These include, for example, history of and previously prescribed medicines and the entire health history like hospital visits, medical results, and correspondence between different doctors. It does not always have to be a completely centralized process, and such data are not always complete within a given center. Sometimes they are scattered, they may be stored in many places. For example, in one hospital there is a part of the data about certain health aspects, and in another there is something else, about a different aspect. This depends on the system adopted in a country. It may also be subject to change or evolution at this time. It may be an ongoing process.

For example, in the UK, where the system works in quite an imaginably standard way, patients could consent to make their health histories available to different hospitals. This fact alone suggests that such information may be shared. Sometimes (supposedly) "anonymized" data were also shared with private companies for research and development purposes. In other places, this may work differently; it depends on the solutions adopted in a given country.

Here we must immediately emphasize that medical data are unfortunately being stolen by cybercriminals. It happens. Sometimes, they also end up on the black market, and their prices fluctuate (it could be $50 for some kind of data). And such private data can be used by cybercriminals for blackmail, or later to try to take over user identities (i.e., identity theft) or accounts. Thus, here the motivation might be financial.

And let's immediately point out that health data are particularly sensitive. Like, they are really sensitive. Often it is impossible to "*change*" them. We can change a password, but the state of health, physiological condition? That is perhaps not as easy to amend, to modify. So, it is imperative that such data are protected. Healthcare systems must, therefore, be protected.

4.1.1 Digitalization and its issues

This computerization, which we mention so often in this book (an important socio-civilization process, a one-way street), includes many medical devices. As we have already said, it can be, for example, a computer tomography (for CT scans) – as the name suggests, the equipment is controlled by a computer. But the same applies to diagnostic ultrasound devices or X-ray devices, or magnetic resonance imaging (MRI), and of course also implants such as pacemakers.

This whole preliminary discussion already leads us to some basic conclusions. In the domain of healthcare systems, we deal with very sensitive objects and data. There are also people interested in acquiring them, or gain access to them. Therefore, these data must be properly guarded and defended. But what exactly are we protecting? First of all, the resources such as medical systems and patient data. Ultimately, it's not just about patients' privacy, it's also about their health and sometimes even their lives.

New medical applications are being created on a regular basis. Services with new, "improved" technologies are also being built (e.g., connected medical devices that we may have at our homes). The fact that computers control diagnostic systems is obvious, because simply speaking, only such products are currently offered on the market. Another thing is the computerization of health data, with the possibility of sharing them. Would it be a good idea to centralize the storage or access to such data? It sounds like a point of risk, but in a sense, such processes might be being built gradually. Once this is done, there may be no way back.

It may be desirable to connect databases, but should it be done? At the same time, it is not at all clear whether the public is provided with sufficiently comprehensive information about the state of cybersecurity of such an infrastructure, about the real risks. Has anyone seen a public, state, systemic report on the analysis of such risks? Thus, how can the citizens trust this process?

4.1.2 COVID-19 as a digital accelerator

On a larger scale, we tested "on the production" how the digitization of healthcare works on the occasion of the many events during the COVID-19 pandemic, including vaccination campaigns. A lot of people, perhaps for the first time, logged into their individual patient account to make an appointment for vaccinations or download a vaccination certificate (which was useful, or crucial, for traveling). In Europe (and elsewhere, e.g., Korea, Singapore, China, the USA) applications were quickly developed to track contacts between people ("digital contact tracing" apps) and to store information about the vaccination status ("vaccination passports"), with the possibility of verifying these data.

Will any of this remain in the future? Will the right conclusions be drawn? Or maybe these installed applications should gain new features, for example, to prove the identity of the user (i.e., be used as a global identity source or proof)? But is it possible to make such unexpected changes? What precedents would it set? What would it normalize for the future? Such questions are very basic to technology, but also to technology policy, and to what societies may expect. In European Union, for example, some exceptional procedures to access user data, created during the COVID-19 crisis, are being normalized,[2] "where the data requested is necessary to respond to a public emergency".[3] And that is only a single long-term effect of the COVID-19 pandemic on laws and technologies.

On the occasion of the pandemic, digitalization in this area has become the focus of public opinion in Europe and worldwide. Only years later will it turn out whether it was a one-off spurt, or whether it will have some far-reaching consequences, will it initiate some processes? Here, it should be noted that much attention in Europe has been devoted to the issue of data protection of such applications created, having COVID-19 crisis management in mind. Even if the European data protection authorities were probably quickly and efficiently approving further ideas for the use of data, which was of course surrounded by opinions and analyses, this raises questions whether systems of this type did not have to "move" to the implementation phase, be accepted, for reasons undeniably political? Were such systems put under a similar scrutiny in other places, like the U.S. or Asia, is another question entirely. It is clear that for example in South Korea or Singapore, the level of digital intervention was significant, including with data revealed about almost-identified individuals and their actions.

The experience of the COVID-19 pandemic is unprecedented for digital technologies, which became an integral part of the policy and crisis response at that time in 2020–2021. However, this was a special situation and we should not expect work in crisis mode to happen more often, or on a regular basis. Or at least we don't wish that to anyone. Political and social calmness and supervision are not only useful and necessary, but also indispensable in digitalization, especially in such sensitive areas as healthcare.

By the way, it is said that in some companies/institutions, COVID-19 was the driving force behind digitization changes. It even functioned as a joke. Hilarity aside, crises always bring about big changes. However, this should not be a standard mode.

4.2 DIGITALIZATION AND CYBERSECURITY RISKS

Digitalization is linked with the emergence of cybersecurity risks. These may be cybersecurity problems due to the fact that a determined actor, when attacking, could do something undesirable from the point of view of those responsible for such a system, users, patients, etc. For example, the attacker can take over (steal) data, paralyze parts or the whole hospital network or systems, or, more broadly, the healthcare system on a national scale (as happened in Ireland or Singapore). Because an important problem of cybersecurity are issues related to the availability of such systems, and even their reliability. In the popular image, the element of confidentiality is often portrayed as crucial, which is of course in this case also related to the problem of availability. Breaches impact on availability.

We will now revisit the discussion about the risk surface. The greater the degree of digitization, the more the risks associated with it can increase, naturally. When we have more hardware or software, there will be more room for problems to happen or arise; and these can cover a wide area, even a whole country, have a substantial range, be serious, have a significant impact. Thinking logically, based on what we have discussed in the previous chapters, there may also surely be some vulnerabilities in such software and systems: in CT scanners, ultrasound systems, hearing aids, in cardiac implants (*pacemakers*). Sooner or later, such vulnerabilities may be identified. And perhaps someone will want to use them. Or at least that cannot be ruled out, although, depending on how such vulnerabilities are exploited, it could have serious consequences for such an actor (e.g., consequences that are discussed in Chapter 7).

There is a well-known case of the Vice President of the United States, Dick Cheney, who in 2007 had the possibility of remote configuration of his pacemaker be disabled. As you can imagine, the vice president is a rather important person. Definitely a VIP (a potentially *high-value target*). It was, therefore, considered that in his case, the systemic weakness of such equipment was too serious of a risk. In this regard, it was concluded that for the reasons of state security, it is justified to exclude the possibility of remote communication (configuration) with his pacemaker. So it was done. And in this case, such a risk can actually be considered as justified.

4.3 RISKS AND THREATS

In the event of a failure, malfunction, or cyberattack, we may have to deal with a degradation of the provision of healthcare services, which can be very painful for the patients. Because they will suddenly be unable to use healthcare services, for example, appointments, treatments (e.g., ransomware infection of systems in hospitals in Ireland in 2021 had an effect on chemotherapy treatments).

Often, medical diagnostics is the first victim: appointments are canceled. In the case of cyberattacks and ransomware, this is also what you might hear about. That after a cyberattack, it is the diagnostic systems that are degraded, they are hit. This is because computer control is important in diagnostics, and sometimes access to patients' medical records, to previous laboratory test results, is also needed. A big problem, and a good reason to exclude such a system from use in the event of a suspected cyberattack, is precisely that today diagnostics rely heavily on computer systems from specific software vendors who are required to maintain these systems under the license, and authorized repair could take a long time. After a ransomware infection or a security incident, such systems are sometimes shut down, just in case, to reduce the risk of spreading the digital infection. Because the possibly needed rebuilding of such a system would take a lot of time. It would also be expensive. Therefore, even overzealousness is justified here as a good practice.

4.3.1 Cyberattacks on hospitals

Cyberattacks on hospitals happen. For example, we can recall the attacks on psychotherapeutic clinics in Sweden, which we have already mentioned in the previous chapter. Patient data were stolen. However, the attacker was so perfidious that he contacted these patients to extort a ransom. He threatened to publish the data, and indeed some of the data were disclosed. There is also a well-known example of a large-scale cyberattack on a hospital in Singapore. The data of more than 1.5 million people were stolen, which is a very large percentage of Singaporeans–including the data of the Prime Minister (which the attackers were specifically looking for). Given the scale of the attack, this naturally posed a broad political problem.

If a large percentage of residents are affected by such actions, then it is indeed a social and, therefore, a political problem (more about that in Chapters 6 and 7). In the case of this attack, it was linked to a group with the support of a foreign state. In the background there were some speculations that it could be Russia.

More generally, there were a lot of cyberattacks on hospitals: in the USA, in France, in the Czech Republic, all over the world. There is no point in listing them all. What they have in common is that they are degrading the healthcare services.

4.3.2 WannaCry ransomware as a driver of cybersecurity funding?

Another important, even historic, incident – which is why it is worthy of note here – was the wave of WannaCry ransomware attacks in 2017, when hundreds of thousands of systems in dozens of countries were affected. From transportation (e.g., railways: railway stations in Germany) to logistics (paralysis of the systems of the global logistics company Maersk). Medical systems have also been affected; they have been infected. Therefore, they were not available – they could not be used, scheduled appointments and treatments were canceled. For example, in the United Kingdom, the state and healthcare later devoted a lot of time to analyzing this problem systemically.[4]

Because of this cyberattack, an additional budget has been allocated to cybersecurity in healthcare. So, paradoxically, did the demonstration of such a large cyberattack contribute to the improvement of cybersecurity, to an increase in expenditure?

It is a paradox that decision makers or politicians perceive such threats only when they come true. When, let us be clear, it is too late. So, to say precisely: when people talk about it, when the problem, which was already widely known at that time, can no longer be swept under the rug. However, this is not a question of cybersecurity per se (although, as we can see, it has an impact on it!), but more a systemic problem related to how the modern State works, what public life or modern politics looks like. It deals with current problems, rather than those "potential and just in case", because it is expensive, while maybe nothing will happen? However, these considerations, while certainly fascinating, are beyond the scope of our book, so we will not continue them.

Let us note, however, that such a cyberattack is paradoxically a kind of opportunity. Because when a catastrophe occurs, there are measures that may (it is worth hoping) contribute to improving the current state and prevent such events in the future.

4.3.3 Cyberattacks on healthcare in Ireland in 2021

As has already been mentioned, cyberattacks on the NHS in Ireland in 2021 reverberated very widely, leading to the paralysis of the healthcare system. It was necessary to cancel a lot of appointments. It was a paralysis as a result of a ransomware infection.[5] It had a significant impact on ordinary residents of the country, which was clearly visible not only in press reports. This problem was long-lasting and could not be ignored, silenced, swept under the rug (and unfortunately this sometimes happens with incidents of this type). Therefore, politicians (ministers and even the prime minister) had to devote time to this problem. Of course, it was reported that cybercriminals are being prosecuted and systems were monitored and access to them was restored. An Irish court even prohibited the publication of data from the attack, but this could not be enforced, naturally (even if procedurally, the decision may have been useful).

This is also a very interesting example of an event where a politician sends a signal to cybercriminals: that their actions are unacceptable. There was circumstantial evidence that these cybercriminals had received these signals. Also as a result of the shock of public opinion in Ireland, but also in the world, they understood how big a problem (and controversy) they had led to and how big the issue had become. Then they unlocked access to the systems. We do not recommend cybercriminals (or anyone) becoming *public enemy number one*. If it is really only about money, then acting in this way may, as you can see, not bring profits.

4.3.4 Other cyberattacks on healthcare centers

History records many cyberattacks on various healthcare centers, on various hospitals. For example, the attacks during the coronavirus pandemic resonated very loudly. These were cyberattacks on vaccination clinics, and before that there were cyberattacks on hospitals. Hospitals, as you can easily guess, during a medical crisis had to deal with increased demand for their services. If there is a crisis that causes an increase in cases (an obvious example here is a pandemic), and there is also another type of event hindering work (such as a cyberattack), then we have two crises at the same time. As you can imagine, this does not make work more efficient. Quite the opposite. As a result of the accumulation of such two crises, the problem becomes much greater. In this case, it must be directly said that people's lives and health are at stake. Cyberattacks at such a time are dangerous. They can increase mortality, even if only indirectly. Epidemics and various disasters are natural incidents, but intentional cyberattacks are deliberate and driven by people.

4.3.5 Will the insurer cover the losses?

Here, it is also worth noting the legal dispute that arose between the insurer Zurich Insurance and the company in the food industry – Mondelez. Well, as part of a very serious cyberattack (ransomware) NotPetya in 2017, the self-spreading worm infected systems and blocked access to them. It was a very broad campaign, which reverberated very widely around the world. Well, the effects of this cyberattack were also felt by Mondelez, whose systems were paralyzed. We are talking about millions of losses. The company had insurance and applied for compensation. An interesting precedent has emerged because the insurer Zurich Insurance refused to cover the losses, citing an exception in the contract relating to "acts of war". According to it, if losses arise as a result of acts of war, the insurer may refuse to cover the costs. This is a standard provision in insurance policies, but perhaps it is not paid attention to, after all, wars do not happen often.

Here, a very interesting question arises, because it is worth considering whether NotPetya was an act of war or a similar phenomenon? At the same time, let us emphasize that Mondelez is based in the United States, while NotPetya was a threat that originated in Ukraine (it was "cyber-detonated" there). A hacked company providing tax filing software was a source of malware propagation (i.e., it happened through these systems). Unauthorized access to this company was obtained and its infrastructure was used. Later on, this worm spread on its own. Although in fact Ukraine was an early target of the attack and potentially it could even be linked to, or classified in, the context of (war) hostilities, because in Ukraine, as you know, we had then (even if creeping, subdued) an armed conflict with the involvement of internal and external actors – Russia's involvement is emphasized here.

Besides – and this is the responsibility for this cyberattack that has been formally attributed (by the USA, Great Britain, the European Union, and others) to Russia, Russian military intelligence, GPU/GRU, and more specifically unit 74455, the Main Center for Special Technologies (GTsST) of the Main Directorate of the General Staff of the Armed Forces of the Russian Federation is being suspected, mentioned here. So, we have a military structure in action. An event during an armed conflict, and with the origin of military structures, military intelligence. So was that a war-like event, or not? Was it an example of "using force" (see Chapter 7)?

We can easily realize that it may have been a military attack, hypothesized, or the use of force in fact, perhaps even an armed aggression if we stretch it further. But: in the context of Ukraine, not the U.S. The question is, then, whether this cyberattack-induced event can be translated to the United States, or, maybe, was it also a military aggression (warfare) against the United States of America? Or at least whether the U.S. has been affected by its consequences? While I do not think that this was a war-like activity with respect to the U.S., when such a case is resolved by the court, it is all about building a convincing, legally sound case. It is imaginable that skilled, well-informed lawyers might eventually succeed here. Who knows what the future is to bring!

There is not much clarity here. This will have to be decided by the court. As we write these words, the case was pending – for another year. It was certainly an interesting scenario and, by the way, it is also very interesting whether an ordinary court in the United States has the right to say that something is related to an armed conflict?

However, in a very similar case, a New Jersey court in the U.S. dismissed such a lawsuit, and the insurer will have to cover the losses ($1.4 billion) of the pharmaceutical company Merck.[6] In the court's opinion, the use of the "war" exception was unjustified. That's why insurers also offer special "cyber insurance" (with similar exceptions) to make it more clear what is insured and what is not Ultimately, in 2023 Zurich Insurance and Mondelez also reached a settlement.

4.3.6 Does cyber insurance make sense?

Here, it is worth considering whether the so-called *cyber insurance* makes sense from the point of view of cybersecurity. Cyber insurance, in simple terms, is a product that covers certain losses resulting from vulnerabilities of systems (but of course those where there were some security measures in place – although these are the requirements of individual insurers, which indeed may have some standard requirements to be met in this space) resulting from negative incidents related to software or hardware (including cyberattacks).

In the current decade, such offers and insurance products are gaining more and more popularity, but there it is not without its controversy. The basic controversy is simply the insurance itself, because it is not clear to what extent insurers have the right competence to identify, recognize, measure, and evaluate the actual risk, and therefore how difficult for them is to reasonably estimate it, and thus the costs of such an insurance product.

It's their problem to resolve this issue. For society and the State, the more important controversy is systemic. It's that if such an insurer covers, for example, the costs of ransomware attacks, i.e., of paying a ransom, for example, it may even lead to an increase in the number of such cyberattacks. There are also signs that cybercriminals have learned, or perhaps noticed, that companies that are insured may be more willing to pay the ransom. Therefore, thinking logically, such a cybercriminal guided by the vision of a profit may be interested in attacking predominantly such companies that are insured. Because they may expect to be paid then. So, we have a paradox here that insurance can make someone a target. That would be quite unfortunate, wouldn't it?

As far as we are concerned, we would not recommend basing cybersecurity in a company or institution solely on insurance. It's not like if someone buys insurance, the systems will suddenly and magically be secured, cyberattack or breach proof. They won't be. Security is a technical, organizational, legal, and partly political issue. Thus, it cannot be so that someone buys an insurance product and thinks that the problem is "solved". It should be emphasized here that such a naïve approach to the problem will end unpleasantly for end users, that is, for the citizens. They are the ones who will suffer. Law and policy should not accept such an assymetrical approach. It would be sweeping the problem under the rug, ignoring it, to the detriment of society. Indeed, ordinary people would suffer because government officials without proper experience and senior business staff would choose the most safe scenarios for themselves. We should avoid such "cybersecurity advisors". But it's understandable that executives are looking for ways to minimize risk – and that's where products like cyber insurance can help. One potential consequence imaginable here is data protection authorities using data protection instruments, like the GDPR fines, to "offset" the assumed cost coverage, so that the risk of financial loss becomes more elusive if a company based their cybersecurity stance solely or primarily on insurance (however ridiculous that sounds)

4.3.7 Hospitals are not treating cybersecurity as a priority – and that is reasonable?

We have said before that the number of cyberattacks on hospitals and healthcare facilities is increasing. Cybercriminals can even treat hospitals as easy targets. Why is that? Hospitals, naturally, do not prioritize spending on cybersecurity and IT, but on healthcare.[7]

Cybersecurity is one of the elements of hospital operation. However, it is not the only one and not the main one. After all, we cannot accept a situation where hospitals would direct most of their resources to cybersecurity. That would run counter to their main area of mandate (or business). At the same time, hospitals must (if only due to the applicable legal provisions) prioritize healthcare and, consequently, still consider the availability of their systems seriously. Thus, such a cybercriminal may assume that such institutions (targets) will be interested in maintaining access to their resources.

Therefore, hospitals might potentially be easy targets indeed, as they direct their resources to other places. So, we have here a tangle of different and complex problems. Healthcare needs to be provided, but nowadays it is also about maintaining the reliability of information systems. However, there will still remain the fact of the existence of actors who are interested only in profit. This makes the problem complex. We have a system that prioritizes the provision of healthcare, in which IT systems are only a secondary element to consider (because the main one is the provision of healthcare services), and on the other side – we have motivated cybercriminals (whose goal is to make a profit; to achieve it – they can cause damage).

During the coronavirus pandemic, this problem has been recognized by many leaders, and in an initiative in which the International Committee of the Red Cross has played a key role, a call has been made to world leaders to give due attention to the issue. It was quite an unprecedented move, although it does not seem to have the desired effect, as it happens with such appeals. We have already talked about political issues and we will continue to talk about them. Here, however, we have a political and humanitarian issue outlined in relation to a social and technical problem. As with many other issues covered in this book, it is increasingly difficult not to consider the big picture when analyzing cybersecurity on a broad scale.

4.4 DIGITALIZATION OF DIAGNOSTICS AND NEW VULNERABILITIES

We have already said that computerization includes diagnostic devices or equipment, and indeed it does. These are devices controlled by computers and if such a computer is paralyzed, the ability to use such devices will automatically be lost. Inevitably, there will be downtime introduced. But that's not all. Because these devices are computer controlled, if cybersecurity vulnerabilities are identified, if they are, say, computers with ordinary Windows operating systems (because that happens), as a result of taking control over such a computer or control system, negative events of a different kind may occur. For example, subjecting the patient to improper practices, therapy (potentially, perhaps, administrating too much radiation in the event of X-rays, administration of incorrect doses of drugs; although safety systems in such applications should exist on many levels as an added protection: the key word here is "should", because whether that's the case is another story) to the detriment of his/her health. Fortunately, until 2023, this had never happened, or at least there is no knowledge of such an occurrence, as a part of targeted measures. Unfortunately, it happened as a result of bad system design (more on that later), which is a telling demonstration of what may go wrong.

4.4.1 Risks of implants

Similar risks are associated with *implantable medical devices* (IMDs), such as *pacemakers*. Such implants are often controlled wirelessly. This happens in this way, for example, when the process of a configuration of such a device takes place, for example, in the doctor's or diagnostician's office. And of course, these implants also have software and settings, similarly like a smartphone, computer, and other devices of this type. There are known demonstrations as a result of which cybersecurity vulnerabilities in such implants could have even led to them stopping to work (e.g., due to battery exhaustion) or to the performance of some undesirable operations (e.g., the administration of strong electrical shocks). It was possible to trigger a program in such a device to apply unforeseen therapy actions, which could end very badly for the patient, even in his/her death.[8] This is what is at stake in the potential hacking of clinical systems, hospitals, hacking of medical devices. The hacking of an implant actually implanted under the skin of a 'volunteer' was already demonstrated,[9] infecting the device with malware. What's more, the self-replication of such malware in RFID-enabled components was also demonstrated.[10] The problem of the possibility, and the consequences, of arranging these "bricks" together is left as an exercise for the reader.

In the event of a suspected breach of cybersecurity, such medical systems (at least hospital diagnostics) must be turned off, and what happened should be analyzed. That's why these downtimes are an absolute must. This is not overzealousness. You have to be sure about the state of the systems in use, because human lives are at stake. That said, you can't just stop a medical implant which is responsible for crucial life functions of the patient.

4.4.2 Data leaks or modification of diagnostics

And here we return to the general problem, because we talked about the fact that data can be stolen. We have said that bad medical therapy can be applied, administered, but there may also be some other consequences. Let's call them more subtle. That is, not so much stealing of data or paralyzing access, but modifying the data. For example, electronic health records may be modified. An extra zero may be added to the figures at the dose of the prescribed medication – which could change the dose of the drug to harmful levels. It could end very badly for the patient, though hopefully such dramatic increases or decreases may be spotted by medical doctors, or nurses, etc. This may also be a modification of the diagnostic configuration. We have already talked about this: for example, too high a dose of radiation could be administered.

These would be attacks on integrity. Fortunately we do not hear about them. However, these are still theoretically possible scenarios and it is prudent to keep them in mind. These would be very serious actions, directly bringing about the risk of loss of health or life of patients.

4.4.3 Cyberattacks on the supply chain

Cyberattacks can occur within the supply chain. It's not like a cyberattack has to start at the top, which is, for example, hitting the hospital system directly. Because there may also be cyberattacks on manufacturers or suppliers of hardware and software, as a result of which such hardware and software would already be delivered in an "infected" form. Perhaps forming a new threat for the future with a "ready-to-use" malware.[11] And this can be a problem, because companies operating on the medical device market are very often relatively small, specialized companies. Their goal is to create a system that will be useful in healthcare, and profitable to them. Very often, they do not have the resources to devote due attention to cybersecurity. At this point, we need to return to the issue of the overall safety of medical devices, because it is a systemic challenge.

4.5 CYBERSECURITY OF MEDICAL DEVICES

The problem of cybersecurity affects hardware and software, but to understand and appreciate why it is so serious, we must realize that it takes a long time to create a medical product. It could be several trials, taking years. Then, we have the development phase, then the testing phase, and the stage of using this final solution. The whole cycle can actually take up to 5–15 years.[12] So, for example, the system used in 2020 could have been created in 2009, and work on the system, which will be ready in 2030, could have started in 2020.

Why is this a challenge? Because maintaining an adequate level of cybersecurity in the case of a product that is over 10 years old is difficult. For example, sometimes there may no longer be security patches for certain operating systems. Good luck trying to find, in 2020, security patches for Windows XP, the operating system of the first decade of the twenty-first century. Software typically eventually goes out of support; that is a fact of life.

4.5.1 Targeted attack on a patient using an insulin pump

In addition, it is very often the case that the creators of systems in healthcare do not pay due attention to certain risks and to certain possibilities. For example, when designing a product, they do not assume the existence of an actor who will want to consciously break the security of said product. Although demonstrations have already taken place showing the theoretical (and practical) possibilities of cyberattacks on many medical components. For example, already in 2011, the possibility of hacking an insulin pump, i.e., a device that automatically administers doses of the drug, was demonstrated. Once it was taken over, a harmful dose was possible to be administered. Insulin pumps are normally used in the treatment of many diseases, e.g., diabetes. They are sometimes equipped with a type of wireless connectivity to modify the configuration. Possible modifications could lead to the administration of too small or too high doses of drugs, which may directly pose a threat to the life and health of the patient. Such cyberattacks can be tailored to specific people.[13] Researchers suggest that the best time to carry them out would be at night, because then the patient might not feel the change in the dose and therefore he/she may not react.[14] Such doses can, therefore, be selected for the individual victim – the patient. Where can the attacker obtain such sensitive information? For example, from the logs from the device itself, and perhaps from the management system of these devices. Assuming that such data are available – a very dangerous cyberattack could potentially be constructed. That's not all.

4.5.2 Targeted attack – battery drain

As a result of a cyberattack on such an implantable medical device, that is, an implant, it may also run out of battery faster than expected. To understand this, it is enough to carry out a simple calculation.

On a "standard basis", medical devices are implanted for many years. They have a certain factory-guaranteed lifespan, related to the battery life, for example, 10 years. This is an estimate of the operating time for the normal mode of use of the device under the assumed typical conditions.[15] If, on the other hand, such a system is hacked (and such capabilities have been demonstrated) and someone takes control of it, the settings could be changed in ways so that the system begins to perform – intentionally – some more energy-intensive operations, such as computational ones, thus accelerating the battery drain.[16] This would be very dangerous, because it could happen in an unexpected way.

Meanwhile, to replace the battery, it is necessary to operate on the patient. Such standard exchanges are planned; they have their own due dates. An unexpected, sudden need for a surgery (requiring surgery on the patient) can be a problem. Now imagine that there are **thousands** of such patients, all requiring urgent surgery, in a short time frame. There are, of course, a limited number of surgeons, surgery facilities, etc. Thinking about the potential consequences is left as an exercise to the reader.

4.5.3 Attacks on medical devices – summary

Such a cyberattack is a kind of philosophical issue, a way of understanding the threat. If it was assumed that the system is to work for some time, then here the attacker would look for the possibility of controlling the attacked system in such a way to break or violate these assumptions, go beyond the "standard defined circumstances". In this case, such an assumption is the battery lifetime, and the instrument violating them – the operations performed on the device. This is the thought process of attackers: they learn about infrastructural and system assumptions and look for conditions for violating these parameters. Very often, as a result of this process, such possibilities are discovered.

4.6 HOW TO SECURE A HOSPITAL

And now, in a few sentences, we will explain how to secure a hospital. But first, a word of caution. We do not think that this book should be the sole and main textbook used on this specific subject, "in production systems". We will only mention a few things that are worth thinking about. However, if a reader happens to manage the cybersecurity of a hospital, he/she should devote much more resources and time to the problem. Hopefully, such a reader knows about it. Our book is not an exhaustive resource on this topic. We speak of certain things because a broader awareness of them may be important. Conceptual awareness can even be useful.

4.6.1 Hardware, software, licenses, updates...

In hospitals, we have hardware, software, and licensing for them, we also have people, hardware and software suppliers, and certain rules and requirements. There is also a finite budget, usually too small in relation to the needs. It is worth taking care of the cybersecurity of all hardware and software, but also making sure that the licenses remain valid, i.e., that there is working technical support (this is also a matter of costs). It is very often the case that the hardware and software in hospitals are not managed by hospital employees, because updates and sometimes even configurations are made by an external company, the supplier. And here we have a problem, because if the license expires, such an external provider will no longer be obliged to make any changes (it will even be against their financial interests).

4.6.2 What happens in the event of a large-scale cyberattack? Scenario of a systemic cyberattack

There is also a systemic problem here, which is not really mentioned very often. Imagine the scale of an entire country, or perhaps even an entire continent, such as Europe. Assume that we have one or more suppliers of a certain medical device. Such medical devices will function in a lot of hospitals. Let's imagine a hypothetical scenario.

What happens if a security vulnerability is identified and it is determined that it is actually a real risk and a real threat, and there is a group that is interested in exploiting this type of vulnerability.

Imagine what happens if, for example, malware is released that spreads automatically.

Such a device at risk must be updated, likely in many places where it is deployed. And this must be done very quickly. However, we have few resources at our disposal: there are one or a few companies that know how these solutions function on the low-level, and thus how the devices based on them actually work. Such companies, automatically "critical" in this situation, obviously have limited resources. Let's suppose they have 20 or 40 employees, and this is sufficient under a "normal situation" in a typical year. If, for example, we assume that we need to make changes in several hundred places, but it is spread over the whole year, then it works well.

But let's imagine that we have an active cyber threat and we need to make changes almost everywhere in a very short period of time, for example within a few days or a week.

It will be impossible. Such a company will not cope with this task, because it is a very non-standard mode of operation, completely different from the one usually provided. This is a systemic threat and there is no easy solution to this problem. There is no economic justification for such a company to maintain the ability to replace all systems in a week, all the time; it is set to do that perhaps a couple hundred times in a year. The easiest method of protection in such a situation would, therefore, be to completely isolate such a system. It will consist of a very strong segregation of networks and systems; making sure that there is no possibility of connecting to such a system from the outside; not using any external peripherals, devices, external memory, no flash drives. But is it feasible? What about configuration data, what about getting results of the tests?

Another possible avenue is, for example, to force such companies to publish all the necessary information, details, and technical documentation required to modify, update, and build the software. Especially with regard to systems that have ceased to be actively maintained and supported by the manufacturer (their lifetime and support has ended).

This is an eminently political problem: there would have to be a law introducing such requirements. So, are there any willing to vote for this to make it happen?

4.6.2.1 Segmentation, segregation, and isolation

In hospitals, there are different types of systems. We have the "business" part, i.e., ordinary computers supporting patient registration or doctors' computers, and the more critical, "production" systems, i.e., more operational ones, computers specifically responsible for handling of medical or diagnostic devices, such as magnetic resonance imaging or ultrasound scanners (USG). The basic assumption in hospitals is to have very strong network segmentation, segregation, isolation, so that there are no easy connections made between different networks and systems. The idea is that if business systems are hacked, it will not be possible to access more critical systems. This is often complicated, because if we have different departments in hospitals, including, for example, one that deals with X-rays or MRI, there is a need to access the patient's medical data in various subdivisions. The network should be built in such a way that there is access to patient data, but that these critical systems are still separated.

So, in hospitals, there are very specific technical challenges and computer security is important, it is important to train doctors and staff (not to connect external devices without a clear need, and only once the device is validated for use), so that everyone knows how things work, what the limitations are and why they are the way they are. Of course, training alone will not help here. However, we wish that your visits to healthcare centers take place where the security is the best.

4.7 LETHAL EFFECTS

Let us return to a dangerous, perhaps even tragic, problem. Well, can there be deaths due to cyberattacks? Can a cyberattack really kill? Healthcare and healthcare systems, as the name suggests, are a health issue. It may also be a matter of life and death, however solemnly it sounds. If computers control sensitive diagnostic devices or sensitive devices implanted in patients' bodies, the question arises: What if something goes wrong?

The question is whether cyberattacks can kill. This question may or may not be provocative. So far, there has been no deliberate fatality due to a cyberattack (although the press often looks for them, which is not surprising).

4.7.1 Bad design – Therac-25 system

However, a known example is the Therac-25 system, where as a result of poor software engineering practices and the creation of a system that had a lot of bugs, mistakes, errors – fatalities occurred. This happened between 1985 and 1987 in the United States. Therac-25 was a radiologic therapy system, i.e., a device that was supposed to treat cancer using beam irradiation. In such systems, it is crucial to aim the beam well, in the right place, and for the dose of such radiation to be of the right intensity and power. Due to software engineering errors and poor user interface, the wrong doses of radiation were administered, leading to a loss of health and death of patients. It was a series of accidents. This emphasizes that software in healthcare systems is a matter of life and death. In the case of Therac-25, however, these were not intentional incidents. These were unfortunate accidents. From time to time, however, we can hear about the fact that a cyberattack, perhaps, led to a death.

4.7.2 Chasing sensation?

There is a peculiar pursuit of such stories. Perhaps this is understandable, because the public is very interested in whether the growing issue of cybersecurity could also be a lethal problem. We are talking about various reports here. For example, in Germany in 2020, where it was suspected that perhaps a cyberattack and ransomware infection led to the death of a patient. In the case in question, the idea was that it was probably due to ransomware that the provision of medical assistance was delayed and the patient died. In practice, no cause-and-effect relationship has been established.

Similar reports were made in the United States in 2021, where a cyberattack resulted in the omission of certain medical readings during labor, a medical problem was not noticed, and the baby unfortunately died. Here we do not know many details, but it also does not seem that demonstrating a cause-and-effect relationship is easy or even possible.

In fact, it is very difficult to establish a link between an event and an effect, in this case a cyberattack and death. In addition, what should be of interest is the question of whether the lethal effects were the intention of the attackers, that is, whether they were intentional or not.

The above situations were real. Aside from them, it is worth considering the theoretical, the hypothetical issues. We have already talked about certain scenarios, like about administering the wrong doses of radiation or drugs, but there are also other risks. Perhaps, if the system is hacked, we can take control of it and falsify some health results. For example, those from computer tomography,[17] in such a way as to lead to a wrong diagnosis and prescribing of a wrong therapy, writing an incorrect prescription. This may harm someone's health or at the very least, it may not help save someone's health.

4.7.3 Careful with reports?

However, it must be said that media reports may exaggerate what actually happened. What is claimed or actually studied.

The results of research confirming the existence of a relationship between the speed of providing health services and the time that must be spent on performing certain activities or configurations on the computer were presented.

In this case, it was found that the increased time for the access to the electrocardiogram (by 2.7 minutes), which must be spent on computer use, is generally associated with increased mortality.[18] This refers to the fact that after a wave of ransomware attacks, cybersecurity was improved, and it was done in such a way that the need to enter passwords, credentials on computers, etc. was built in (these are standard security measures). Thus, these studies would only state that there is a relationship between the length and time taken by some operations on the computer, and the fact that some things will take more time, and, as a result, medical services will be provided to the patient a bit later.

However, this cannot lead to the conclusions that, for example, "ransomware kills", because it is rather a matter of the user interface and how it is designed. It is obvious that in computer systems, there is a need to provide some authentication functionality, to prevent unauthorized users from using such a computer. Some cybersecurity fundamentals simply have to be present. However, we cannot say that the incorporation of protections leads to death. We can only conclude that the design of the user interface has an impact on the ease and time consumption of such a solution.

However, studies of the safety of medical devices as well as systemic threats are important. And there is still hope that not only will the cybersecurity risks be identified, but also that systemic problems will be identified. That is, risks that arise from the very way devices work, function, from their design. So, for example, we have a pacemaker and it works in such a way that from time to time it corrects the work of the heart. If someone takes control of the configuration of such a pacemaker, then he/she can make a bad correction, which can be functionally equated with unwanted electroshocks administered.

We mentioned that often medical devices are controlled by standard operating systems, ordinary computers. However, sometimes these need to be specialized. And here we already have a certain way of reasoning.

One might say – philosophical, and it is similar to the way of reasoning in the previous chapter.

Since such a system is nonstandard, it cannot be hacked as easily as standard ones. Therefore, understanding such a system and coming up with a method to break such safeguards would require time and cost (you even need to have access to such a system, e.g., to acquire it). This might not be available to all the potential attackers.

4.7.4 Why kill with a cyberattack?

The question, however, is why allocate such funds, outlays, incur the costs, if there is no obvious return on such an investment (we are talking about a financial return)?

A political effect as a result of a cyberattack with fatal consequences would be decidedly negative, serious, dramatic. If anything affects the health or life of people, it arouses great interest of the press, public opinion, and politicians. Rightly so. And later, perhaps, the interest of diplomats or even the military. Such an interest is not in the interest of for-profit cybercriminals, because it means problems for them. Perhaps, however, there are groups and actors who may be interested in gaining such abilities. Not for the financial profit. However, this is a separate problem, and this is what we will talk about in Chapter 7.

4.7.4.1 Is it easy to detect death due to a cyberattack?

Let's outline the issue. Let's call it – a problem of detecting cyber threats with a lethal effect.

If we can imagine a cyberattack and taking control of an implant that is embedded in the body, then the question arises: what happens when death occurs as a result of the malfunction of such an implant? Such a case will be investigated. The question, however, is whether such an investigation includes the cyberattack hypothesis. It seems that this does not necessarily have to be the case. In any case, there is no certainty that anyone is looking for such events, indeed. In this way, fatalities remain a vague, statistical problem, blamed on failures or malfunctions, a hardware problem or a configuration program. But – something related to the standard scope of functioning, not to deliberate action.

It is, therefore, not at all clear whether it would be easy to identify, detect, and confirm a deliberate fatal cyberattack. So it's a bit of a paradox that there are health devices and we have a growing problem of cyberattacks, and it's not clear whether it would be possible to easily detect that a cyberattack is responsible for a lethal effect, for example as a result of hacking a pacemaker. Is the cybersecurity of such medical devices taken seriously enough? Unfortunately, we do not have good news, because it seems that "manufacturers do not take into account the possibility of such attacks when developing such devices".[19] How could, then, a signature of operation resulting in potentially lethal effects even look like? Chances are that it would necessitate first to exclude the first assumptions about software, configuration, or hardware malfunction. Only afterward could the hypothesis of intentionality be verified. Unless, of course, someone in the first layer of analysis decides not to classify something ambiguous as a typical or usual malfunction.

4.8 OKAY, BUT CAN A CYBERATTACK KILL?

We will summarize this chapter by returning again to the possible effects of a deadly cyberattack. Let's recall that we are considering a provocative question: can a cyberattack kill? This question was already raised, but the provided answer was suggestive.

This time we will answer this question directly: yes, a person can be killed by a cyberattack. A scenario follows.

4.8.1 Cyberattack scenario with lethal consequences – can such a logic bomb be detected?

As we have already mentioned, there are potentially such possibilities. Taking control of the medical diagnostic system and for example, administering too high a dose of radiation to the patient may be possible. It may also be possible to take control of the implant in such a way that as a result of identifying *a specific* implant (even a specific person or group of people, for example by inspecting the serial number of the hardware), malware would be activated that would send a malicious instruction.

Another hypothetical scenario could even be a very broad cyberattack. Let's imagine the execution of a cyber operation on a larger scale.

Let's consider a hypothetical scenario where there is a mass infection of such implants. Such implants are computers. Computers, as it is already clear, have clocks. Therefore, it is possible to design, theoretically, malware in such an implant that it activates itself at a certain time, on a specially selected day. What if we have several thousand patients-users and at the same time, a malicious procedure is launched in all of them? In extreme cases, this could lead to thousands of victims. This would be a very perfidious and malicious cyberattack, and its effectiveness would unfortunately be potentially high. This situation would be much more serious than if we had such deaths occurring in an uncoordinated manner, one after the other. Because if we were dealing with isolated cases, someone would probably start investigating them and the problem would be identified, eventually the cause would be discovered, there would be a chance to remedy the problem. However, if we have several thousand attacks, all executed at once, there is no possibility of a quick response, and the investigation would require time.

In fact, we have considered here the use of embedding a *logic bomb* into such an implant. Logic bomb, i.e., a malware that activates under certain circumstances, such as at a certain time. It was explained that it was not clear whether such attacks could be detected. However, if we had several thousand failures that occurred around the same time, it would be a very strong indication that this is not a coincidence. A simple failure on such a scale, with such a coordinated effect, would be statistically improbable.

4.8.2 Coordinated battery drain of a medical implant? A scenario

Now let's consider a hypothetical disruptive scenario where, let's say (a numerical assumption for visualization) 10,000 implants of patients are infected as a result of a cyberattack – and that their batteries (artificially caused) run out on a specific day, such as January 31. Would it be realistic to make so many unplanned, perhaps lifesaving, device replacement procedures in one day? Of course, it depends which country we are considering (some would fare better than others), but there are many justified doubts here, so for the sake of simplicity we will say: of course not.

At the same time, it would not only be a paralysis of health services. There is a really high risk of lethal effects here. Fortunately, so far, this scenario is purely hypothetical. Let's hope that this will not change. Another thing is that the actions described in this scenario would have to be deliberate and definitely not profit-driven: such a person, or persons, would want to kill. We do not know of any cybercriminal or state groups with such motivations today. That would be a very specific intention. Very dangerous, with the potential to destabilize the political and security situation (more on this in Chapters 6 and 7).

However, cybersecurity of medical devices is not a topic for jokes. In 2017, the FDA (Food and Drug Administration) announced that 465,000 pacemakers had to be withdrawn because a serious safety problem had been identified that could have potentially allowed the malicious actor to drain the battery (earlier than assumed) or even force certain side effects on the pacemaker.

The remote, wireless ability to configure such devices is useful for patients, because if we need to update the operating mode, we do not need to perform a surgery – we can do it remotely. So it is useful, although the price is some added risk (as the story of Dick Cheney mentioned earlier indicates, for some patients such a risk is unacceptable).

We will end this chapter with these optimistic scenarios. We will revisit the issue of lethal effects in the chapter about the critical infrastructure and the one about cyberwar.

NOTES

1 See. https://www.oxfordlearnersdictionaries.com/definition/english/infrastructure?
q=infrastructure
2 Article 15 ("Exceptional need to use data") of the Proposal for a Regulation of the European Parliament and of the Council on harmonised rules on fair access to and use of data(Data Act), https://eur-lex.europa.eu/legal-content/EN/TXT/HTML/?uri=CELEX:52022PC0068&from=EN

3 Ibid, article 15(a).

4 UK Department of Health and Social Care, *Securing cyber resilience in health and care. Progress update October 2018*, https://assets.publishing.service.gov.uk/ government/uploads/system/uploads/attachment_data/file/747464/securing-cyber-resilience-in-health-and-care-september-2018-update.pdf

5 PwC, *Conti Cyber attack on the HSE. Independent post Incident review*, 3.12.2021, https://www.hse.ie/eng/services/publications/conti-cyber-attack-on-the-hse-full-report.pdf

6 A. Vittorio, *Merck's $1.4 billion insurance win splits cyber from 'act of war'*, 19.01. 2022, news.bloomberglaw.com/privacy-and-data-security/mercks-1-4-billion-insurance-win-splits-cyber-from-act-of-war

7 L. Gisel, L. Olejnik, *The potential human cost of cyber operations*, report of the International Committee of the Red Cross in Geneva, 2018.

8 Patel, Z., Velankar, Y., Trivedi, C., & Oza, P. (2023). Wireless Implantable Medical Devices Security and Privacy: A Survey. In *Smart Energy and Advancement in Power Technologies* (pp. 69–87). Springer, Singapore.

9 Gasson, M. N. (2010, June). Human enhancement: Could you become infected with a computer virus? In 2010 *IEEE International Symposium on Technology and Society* (pp. 61–68). IEEE.

10 Rieback, M. R., Crispo, B., & Tanenbaum, A. S. (2006, March). Is your cat infected with a computer virus? In *Fourth Annual IEEE International Conference on Pervasive Computing and Communications (PERCOM'06)* (pp. 10-pp). IEEE.

11 Symantec, *New Orangeworm attack group targets the healthcare sector in the US, Europe, and Asia*, April 23, 2018, https://symantec-enterprise-blogs.security. com/blogs/threat-intelligence/orangeworm-targets-healthcare-us-europe-asia

12 P.A. Williams, A.J. Woodward, *Cybersecurity vulnerabilities in medical devices: a complex environment and multifaceted problem*, "Medical Devices (Auckland, NZ)" 2015, no. 8, p. 305; European Society of Radiology (ESR), *Renewal of radiological equipment*, "Insights into Imaging" 2014, no. 5, pp. 543–546.

13 T. Levy-Loboda, E. Sheetrit, I. F. Liberty, A. Haim, N. Nissim, *Personalized insulin dose manipulation attack and its detection using interval-based temporal patterns and machine learning algorithms*, "Journal of Biomedical Informatics" 2022, vol. 132, 104129.

14 Ibid.

15 Kaspersky ICS CERT, *Abbott recalls pacemakers due to cyberattack risk*, 09/04/ 2017, https://ics-cert.kaspersky.com/publications/news/2017/09/04/abbott-recalls-pacemakers-due-to-cyberattack-risk/

16 X. Hei, X. Du, J. Wu, F. Hu, *Defending resource depletion attacks he implantable Medical Devices*, in: *2010 IEEE Global telecommunications Conference GLOBECOM 2010* IEEE, 2010; S. Das, G.P. Siroky, S. Lee, D. Mehta, R. Suri, *Cybersecurity: the need for data and patient safety with cardiac implantable electronic devices*, "Heart Rhythm" 2021, vol. 18, no. 3, pp. 473–481.

17 Y. Mirsky, T. Mahler, I. Shelef, Y. Elovici, *CT-GAN: Malicious Tampering of 3D Medical Imagery using Deep Learning*, in: *28th USENIX Security Symposium (USENIX Security 19)*, 2019, pp. 461–478.

18 S.J. Choi, M.E. Johnson, C.U. Lehmann, *Data breach remediation efforts and their implications for hospital quality*, "Health services research" 2019, vol. 54, no. 5, pp. 971–980.

19 V. Hassija, V. Chamola, B.C. Bajpai, S. Zeadally, *Security issues in implantable medical devices: Fact or fiction?*, "Sustainable Cities and Society" 2021, vol. 66, no. 2.

Chapter 5

Cybersecurity of critical infrastructure

5.1 VULNERABLE PART OF THE STATE

For the purposes of this book, we will regard as critical infrastructure the critical elements of the State infrastructure necessary for the functioning of the State and society (population). This fairly broad definition includes elements such as energy, transport, healthcare (the subject of the previous chapter), industry, water treatment infrastructure, or important institutions responsible for the monetary security of the State (financial system) and other sectors important for the State.

Such an infrastructure is critical, because it is necessary for the functioning of the State, the society, sometimes even for the existence of the civilian population. In simple terms, life without certain services would be much more difficult, and perhaps even impossible in the modern world. It is difficult to imagine functioning in conditions of unreliable access to electricity or running water. The standard of civilization is that this access should be reliable. Similarly with access to universal healthcare, although here different countries have different internal conditions or constraints, for example, it might be expensive. We will focus here on the issue of cybersecurity of individual elements of critical infrastructure. We will select a few of them and discuss them as *case studies*. We will talk about cybersecurity, i.e., both the security of information systems and possibilities of compromising security, i.e., carrying out cyberattacks, and we will list what the consequences may be. Of course, we will discuss well-known examples of such cyberattacks. These are instructive, because we can draw many conclusions from them for the future.

As we have already discussed, cyberattacks can be classified as attacks on confidentiality, integrity, or availability. This chapter will talk about systems in broad terms. A cyberattack on the availability of a specific server, such as a power plant website, will obviously have no effect on the consumers because those really important systems should be isolated. Therefore, a public website disruption will be a "cyberattack", but only on

DOI: 10.1201/9781003408260-5

the website, and not on the critical infrastructure itself, i.e., on the production of electricity or its distribution. This is an important point, because it will protect us from sensational reports exaggerating certain events that actually may not have any meaning. They can, however, arouse anxiety in the society, to which the media "handling" of such an incident sometimes contributes significantly, but this is not the place to consider information operations.

5.1.1 A different classification of cyberattacks

When it comes to cyberattacks on critical infrastructure, it is worth distinguishing cyberattacks according to a slightly different classification than before. These are cyberattacks on accessibility, but not only. We can distinguish: destructive attacks, which may even aim at the physical destruction of infrastructure, and disruptive attacks, which aim to paralyze the provision of service. This could be, for example, a (temporary) interruption of the power supply or a disruption of work of a factory. At the same time, it is conceivable that a destructive cyberattack can also have disruptive effects. However, causing physical destruction is not always necessary to cause interference with the operations of its target. As we have already pointed out, a cyberattack on the so-called business network of an infrastructure operator usually does not reach critical elements of the infrastructure. For example, if we attack the business network of a nuclear power plant, it will almost certainly not involve any access to further, more sensitive elements, such as monitoring or the core of such an infrastructure.

The same will apply to other infrastructures, such as energy elements, transport or pipelines, gas pipelines. A very good example here is the cyberattack on the operator of the Colonial Pipeline in the United States. The 2021 cyberattack targeted the business network itself, and therefore the ability to process orders. However, this led to the shutdown of the entire pipeline. Although it was not formally necessary to do it, it was done for business reasons. And this is an interesting case in which an attack on the business part, i.e., the non-critical part, actually led to paralyzing the operation of the pipeline – to its shutdown. However, this was a conscious decision of the operator, motivated by financial reasons. Notably, however, this cyberattack has led to increase in fuel prices: as a result of the pipeline shutdown in early May, the price per gallon of gasoline increased by 4 cents in the affected areas for the rest of the month.[1]

5.2 EXAMPLES OF CYBERATTACKS AGAINST CRITICAL INFRASTRUCTURE

Let us now turn to concrete examples from specific areas. First of all, let's discuss the issue of electricity, energy, generation, and distribution.

5.2.1 Energy

Let's start with a possible cyberattack on a power plant. It can be a hydro-electric power plant, a wind farm, a power plant based on burning coal, a nuclear one. For us, it doesn't really matter much. Suffice to say that a power plant is a very complex hardware and software environment, and within it we have all sorts of electronic equipment and all sorts of software. Important note: some power plants are highly dispersed, such as wind ones. A cyberattack at another layer, such as a means of communication, can sometimes involve many, perhaps even all of important nodes. This happened in 2022, when access to approx. 5800 wind turbines in Germany was lost,[2] which was caused by problems with communication via satellite internet, as a result of an attack on the provider's infrastructure.[3] This highlights how fragile such an infrastructure may be in practice.

At the same time, the details of what hardware and software are used in a specific place are rarely publicly disclosed. This is understandable, as many things concerning critical infrastructure issues are classified. States treat the list of elements considered as "critical infrastructure" as classified. The EU NIS Directive[4] refers to operators of critical infrastructure as an 'operator of essential services' (Article 4(1)) and it is an entity providing a service which is essential for the maintenance of critical societal or economic activities' (Article 5(2)(a)). At the same time, critical entities are defined in the NIS 2 Directive, where "critical entity" (Article 2(1)) is identified by each EU country and includes, for example, "energy companies", "distribution system operators" (energy), "district heating", "central oil stocks", "gas supply companies" (Annex I). It also covers digital infrastructure, certain public administrations, banking, financial market infrastructure, transport (Annex I). And this is the critical infrastructure as defined in a binding legal document: entities important for the existence of the State and the population.

5.2.1.1 Nuclear power plants

In the past, there have been quite a few reports of cyberattacks on various types of infrastructure, such as power plants, and also on nuclear power plants. These were usually cyberattacks that could only reach the business elements of the network, i.e., they did not have infrastructural consequences. It is rare to hear publicly about cyberattacks that have actually affected the infrastructure. There was one case of an unidentified power plant in the United States in 2017 that was reportedly shut down as a result of a cyberattack. However, no detailed information about this has ever been revealed, so we are only mentioning further speculation regarding this rumor.

In 2003, Slammer,[5] the first worm capable of rapid propagation, made its way into the decommissioned Ohio Davis-Besse nuclear power plant, which led to the loss of control over the digital radiation and temperature sensors for several hours, although analog sensors were still working. Of course, this was not a targeted cyberattack. The Slammer worm selected potential targets pseudo-randomly, infecting all the vulnerable ones that could be found. Its creators, however, made mistakes that slowed down the spread of the worm: this process of pseudo-random selection had flaws, its quality was poor.

5.2.1.2 Cyberattacks on energy distribution in Ukraine

Against this background, the events in Ukraine in 2015, 2016,[6] and 2022 (during the war) stand out. These were, in fact, the first such largely unprecedented cyberattacks.

Those that took place in 2015 and 2016[7] actually led to the interruption of electricity distribution – it did not reach the end users. Several hundred thousand people lost their power supply for several hours. The operation in 2015 was a very large-scale cyber operation. It began in the spring of that year. Security was breached; attackers gained and made their access firm, attaining an access capability. This is how the position within the systems was established – so that it would be possible to run the *effects operation* (more about it in Chapter 7), to turn off the electricity in December 2015. Three power distribution centers were disconnected, corresponding to dozens of power substations. It was a very complex operation. It all started with sending a phishing e-mail, and then there was taking over control: gaining access to the internal VPN and ultimately access to control panels.

It should be clear that today's level of computerization means that energy distribution is controlled digitally, and even remotely. So it may be possible to reach such a system from the outside, access the control panels and simply cause a "*disconnect*". However, this is not all, because in the situation of cyber operation in Ukraine, the power switches were blocked by software – overwriting the hardware's firmware. Firmware, i.e., low-level control software. This was done in order to block the equipment and prevent easy switching on of the current, also via software. The system was paralyzed: the IT system with which the equipment was controlled was shut down and destroyed. This resulted in the need for manual repair, and thus for visiting such a substation, physically. As part of this cyber operation, the telephone line was also overloaded so that customers could not get through and report electricity shortages.

In 2016, this action was repeated (whether this can be called an "attack" will become clear in Chapter 7 on cyberconflict). But this time a more automated system was used. So, a malware has been created that does certain things by itself, automatically. As you can see, progress in this area is gradual.

5.2.1.3 What happens when the power is switched off

Once the electricity is turned off, what actually happens in such a situation? If we remotely shut down the electricity in a large agglomeration, in a large city, it is conceivable that this could undermine citizens' trust in the government (although it may not be immediately clear how the loss of energy supply occurred) and, therefore, have a psychological effect. If only because nowadays access to electricity is a standard and it is simply something that is expected from the State. Therefore, it can also be an element of an attack on the whole State, on trust in the State, a psychological operation.

5.2.1.4 An attempt to turn off the power under wartime conditions?

In 2022, under wartime conditions, Russian cyber operators sought to repeat such cyberattacks and did so with a new version of the automaton, a tool known as Industroyer2. Nine power substations were successfully infected. However, these were not disabled because the cyberattack was detected and neutralized. This underscores the great progress in system defenses that has been made in the seven years since the first attack in 2015.

5.2.1.5 How to protect the system

It is worth considering how we may protect against such a situation. From the previous subsection, it follows that successful defensive actions can be done even under wartime conditions. But the problem of cyberattacks on critical infrastructures can be systemic.

Various types of studies suggest that the State should use several operators of electricity production and distribution, because such separate companies or operators tend to utilize different types of hardware and software, from several suppliers. Thus, if a cyberattack targets the infrastructure of a specific operator, such an operation will target specific types of hardware and software. The rest may remain to be safe or at least not be given any time by the attackers, because that would increase the cost of a cyberattack.

It is the problem of avoiding a *monoculture*, i.e., a situation where there is only one vendor of hardware and software, because the strength of cyberattacks lies precisely in *scalability* and coordination. An ideal cyberattack would be possible if we had a monoculture infrastructure: the same hardware, the same software. Then, it is enough to find a vulnerability perhaps in one part of such a system. And then, everything can be reached with a "single" cyberattack, very quickly. The visible effect would be a *cascading* paralysis of the infrastructure. Everything would stop working, in a short time, an intentionally caused blackout (*in extreme circumstances*). This is a worst case scenario. Good segregation of the network and ensuring that there is no monoculture of one supplier allows preventing its implementation.

Admittedly, 2022 has shown how much progress has been made in the field of cyber operations targeting critical infrastructure. At that time, the existence of cyber tools has been discovered[8] and revealed that destructive actions could be carried out against devices from various vendors.

Creating such tools in this way is laborious and expensive. Someone must have done it on purpose. Fortunately, these cyber tools were not employed in practice, as they had been detected before that could happen. The described situation showed great progress both in the development of tools and in the detection of operations. We may assume further progress in this space.

5.2.1.6 Blackout as a result of a cyberattack? Scenarios

Another "nightmare" scenario is a cascading shutdown of energy production or distribution, constructed in such a way that it would lead to a widespread blackout, over a large area, perhaps covering the entire country. This could mean huge costs, even in the order of several hundred billion dollars, if such a blackout would be long lasting (and it may not necessarily be simple to restore the energy system in such a case). The social costs would also be enormous. But how can such a cascading power outage be brought about? We will present here several possible scenarios. All of them are, so far, only theoretical, hypothetical.

One way is to cause electricity fluctuations in the network in such a way that the network simply gets overloaded. This can be achieved, for example, by physically destroying dozens of selected high-voltage transformers in such a way that they would be difficult to repair, which would make such a blackout long. The urgent need to replace dozens of high-voltage transformers may not be taken into account in a risk management situation (crisis situation). Of course, one might have dozens of transformers "in stock" so that they can be quickly replaced, but this means high costs. In risk management, the so-called *n-1 rule* is often employed.[9] It assumes that the whole system must operate in a situation where an element of the system is disconnected, say when the operation of a particular power plant or some other element in such a power plant is lost. But what if a cyberattack disconnects more elements, a cascade, at the same time?

5.2.2 Scenario: Physical destruction of the transformer

The question also remains, is it possible to physically destroy energy transformers with a cyberattack? Potentially, yes.

According to technical standards, the expected lifetime of the transformer is 180,000 hours (21 years). Thus, we can imagine that under standard conditions, the transformer needs to be replaced from time to time. But it's not like we have to replace a few dozen or a few hundred of these, at once, in one day, because there is this guarantee that on average it is necessary to do it about every 21 years. So the purpose of such a cyberattack could be to use these assumptions that the transformer is to operate for a *guaranteed period* in conditions of uninterrupted operation *"in a normal situation"*. This can be achieved, for example, in such a way that a cyberattack will lead to overloading such a transformer. Thus *we are questioning the assumption* of operating in a "normal situation".

There are many possibilities here to identify weaknesses of the transformers. Specialists know this. According to such a potential scenario, the attacker would target a thermal protection system that prevents the transformer from overheating.[10] There is software access to it. And here, theoretically, let's assume that the attacker knew the system and its vulnerabilities well enough to be able to reset the firmware, such software – to disable these protections. For example, in such ordinary (safety) fuses (*breakers*) operating in normal conditions, it is possible that the overload management is activated in the event of an overload of 150% above the norm. That is, for example, if too much current is transmitted, that is, energy of too high an intensity. Imagine an attacker modifying the transmission in such a way that this value rises to 300%, but there will be no shutdown for security reasons – because the security system has been disconnected (by a deliberate, intentional action of attackers). So we are dealing here with the disconnection of security systems. And here let's return to the said technical standard of transformer safety, because it predicts not only the lifetime of the transformer, but also relates these parameters to certain elements of the transformer, specifically – to hardware insulation. The standard lifetime of such a transformer is 20.5 years – under certain assumptions, for example, that the transformer operates at a constant temperature of 30 degrees Celsius (on average).[11] Thus, we already see some way to have a negative impact on such a transformer. It is necessary to lead to a situation in which the operating temperature will increase significantly (and the safety systems will not work, because they have been "disconnected"). According to the standard, it is assumed that such a transformer loses 1–4% of its lifetime with a constant overload lasting almost two hours. However, if the overload is associated with an increase in operating temperature to 160 degrees Celsius, the rate of loss of insulation strength (i.e., insulation damage) will increase significantly and it can completely fail in less than 48 hours. At the same time, in a situation where for every 25 minutes of such a continuous operation, 4% of the expected lifetime of the transformer is lost, it can be destroyed in about 10 hours.[12]

The whole cyberattack would consist in modifying the software elements controlling the equipment in such a way as to significantly shorten the lifetime and, as a result, lead to physical damage with disconnected security systems. There would be physical degradation, destruction of such equipment. If this is done in a quick succession to multiple transformers, it can paralyze the entire energy system.

According to existing studies, the cyber-shutdown of a number of key transformers could lead to a major blackout in the UK, which could affect millions of people, as some substations are crucial (some are more important than others) to the power system, and shutting them down would have very serious consequences.[13] Fortunately, carrying out such an operation is not so easy.

The Russian war that erupted in Ukraine in 2022 demonstrated cyber-attack attempts on the electricity system. These were unsuccessful. However, the kinetic strikes (with missiles) did cause severe damage and service outage. This highlights that cyber and kinetic activities may serve similar purposes. More details about this important topic are given in Chapter 7.

5.2.2.1 Practical demonstration of physical damage

The question also arises as to whether physical damage has ever been caused. In 2007, such a test study was conducted in the United States under control conditions. The control of the electricity generator was manipulated. And in fact, it was possible to cause real damage – the power generator caught on fire.

At this point, this should no longer surprise us. We know that the power distribution system can be paralyzed, that physical damage can be caused. However, the larger world learned about such real consequences relatively recently, when in Ukraine people were successfully cut off from electricity. However, such cyber operations are by no means commonplace. They are exceptional.

5.2.2.2 Skepticism about reports is recommended

We must also devote time here to more *philosophical* issues. Well, there are real reports about the power outage as a result of a cyberattack. So we already know that it is possible, because it happened. Therefore, the very idea that a cyberattack can turn off the electricity has penetrated into the public consciousness. The general public and the public opinion is aware of it. Over time, as it became even more popular, people were seeking information on this subject. If something is theoretically possible, and even has happened, maybe it will happen more often, remaining a constant threat? This is a disastrous, flawed logic!

One of the effects of this reasoning is that if, for example, there is a blackout or power outage, which may have a quite an ordinary background (e.g., natural, accidental), often the media, or the public, might suspect that it could have happened as a result of a cyberattack. So wild speculations and even quasi-conspiracy theories arise (that's just the power of rumors). This was the reaction to the lack of electricity in Venezuela in 2019,[14] where there were even insinuations about the participation of some foreign state. There has been similar speculation in relation to power outages in the United States, Iran, and elsewhere. It must be made clear that in the vast majority of such situations, the answer is: "*No, this power outage, this failure did not occur as a result of a cyberattack*". Why? Firstly, because it is not easy to carry out such a cyber operation, and secondly, it takes time to say that the loss of electricity is the result of a cyberattack. So if there is a speculation, for example, that "something is not outside the realm of possibility", it does not mean that it happened. Let's watch carefully who spreads such reports. How can such a person know about it, especially so quickly? What is the credibility of such a person? Maybe none, for example, if it is a "*chief expert in everything*" (or a specialist, but from a very different area), and is burdened with a history of previous various types of mishaps, or even misinformation (this is dangerous, especially if it is a well-known person, a popular one, because rumors nowadays can spread very quickly).

Perhaps, in fact, nowadays it should truly not be ruled out that the loss of electricity could have occurred as a result of a cyberattack, as one of the potential scenarios, but this does not mean that such suspicions are serious, exclusive, conclusive, and unique. It only means that a risk is simply not excluded. That it is taken into account as one of the hypothetical scenarios. That's it, and that's reasonable – because usually these suspicions are not justified but that requires an analysis, investigation. At the same time, cyberattacks on a power plant or a nuclear power plant "sell" well in the public, because it creates a sensation. But in most cases such cyberattacks do not matter, they did not even happen.

5.2.3 Water treatment/sanitation systems

As is the case with electricity, water treatment systems are an area of much speculation. Theoretically, the possibility of cyberattacks against these systems was considered. There are not many example cases, although some events have indeed been recorded. For example, in Israel, when possible attempts at cyberattacks, probably from Iran, were analyzed and it was assumed what could go wrong if such cyberattacks were successful. There is a known case of apparent taking control of the water treatment system in Ukraine, as well as in other places, for example, in the United States, Florida, where the person who gained control of the control panel allegedly even tried to change the chemical mixture during water treatment in such a way that certain chemicals would be in excess (Information revealed subsequently undermined those initial allegations, made by authorities). This is one of the main problems with cyberattacks on such critical infrastructure elements as water treatment systems. By changing the chemical composition, we can potentially poison a wide population. And this is a very big problem, because it could, theoretically, let's emphasize that, lead to the loss of health or even life of people on a large scale.

This will be discussed in more detail in Chapter 7 on cyberwar, but here we will make an important remark.

It's not like such a cyberattack would be "legitimate". Even if external state actors, i.e., some cyber operators of the government or military, wanted to carry out such a thing, they must be aware that they would be violating international treaties designed to protect civilians. Attacks on the infrastructure necessary for the existence of civilians are illegal, which should be respected by any responsible state. So much for international law, because it is also clear that cyberattacks are illegal from the point of view of national laws (although this can be difficult to enforce when, e.g., the attackers are in another country).

Here, however, let us point out that it is not necessarily the case that in the event of a change in such a chemical composition of water, there must actually be a real risk of poisoning. Various types of chemicals are indeed used to treat water, but as you can imagine, if we "turn the lever" or change the configuration, we will not necessarily lead to a poisonous mixture – if only because there are some prosaic and obvious limitations. That is, physical limitations. It may happen that such a chemical element will simply physically run out in the tank; that is, it will not be possible to lead to widespread poisoning, because such chemicals will run out. However, it may also be that such water will then be poorly treated, which means that it will have undesirable biological parameters. This is a different kind of problem (and still a problem).

There is also a general issue of intention, because if someone does something like that, it is obvious that they have some bad intentions. They want to cause harm, perhaps lead to the loss of health or life of people. It is a serious matter when civilians are targeted. To say the least, this is unacceptable!

5.2.4 Gas and oil

There are groups interested in and specializing in cyberattacks on gas infrastructure. With regard to the technological issues: gas distribution systems are very complex. They have completely different hardware and software in different elements and layers of such a system. Thus, there are potentially many different points of vulnerability that can be attacked. In principle, everything depends on the creativity of the attacker, but it requires dedication of resources.

For example, Shamoon worm was released in 2012 (affecting about 30,000 systems), followed by Shamoon 2 in 2016,[15] which was basically aimed at the infrastructure of one company – Saudi Aramco. And it led to paralysis of operation. Gas and oil production was not affected, but the company's operations encountered many problems.

5.2.4.1 Siberian pipeline – give it no credence

It is also worth adding here a more speculative example of a so-called urban legend. Well, sometimes the so-called cyberattack on the Siberian Pipeline in the 1980s is mentioned. Apparently, the alleged CIA operation led to the embedding of infected software, which at some point activated and led to the explosion of the pipeline. There is a problem with these reports, because nothing confirms them, and it is not at all clear whether it could have been technically possible at all. It is a story, spread in certain circles, by perhaps less knowledgeable people.

5.3 SECURING CRITICAL INFRASTRUCTURE

Securing critical infrastructure is based on good practices of maintaining IT and OT (*operational technology*, including control systems, etc.), isolation of networks, monitoring them, maintaining the ability to monitor the control layer of equipment. It stems from the need to know what works within the system and the need to maintain such a system.

Industrial systems are also increasingly digital and difficult to maintain, and the passage of time adds to that. This is due to the fact that once implemented, a system can be used for up to 20 years. It may no longer be maintained by the manufacturer (e.g., the operating system provider), for example, security patches are no longer released. Therefore, it is necessary to design systems and networks in such a way that there is no easy access to such potentially vulnerable and sensitive systems, because these often supervise very important, complex processes.

There are other challenges in installing updates in this environment. For example, updates always require testing to protect industrial automation from failure, which would incur, for example, high costs and downtime. Therefore, it is also necessary to determine whether new software versions do not have a negative impact on systems, for example on absolutely critical ones – *safety instrumented systems* (SIS): physical, chemical, manufacturing, management of turbines, etc. Some industrial environments must operate continuously (24/7/365) and there are only certain moments of planned downtime when major changes can be made, for example two weekly windows a year. And if the software that is used is no longer supported, creative thinking is needed – isolating such systems more strongly, implementing network filtering rules (because even these components probably need to be controlled remotely).[16] The inability to shut down systems during operation is a common problem; it also affects large scientific undertakings. For example, the Large Hadron Collider at CERN, Geneva, where certain changes and modifications are impossible (or difficult) during operation, especially when the particle beam of protons is in a 27-kilometer ring of the circular accelerator. For example, because human access is practically impossible due to the radiation that occurs at that time (which would have harmful consequences for health). That is why planned downtime and interruptions are made. Then one can make corrections, modifications, alterations, repairs (of hardware, software, etc.). Such a scientific environment is basically an industrial setup, because there are a lot of control systems (accelerator infrastructure, detectors, their components). At the same time, it cannot be allowed for someone unauthorized to gain low-level access to critical resources in such a sensitive and valuable infrastructure, to such an equipment. This would no longer only be a cybersecurity problem and a risk to infrastructure, to research – but it could also damage the attack victim's reputation.

5.4 HACKING PHYSICAL ELEMENTS

For some time, advanced threats facing industrial automation systems and components have been considered, for example, *programmable logic* controllers (PLC), SCADA (*supervisory control and data acquisition*). These are the digital elements that control industrial processes (turbines, valves, bulkheads, pumps, chemical or physical process supervision, etc.) and are often critical for the very safety of the manufacturing process, production, as well as for occupational safety: for the health of the personnel. So it is necessary to protect them – isolation from threats, installation of updates, etc. Work is also underway to investigate what could go wrong in order to be aware of the risks, to anticipate them, to be able to secure such a system.

It's also a cybersecurity philosophy: thinking about what could go wrong and how to prepare for it.

5.4.1 Ransomware for industrial systems and PLC worm

One hypothetical scenario considers ransomware in PLC components, i.e., physical devices, sensors, surveillance and control systems. We have already talked about ransomware, albeit in a different context. As we can imagine, the "ransomware for industrial systems" scenario would paralyze the system until the ransom is paid (unless, e.g., it was a military attack during a war, and the sole goal was the paralysis – more on this in Chapter 7). It is not entirely obvious what the consequences could be, because perhaps the inability to control an important process could even lead to a catastrophe (physical destruction). However, such paralyzing tools must be considered today. For demonstration and scientific purposes, such ransomware (LogicLocker) has already been created for various types of PLC systems,[17] and in the case of another (ICS-BROCK), the "*combat capability*" to paralyze the industrial system was tested[18] (on the example of the environment of the object controlling the water treatment system). In this case, such a tool could not only paralyze operations and normal work, but also take active measures in the event of non-payment of the ransom, causing physical destruction, bringing a threat to life and health of the personnel, which in itself is dangerous. If such ransomware infects firmware, it will not be detected by the antivirus (such software does not have a "visibility" in such low level layers). And such malware can be expanded with additional functions, for example, automatic propagation within the network of an industrial system. It would be sufficient to build in the worm function into the malware.[19]

5.5 PHYSICAL EFFECTS

We have already talked about physical damage scenarios and even demonstrations of physical damage to a power generator. In a similar way, attacks can be carried out on the control systems of other physical elements such as pumps, windmills, or turbines. For example, it is possible to potentially change the parameters of their work or even to alternately change the frequency of their work in a way that would lead to their degradation and, as a result, physical destruction. The effects of such a cyberattack or a cyber operation would be physical.

5.5.1 Stuxnet

There was the case with a large (probably) military cyber operation, called Stuxnet (after its discovery) in which the frequency of centrifuges at the Natanz uranium enrichment facility in Iran was changed, tampered with.

Stuxnet is, in a way, a very fascinating piece of software. It worked automatically. Once it entered the internal systems of this uranium enrichment facility, it automatically identified and found the targets, infected them, and physically affected the frequency of the centrifuges – alternating those frequencies. This led to their physical wear, to destruction. In a sense, we discussed a conceptually similar way in relation to the case of violation of the safety of transformer operation. But this one actually happened. How come it worked? Well, such centrifuges in question have a certain lifetime and changing alternately the frequency of operation is not something standard – it led to their physical degradation. It is not clear what the political objectives of this cyber operation were. It was one of the most famous cyber operations in history and will remain so for a long time, probably forever.

5.5.2 German steel mill

Another example of physical damage affected a German steel mill; we do not know exactly which one, as it was not disclosed. However, there was some kind of explosion there, although it is not known under what circumstances; not much is known about this case.[20] There is a possibility that it was a cyberintelligence operation and this explosion was an "accident at work", i.e., it was an unintentional action. Accidents happen, including during cyber operations. Even more so when these are conducted in sensitive environments like the industrial ones.

Here it is also worth mentioning a very dangerous software created (according to the indications of companies and the Western countries) in Russia. It targeted certain elements of physical control, specifically Schneider Electric's Triconnex safety systems. This malware was called TRISIS/Triton[21] and its capabilities included disabling safety capabilities on systems in such a way that if such a physical system were to operate uncontrollably, the safety system might not work. Because it would be turned off! So, again, it is also an almost practical implementation of the hypothetical transformer scenario that we described earlier. A very dangerous situation combined with physical destruction could occur. Perhaps, even leading to the loss of life. Why was such a tool created, with such capabilities? This has not been established.

5.6 TRANSPORTATION SYSTEMS

Transportation systems, i.e., railways, ships, buses, trams, metro, but also, for example, control systems in airlines and their entire infrastructure, such as ground stations in control towers, air traffic control systems – all this is based on control systems. By taking control of them, we may hypothetically lead to dangerous situations. Even if only to the need to turn them off to investigate what happened.

Fortunately, there has never been any actual transport disaster in connection with a cyberattack. According to the Belarusian Cyberpartisan group, in 2022 the group supposedly disrupted railway traffic in Belarus, more specifically – the movement of trains with the Russian army was affected – and in fact some kinds of problems indeed took place there. But there are no independent reports on this topic; hence, verification is difficult, especially in the conditions of the ongoing armed conflict, where we had many manifestations of the so-called fog *of war*. We do not exclude it, but it is simply impossible to verify independently from the outside, especially during the still sensitive period in the region. There are also known situations when there were railway downtimes.

There are also – more theoretical – considerations about breaching or bypassing security boundaries of systems in an aircraft. Indeed it is important to consider exactly what these systems need to be protected against, due to the fact that planes are equipped with electronic hardware elements that may adversely affect flight operations in the event of their violation.[22]

In the more than a hundred years of automotive history, there is also something new, i.e., cars with a certain autonomy or perhaps one day even "self-driving" (with full autonomy) cars. Such solutions are based on the so-called artificial intelligence, sensors, and control systems. Potentially, by breaching security in some way or finding vulnerabilities in the software (or the way the sensors work), control could be taken over such software and that could lead to dangerous situations. Besides, there are known cases in which the control of such a car was remotely taken over and it was even possible to cause its sudden braking,[23] which could end very badly on the highway. By the way, in 2008, a 14-year-old boy was detained in Poland for modifying the TV remote control so as to remotely impact tram control systems. Perhaps it was fun, but it led to unexpected incidents, including derailments[24] and even injuries to people due to sudden braking and collision of trams. In this case, however, the impact was at a short distance. As we can imagine, he had to be relatively close to the sensor, it was not a remote operation via the internet. But Russian military intelligence also performs the so-called close *access* cyber operations. What happened to the then-14-year-old afterward is unclear.

5.7 WHAT DO THE STATES DO ABOUT IT?

What should States do with such cyber threats, risks, dangers? Nowadays, a lot of resources are devoted to ensuring the cybersecurity of critical infrastructure. It is also a diplomatic issue. The President of the United States in 2021 warned the President of Russia not to carry out cyberattacks on critical infrastructure, as this would be interpreted as a very serious incident and could have consequences. The President of the United States was forced to do this because his country's public opinion was increasingly concerned with cyberattacks and the ransomware problem in general. Since there was pressure, action had to be taken. With regard to cyberattacks on Russia in connection with the war in Ukraine, the Russian Ministry of Foreign Affairs noted cyberattacks on Russian critical infrastructure and did not rule out "targeted responses" to such cyberattacks "in accordance with international law".[25]

5.7.1 Europe, USA

At the beginning of this decade, the European Union was a bit better prepared in this context compared to the United States. At least that was the situation in 2022, in legal terms. In the European Union, the Network Security Directive, which takes into account the cybersecurity of critical infrastructure, for example, enforces the sharing of information. As we write this, an amendment to this directive is prepared.[26] There will probably be further such regulations. We have already referred to the above-mentioned directive, on the occasion of the definition of an essential service, let's add here that it defines requirements in relation to the security of critical infrastructure, including transport. It includes the need to monitor the cybersecurity of such systems, cybersecurity tests, as well as the need to specify the list of critical infrastructure elements and the parameters to be monitored. It imposes an obligation on the operator of the critical infrastructure, generally the operator of *essential services*. These existing requirements for reporting cybersecurity incidents relate to actions with measurable and significant effects, for example, they refer to a specific extent of downtime if they affect a significant percentage of consumers. At the same time, such measures mean that in most cases it may not be necessary to report such incidents at all if the range of necessary effects is high, and such events are extremely rare. However, these are the arrangements of individual European Union countries.

The U.S. is catching up with Europe, with an executive order published in 2022 that requires companies to share information about incidents.[27]

These works adapt solutions from the EU, which is why we focus on the initial proposals in this book. It is expected that such readiness will expand to other places in the world, too. Different rules are surely to come as well.

5.8 THE KEY CIVILIZATIONAL ISSUE

Critical infrastructure is a key issue of continuity, existence, or even survival of the State and its society, its population. It is pretty obvious that the functioning of the society requires the operation of the water treatment and supply system, as well as the generation and distribution of electricity. These are the requirements of a civilization. It is also hard to imagine that remote disconnection of heating can be tolerated in a country where winters are cold. A similar situation has already occurred in Finland[28] during freezing weather. The *distributed denial of service* attack temporarily blocked the heating system, but led to an "infinite loop" (executing the same actions continuously, such as calculations) in which the system was unable to return to operation on its own. Fortunately, this effect was temporary, because normal operation was quickly restored. But what if it happened in tens or hundreds of thousands of homes across the country? In this case, it is worth taking care of a basic and serious approach to cybersecurity, because surely we cannot take seriously the advice to equip ourselves with additional blankets just in case of a cyberattack. That would be ridiculous.

We will end this chapter with a question about the possible consequences of cyberattacks paralyzing the infrastructure. What could be the consequences? These could be serious repercussions, diplomatic, political, and even in connection with the security of the State – of a military nature. It can even lead to war in extreme cases. We will devote more consideration to this in Chapter 7.

NOTES

1 T. Tsvetanov, S. Slaria, *The effect of the Colonial Pipeline shutdown on gasoline prices*, "Economics Letters" 2021, vol. 209.
2 L. Holzki, L.-M. Nagel, M. Verfürden, K. Witsch, *Massive Störung der Satellitenverbindung: Enercon meldet fast 6000 betroffene Windanlagen*, 28.02.2022, https://www.handelsblatt.com/unternehmen/energie/erneuerbare-energien-massive-stoerung-der-satellitenverbindung-enercon-meldet-fast-6000-betroffene-windanlagen/28114360.html
3 Nordex Group, *Nordex Group impacted by cyber security incident*, 2.04.2022, https://www.nordex-online.com/en/2022/04/nordex-group-impacted-by-cyber-security-incident/
4 Article 4(4) of Directive (EU) 2016/1148 of the European Parliament and of the Council of 6 July 2016 concerning measures for a high common level of security of network and information systems across the Union (OJ. EU L 194, 19.7.2016, pp. 1–30).

5 D. Moore, V. Paxson, S. Savage, C. Shannon, S. Staniford, N. Weaver, *Inside the slammer worm*, "IEEE Security & Privacy" 2003, vol. 1, no. 4, pp. 33–39.

6 D.E. Whitehead, K. Owens, D. Gammel, J. Smith, *Ukraine cyber-induced power outage: Analysis and practical mitigation strategies*, in: *2017 70th Annual Conference for Protective Relay Engineers (CPRE)*, IEEE, 2017, pp. 1–8.

7 A. Greenberg, *New clues show how Russia's grid hackers aimed for physical destruction*, 12.09.2019, https://www.wired.com/story/russia-ukraine-cyberattack-power-grid-blackout-destruction/

8 Dragos, *CHERNOVITE'S PIPEDREAM malware targeting industrial control systems* (ICS), 13.04.2022, https://www.dragos.com/blog/industry-news/chernovite-pipedream-malware-targeting-industrial-control-systems/; N. Brubaker, K. Lunden, K. Proska, M. Umair, D. Kapellmann Zafra, C. Hildebrandt, R. Caldwell, *INCONTROLLER: New state-sponsored cyber attack tools target multiple industrial control systems*, 13.04.2022, https://www.mandiant.com/resources/incontroller-state-sponsored-ics-tool

9 EECSP, *Cyber Security in the energy sector. Recommendations for the European Commission on a European strategic framework and potential future legislative acts for the energy sector*, 2017, https://ec.europa.eu/energy/sites/ener/files/documents/eecsp_report_final.pdf; Y. Lin, Z. Bie, *Study on the resilience of the integrated energy system*, "Energy Procedia" 2016, vol. 103, pp. 171–176.

10 C.W. Ten, K. Yamashita, Z. Yang, A.V. Vasilakos, A. Ginter, *Impact assessment of hypothesized cyberattacks on interconnected bulk power systems*, "IEEE Transactions on Smart Grid" 2017, vol. 9, no. 5, pp. 4405–4425.

11 Ibid.

12 Ibid.

13 E.J. Oughton, D. Ralph, R. Pant, E. Leverett, J. Copic, S. Thacker, R. Dada, S. Ruffle, M. Tuveson, J.W. Hall, *Stochastic counterfactual risk analysis for the vulnerability assessment of cyber-physical attacks on electricity distribution infrastructure networks*, "Risk Analysis" 2019, vol. 39, no. 9, pp. 2012–2031.

14 S. Valderrama, *Venezuela blames 'attack' as another crippling blackout hits*, 25.03.2019, https://www.reuters.com/article/us-venezuela-politics-blackout-id USKCN1R62A7

15 R. Falcone, B. Lee, *Shamoon 2: Delivering Disttrack*, 27.03.2017, https://unit42.paloaltonetworks.com/unit42-shamoon-2-delivering-disttrack/

16 NIST, *Guide to Operational Technology (OT) security*, 2022, https://nvlpubs.nist.gov/nistpubs/SpecialPublications/NIST.SP.800-82r3.ipd.pdf

17 D. Formby, S. Durbha, R. Beyah, *Out of control: Ransomware for industrial control systems*, in: *RSA conference 2017*, 2017, vol. 4.

18 Y. Zhang, Z. Sun, L. Yang, Z. Li, Q. Zeng, Y. He, X. Zhang, *All your PLCs belong to me: ICS ransomware is realistic*, in *2020 IEEE 19th International Conference on Trust, Security and Privacy in Computing and Communications (TrustCom)*, IEEE, 2021, pp. 502–509.

19 R. Spenneberg, M. Brüggemann, H. Schwartke, *PLC-blaster: A worm living solely in the PLC*, "Black Hat Asia" 2016, vol. 16, pp. 1–16.

20 R.M. Lee, M.J. Assante, T. Conway, *German Steel Mill cyber attack*, 30.12.2014, "Industrial Control Systems" 2014, vol. 30, no. 62.

21 Dragos, *TRISIS Malware. Analysis of safety system targeted malware*, 2017, https://www.dragos.com/wp-content/uploads/TRISIS-01.pdf.

22 United States Government Accountability Office, *FAA should fully implement key practices to strengthen its oversight of avionics risks*, 2020, https://www.gao.gov/assets/gao-21-86.pdf

23 A. Greenberg, *Hackers remotely kill a jeep on the highway – with me in it*, 21.07.2015, https://www.wired.com/2015/07/hackers-remotely-kill-jeep-highway/

24 John Leyden, Polish teen derails tram after hacking train network, 11.01.2008, https://www.theregister.com/2008/01/11/tram_hack/

25 Министрерство иностранных дел Российской Федерации, *Ответ специального представителя Президента Российской Федерации по вопросам международного сотрудничества в области информационной безопасности, директора Департамента международной информационной безопасности МИД России А.В.Крутских на вопрос СМИ об атаках на объекты российской критической инфраструктуры (Ministrerstvo inostrannyh del Rossijskoj Federacii, Otvet special'nogo predstavitelja Prezidenta Rossijskoj Federacii po voprosam mezhdunarodnogo sotrudnichestva v oblasti informacionnoj bezopasnosti, direktora Departamenta mezhdunarodnoj informacionnoj bezopasnosti MID Rossii A.V.Krutskih na vopros SMI ob atakah na ob"ekty rossijskoj kriticheskoj infrastruktury)*, 9.06.2022, https://www.mid.ru/ru/foreign_policy/news/1817019/

26 Directive (EU) 2022/2555 of the European Parliament and of the Council of 14 December 2022 on measures for a high common level of cybersecurity across the Union, amending Regulation (EU) No 910/2014 and Directive (EU) 2018/1972, and repealing Directive (EU) 2016/1148 (NIS 2 Directive)

27 See President of the United States (2022), Executive Order on Improving the Nation's Cybersecurity, https://www.whitehouse.gov/briefing-room/presidential-actions/2021/05/12/executive-order-on-improving-the-nations-cybersecurity/

28 Metropolitan.fi, *DDoS attack halts heating in Finland amidst winter*, https://metropolitan.fi/entry/ddos-attack-halts-heating-in-finland-amidst-winter

Chapter 6

Cybersecurity of a State

6.1 WHAT IS THE CYBERSECURITY OF A STATE?

This chapter will be slightly different from the others. We will ask here the question of whether it is possible to hack a State. However, let's answer the question at once: that yes it is possible, in this age, it can be done. But what does it really mean?

The State can be hacked. If merely due to the fact that more and more elements of the State are being digitized. They are available online – this digitalization is progressing. Therefore, the risks are increasing. But the possibilities, and the nature, of hacking a State can be understood in many ways, at different levels. It can be hacking – with the help of various techniques – of State systems. It can also be hacking citizens or their accounts (on a large scale), both private and business (within the State infrastructure). This is especially true of hacking the resources and devices of officials or politicians.

It may also be the effect of a cyber operation on a national scale, perhaps an interference in internal political affairs, an intelligence operation, and who knows, maybe even a military one.

6.1.1 Cybersecurity of citizens, or described more broadly

As we know from the first chapter, the cybersecurity of the State at the most general level could be understood as the cybersecurity of companies, institutions, and citizens, all taken together (and possibly even measured, in some way). Understood holistically, i.e., coherently. However, it is difficult to imagine that such a vague definition would be useful in practice. In this chapter, we will refer to the issue of cybersecurity in the context of State institutions in the *strict sense*: State systems, perhaps databases, infrastructure, politicians, officials, the internal political system as a whole, too.

Of course, in some countries social security and care, the healthcare system is also a State element, but here we will not consider it (we have already devoted a whole chapter to healthcare). Within the framework of the cybersecurity of the State, issues of both internal (domestic) and external national security are also important, and so are military issues (this, however, will be the subject of the next chapter).

Basically, we will not talk about defense against cyber aggression. We will only mention things that are very close to this matter: external interference through cyber operations in the internal political situation. More serious territory is covered in Chapter 7.

6.2 COUNTRIES HAVE ALREADY BEEN HACKED

States or their components, the vulnerable ones, have already been hacked. Institutions, people, officials, politicians, all that, and in many places around the world. It can be said that attacking these elements was precisely the hacking of the States as they are the object of State matters. These are areas such as the political situation or actions with an impact on it, whether direct or indirect, with interference in local State affairs. The impact on the internal political situation may even constitute issues of State sovereignty violation, or worse.

Cyber operations against States, such as meddling in the electoral process or system, are also a **new geopolitical reality**, a new risk that we must be aware of. It is natural and understandable, when the purpose of an operation is to obtain information, to use intelligence operations – what may even be seen as legal (more precisely: not strictly illegal) under international law; even employing what is colloquially called cyberattacks, although in this case a much better term is indeed "cyber operation" (more about this distinction in the next chapter). But actions that can (potentially, accidentally, or intentionally) have an impact on the political situation, including elections, take on a completely different dimension. Then these are more aggressive actions, perhaps even a violation of the sovereignty of the State or an interference in domestic affairs. Such events happened in the United States (2016), or in France (2017), which are the events best known and understood.

6.2.1 Cyber operations against the U.S. political system (2016)

Let's start with the most well-known example, i.e., cyber operation in the U.S. presidential election in 2016, the related publication of data and harnessing them in an information operation aimed at a specific candidate (and, more broadly, against the Democratic Party). It was a very clever operation that highlighted that the hacking of politicians, diplomats, or other people associated with the State had become a reality.

6.2.2 Elections, intelligence, and human nature

It is understandable that in the case of elections or in the period outside the elections, external actors are interested in what is happening or may happen in the future in a country. This is the subject of intelligence activities, and for some time also cyberintelligence operations.

Against this background, the events of 2016 in the United States were of a slightly different nature. Cyberattacks have occurred, but they have been harnessed into an active cyber operation enabling information activities. The data leak was carried out in such a way that the public became interested in this topic. It was not difficult, because it happened for the first time, previously awareness of the problem was not widespread, and the media treated this topic as a sensation.

6.2.3 Intentional leaks and their effects

The leaked data were constantly harped on about by the public, including the media. They were analyzed, described very accurately. It is difficult for the media to pass up, ignore such an opportunity; after all, an insight was gained into the internal politics, into the political "backrooms", potentially into "scandals" or at least into the impression of their existence. For example, to consider it in a simple way: if there is a leak, and of non-public data at that, surely there "must" be something compromising inside, right? Because otherwise there wouldn't be a leak, the reasoning goes. In this sense, *the very fact of a leak can be compromising* – even if there is nothing actually concrete inside, it can be used for information or propaganda. All the more so when there is a lot of such data, because then perhaps no one will thoroughly analyze all of them, especially when there is time pressure (this motif was important in France in 2017).

In the U.S., this led to significant losses, and it all started with the hacking of one person – John Podesta, a politician involved in the election campaign of the Democratic Party. By clicking where he shouldn't, he consequently did something he shouldn't. This person was, of course, deceived. It doesn't matter much if he did it out of ignorance or out of haste. As a result, his data, his e-mails were seized. These data were then used very creatively. This probably had some impact on Donald Trump's victory in the presidential election in 2016. Not necessarily on the result itself. However, during the entire period of his presidency, these past events were recalled, analyzed, and reproached.

So there is no doubt that the cyberattack directly affected the internal situation in the United States. Regardless of whether it is considered to have actually determined the outcome of the 2016 elections. This cyber-enabled information operation was quite a 'success'.

6.2.4 Cyber operations against the political system in France (2017)

A similar type of cyber operation was an action with elements of information operation in France, during the election campaign for the presidential election in 2017, when data from Emmanuel Macron's headquarters were stolen, and captured. These data, as in the United States, were leaked to the public – then analyzed, and caused confusion, although on a much smaller scale. They were not covered by the large media. If only because the leak came relatively late, but perhaps also because of a certain kind of greater maturity of the local media in France? Alternatively: a lack of incentive to cause issues for the leading candidate, including with data of such an unknown provenance and unclear intention.

In any case, even if this leak led to losses, they were small. Besides, there was no way that such an incident could affect the outcome of the elections in a country like France. If only because the public opinion and the mainstream media were more favorable to Emmanuel Macron than his opponent Marine Le Pen from the far-right option. It wasn't like in the U.S. where the race was even. And such an operation could not have realistically affected the outcome of the presidential election, but hypothetically it could have been relevant for the subsequent parliamentary elections (in practice, however, it seems that it wasn't, moreover, the party of the victorious president Macron won in them too; but this can be known only after the fact!).

6.2.5 Cyber-enabled information operations aimed at the electoral process

Despite the small effects, however, it highlights the fact that cyber operations with elements of information operations are a new geopolitical reality. These cyber operations were the actions of external States, namely, the civil or military services of the Russian Federation. Such attribution was made by the Western countries.

6.2.6 Hacking social media accounts – a preface to an information operation?

In this context, it is worth mentioning incidents of different and more general nature. The risk of social media accounts of politicians, journalists, analysts being hacked. It is also, in general, hacking of e-mail accounts and taking over their contents, revealing the contents. Such actions may be carried out within the framework of information operations.

As is easily imaginable, hacking a social media account that is followed by many people (it could be the social media account of a politician, journalist, analyst, or other public figure) can be a good *investment*. Such an account can be an excellent centerpoint for spreading "Fake news" (or propaganda) or a kind of political spin, implanting a specific narrative, a message, an information content, a history, and generally causing a stir, trouble.

Furthermore, domestic constraints play an important role, too. If such an attacked State is, for example, characterized by significant internal polarization, it is conceivable that at least one party to the political dispute will be interested in using such informational content. For example, out of ill will or in connection with one's own political beliefs, or simply to galvanize support. Some part of the public may believe in such *manufactured content* if only because someone is hostile to a particular person or political option represented by that person, so out of a sheer choice. That's how and why it works. It's because of the fact that there will be many people who will "*buy*" it, accept it, be receptive to it. And if such people are sufficiently "*fixated on certain theses*", or concepts, then they may never even believe the potential future explanation of the true nature of these actions (that is, the result of an account hack).

The situation of strong polarization is a circumstance extremely conducive to information and propaganda operations. It is understandable that external adversaries can be interested in exploiting such internal conditioning. After all, it's their job, they do it for a living, certainly not because they are for or against some weird party or a concept in a (to them) foreign country, right?

6.2.7 Professional cyber operations

Usually, if we are dealing with a cyber operation or information operation for which an external State is responsible, it is carried out by professionals. They don't necessarily "support" someone or are "against" them. They don't necessarily have particular views as much as they are professionals and have their specific goal: professional, political, intelligence, perhaps military. It can be, for example, to cause doubts or even scandals, or to lead to internal divisions in the target State or maybe even to provoke a conflict between States.

We have covered information-operations in Western countries, like in the U.S., France. It is interesting to consider the cases in Central Eastern Europe, which is close to the war-affected Ukraine territory. In this sense, the activities of the so-called UNC1151 group[1] and the so-called "Ghostwriter" campaign, attributed to the services of Belarus (according to public reports, cooperation with Russia may be possible here), must appear very differently in Poland or Lithuania than, for example, in France (considering the events in 2017, specifically). For example, because the election campaign was underway in France, even if there was absolutely no chance that the election result could be changed due to such a data leak (Emmanuel Macron had a definite advantage). It should be additionally emphasized here that Macron's staff handled this event quite efficiently, too. The problem was immediately publicly addressed, strongly stating that the content was stolen. Importantly, this was done before the electoral silence period in France.

This is probably how this kind of information operations should be handled. Some authoritative source of information must respond quickly and efficiently. The fascinating question is under what circumstances and how to do it. As we will talk further, securing the electoral headquarters is a complex strategic issue. But – this is still very different from the situation of a potential interstate conflict.

6.2.8 Cyber operations and the situation at the Polish–Belarusian border in 2021

A special case in Central Europe, which in this decade is gaining great importance in connection with the Russian invasion of Ukraine of 2022.

From today's perspective, it is difficult not to try to seek or identify links with cyber operations against Poland and Lithuania (and more generally, this region of the world), attributed to Belarus, with other activities in connection with the events on the eastern border of Poland,[2] described as "hybrid operations", and perhaps even some military operations in Ukraine. At that time, in 2021, the uniformed services of the Belarusian State were involved. Such a link would make the activities on the eastern border of Poland much more serious. In connection with the escalation of events in 2022 – in such a situation, it would be of great importance for NATO, too, for Europe and for the USA. This may be seen in light of other events potentially aimed at increasing conflicts, explained in Chapter 7.

6.2.9 The case of Taiwan: Outreach and the man from nowhere

By correctly designing the election campaign and information and PR activities on the Internet, a completely unknown person (the so-called man from nowhere) was promoted in Taiwan to such a level that he actually managed to win the election in one of the cities. Cyber operators from China were apparently of help in this.[3]

6.2.10 Attacks elsewhere

Note that various types of cyberattacks on the electoral system occurred in other places too; for example, in Russia (as claimed by the authorities) and in other countries of the European Union. In a sense, they have become a sign of our times.

It happened in the United States, it happened in France, that's why to a degree it's looked for everywhere. The cybersecurity of electoral systems and voting machines in the countries where they are used is analyzed.

However, the assumed scenario in relation to cyber risk for specific country X cannot always be easily translated into a real scenario in another country Y. Such analyses, based on the "copy-paste" method, are not of great value. If only because the domestic situations in countries may be very different, not even speaking about the technical-legal process of actual elections.

6.3 ELECTRONIC VOTING AS A SYSTEMIC VULNERABILITY OF A STATE

The background to cyberattacks on election systems and campaigns is broader. Curiously, these cyberattacks coincided with years in which the digitization of the voting system in Switzerland was to be finalized. However, these events have led to the slowdown or suspension of such work.

Swiss aspect is important to note. It is not surprising that such an idea was even considered there: in Switzerland, the construction and implementation of such a system makes sense. If only because Switzerland is a direct democracy that relies heavily on referendums, of which there are many throughout the year. People have to vote often, on many things. From the typical elections, to the right to hang laundry out of the windows facing streets in a particular city (well, maybe not necessarily with such a precision of choices, but you get the idea).

However, in the majority of countries, voting takes place so rarely that the digitization of this element of the functioning of the State does not have such a good, reasonable justification. On the contrary, it would mean introducing additional risk points where the actual gains were unclear (this would be digitalization for the sake of digitalization). In fact, it would not really improve much if elections are held so rarely. In practice, it is not a big problem to go and vote physically (mark the vote with a pen on a piece of paper). The cost-benefit case, including the risk, is evident here.

Electronic voting is a major technical and social challenge in which many problems have to be addressed, mitigated, and solved. Many assumptions, sometimes contradictory, need to be reconciled, at the same time. For example: there is a need to count the votes correctly, but in such a way as to ensure the anonymity of voters. So it cannot be possible to determine who voted, and how.

Because deanonymization and assigning the method of voting to specific people should not be possible for State services. Unless we absolutely trust officials and current or future ruling politicians. So, where there is a lot of trust of citizens in the State and its institutions, it could theoretically work. But in other countries, not necessarily.

It would, therefore, be necessary to build the system in such a way that it would be impossible to determine who voted and how, using IT, advanced mathematics, or technology. That is, to guarantee (i.e., not just assume) complete anonymity. This would be difficult, though probably possible (but at great cost and time, assuming it is done reliably; whether we can make this assumption depends on the particular country).

However, this aspect is very easy and cheap to achieve with pen and paper, when voting physically behind a curtain.

Unless, of course, the law was changed in such a way that it would simply be mandated to limit the anonymity of voting where it could be done in practice. Well, guarantee anonymity, just using "legal" tools. This is called anonymization on paper, i.e., the statutory, official recognition that a certain way is by definition anonymous (similarly, e.g., weather conditions could be voted for the next week. You get the idea). However, it is difficult to say whether this would guarantee the trust of the voters, the citizens in such a system. However, this would certainly not be a practical-legal guarantee, but a more statutory declaration (on paper).

Let's also consider what potential aims may be pursued by politicians or candidates who propose electronic voting, voting via the Internet, etc. We know how the digital environment looks like today. We can do shopping online, e.g., buy shoes. But securing an online shop (e-commerce) and elections are completely different issues. The risks, the threats, vary greatly. For example, military intelligence is unlikely to target an ordinary online store. Proposals to conduct elections via the Internet modeled on online shopping (or other related examples of the kind) must, therefore, be considered a harmful demagogy, proving at least the incompetence of the originators.

6.3.1 Transparency issues

A completely different problem is that such a complex IT system, using advanced cryptographic, IT, and mathematical methods, would be difficult, in fact very difficult, to explain to citizens. That said, the operation of a conventional system is easy to explain. We just have a piece of paper, a pen, a system of counting votes and that's it. Everyone will understand that.

However, explaining how a complicated, digitized system works, to the members of society, would be much more difficult. These are obviously issues of basic citizens' trust in the State and in the electoral system. Are the votes real? Are they rigged? Should the end result of the election be trusted? This is ultimately a matter of State stability.

6.3.2 Tread carefully with digitization

Therefore, we should make it clear that it is better not to digitize certain sensitive areas. Such as the electoral system, the key and delicate fabric of election systems. Of course, perhaps someone might have some interest in pursuing this. But this is not necessarily in the public interest. Let's not rush to it. It's best to leave it as it is. Not everything needs to be modernized. Elections and the electoral process are an example of a system that is better not to be converted into an electronic system, because it is a matter of public trust in the political representation of the society.

Of course, this can be done. There is also no certainty that if this is done, something will *immediately* go wrong, that a catastrophe will happen *unavoidably*. This will simply be *another* point of risk – technical, social, and political at the same time. A fascinating question would be whether, if someone, somewhere desired to digitize elections, would any political force take the risk of possible abuses on their banner? To question such a system as part of their political program, proposals put forward for considerations? Or could a different political force even challenge the results of such an election?

Again, a simple solution to this problem is to apply the golden rule: "*if it works, do not touch it*".

6.4 A GENERAL SCENARIO – CYBER-ENABLED INFORMATION OPERATION

Now it is a good time to use the information laid out so far to systematize it. Here we outline a hypothetical and theoretical scenario that can be *used indefinitely* in relation to any country. It's an "automaton", a scenario that could always work, some kind of a perpetuum mobile. In this scenario, we consider hacking political systems in order to pressure politicians and the public. The attack begins by hacking the devices of politicians (business or private), their families, their friends, perhaps the electoral staff. The next steps are:

- theft of information,
- their disclosure in a strategic way (in various doses of different sizes, kinds, nature, at specific moments),
- making the audience interested in them (this group includes users of social media, forums, recipients of traditional media and the media themselves, political competitors, various others).

It may also be combined with a coercive element (direct or indirect) aimed at some State structure or parts of the political theater, or even some individuals. This is a scheme of a cyberattack combined with an information operation, which is of a very political nature, so to speak. To a degree we have already seen the implementation of a similar scenario, for example, in the United States, in France.

In general, it can be difficult to protect against such a scenario. If only because the public is often very interested in reports from inside the political world, as well as in possible details, flavors from the "political backrooms". It's like an "infotainment", sort of. If we can be interested in the lives of celebrities, TV actors, we can also get excited about other public figures and their (mis)adventures, actions, activities. So, as we have already discussed, the public may naturally be interested in such data leaks. This is, therefore, a favorable ground for them to happen.

Even the various political parties or players may also be interested in a cyberattack on another particular political party or a player. If only to use such a "gift" politically, obviously. Even if it was the result of the actions of cyber operators from foreign countries. That would, of course, assume a sad reality of a zero-sum game in a political environment of a particular State. It would, of course, not be recommended. But the facts of life are that leaks sometimes happen.

Indeed, there should be a cross-party (in the U.S.: a *"bipartisan"*) agreement not to use such hacked content in this way, especially if there is a credible suspicion that these are actions of foreign countries aimed at destabilizing the political and social situation in the country (especially during the election campaign). Realistically, however, let us recognize that it would be difficult to obtain such an agreement, in many countries. A sad fact, but a fact. While this book is about cybersecurity – let's be realistic.

6.5 HOW COUNTRIES PROTECT OR DEFEND THEMSELVES

Countries defend themselves by developing cyber capabilities. They may protect (or should do so) their officials, politicians, etc. There is no reason to repeat how to protect ourselves from a user's perspective, because we have already written about it. The State should identify good recommendations, issue them regularly, and enforce their application. Someone should work it out, someone else should enforce it.

6.5.1 EU GDPR, NIS – when it is worthwhile or necessary to act

It is worth noting, however, that countries in Europe (a model case in terms of legal requirements) comply with obligations resulting from, for example, the General Data Protection Regulation (GDPR), and also implement the Network and Information Security Directive (NIS). Then it is a matter of corporate compliance, and in such a company whole processes are built around it.

Policymakers and regulators may hope that as a result of this process there will be improvements on a national scale. It is not unreasonable.

6.5.2 CERTs and other institutions

CERTs, or computer emergency response teams, work in almost all countries and in various domains. Such structures also operate at institutions or other entities, e.g., financial, with elements of critical infrastructure (e.g., energy system). CERTs also operate at the government and military level. These are specialized analytical and advisory teams that are very much needed and must be maintained, taken good care of, developed. Because in fact they deal with the specific, actual work requiring special expertise and knowledge. Often much more important work than the one performed by the so-called high officials, who, by the way, can be quite arbitrary, random, people themselves. It is becoming more and more difficult to find specialists.

Nowadays, cyber components in the police are also being developed. And it is not surprising, because cybersecurity and data loss or other negative consequences for citizens are a growing social problem. Certain competences and capabilities must be present in the police services. Due to the fact that the scale of cybercrimes is growing, these capabilities are being developed, or at least awareness is being built, also within other State institutions such as courts or prosecutor's offices. If only because there are more and more cases related to cybercrime, ordinary crimes also often involve electronic devices to some extent. Such cases need to be handled properly; there must be people who understand this area.

6.6 IS IT POSSIBLE TO SECURE THE STATE?

Elements of the State can, and must be, secured. These are changes at the legal level (e.g. laws), of technological standards, as well as of the technologies themselves. This may need thought, vision, the right budgets, and willingness to act. Even if some of these activities are not spectacular, and difficult to present to the public.

6.6.1 Elections

As an example worth repeating, a fundamental element in increasing the cybersecurity of elections[4] is the non-implementation of the electronic election system like e-voting (electronic voting) or i-voting (online vote). This is a rare case where *not doing* something increases the cybersecurity. It is enough to not implement digitization to increase (well, maintain) the cybersecurity of elections, although this is not provided for by any national cybersecurity strategy and nowhere has it been recognized as an element of security.

However, it is worth realizing that even in the case of offline, non-digital elections, the importance of cybersecurity is considerable. Especially of some of its elements. For example, in relation to institutions managing elections (like vote counting process) or in the case of sending data about elections (votes, results), or even when announcing the results (giving wrong results, for any reason, could lead to chaos on a national scale). Still, if we have everything on a piece of paper, in theory, it will always be possible to refer to some basic source data, if only to cross-check the counts. So even if someone hacks, i.e., gains unauthorized access to some systems, and interferes with data during or before their transmission, e.g., by changing the proportion of votes, it will always be possible to re-count them to determine the actual result.

6.6.2 Political parties

Is it possible to secure a political party? Two issues are worth considering here: security in the general case (continuous operation), and a cybersecurity strategy for the election campaign time (i.e., staff). These are different issues. First, we will discuss a general issue in relation to a political party.

Political parties are people, and more broadly, party infrastructure consists of, for example, buildings, systems, electorate. However, these are still mainly the "live" politicians, their personal base, e.g., assistants, the data. Here there are issues of security, personal cybersecurity and access rights to information, to data. For example, when the password to a social or e-mail account is shared with several people, there is an increased risk that if at least one such person is hacked, some sensitive data will leak, e.g. a bill, opinions, findings, plans, strategy. Here, therefore, a lot depends on the personal cybersecurity of such people.

It is worth emphasizing the role of multi-factor authentication once again. For example, when a *universal second factor authentication* (U2F) key allows logging in to systems using the second login factor (i.e., even if someone steals the username and password, they will not gain access to the systems). There are many more such rules, good ideas. For example, if a person's computer is infected with malware, then the issue of securing the password will not be that important. Someone who gains control over such a computer will have access to everything, anyway. It is, therefore, a complex problem. Time must be devoted to it, as well as appropriate resources, and the chosen solutions must be related to the current risks. Also to those specialized ones concerning political parties specifically.

Political parties typically have some kind of information systems. Someone has to manage and administer them. It is best to involve an external company to the task, because it is difficult for political parties to maintain their own IT teams. This means that there should always be someone who knows more than the others. Someone who is responsible for the topic and does it not necessarily because of the personal political views but because these are his obligations under the contractual agreement for which remuneration is received. At the same time, such a person does not necessarily have to have extremely advanced technical skills, and a whole team of specialists is not always needed.

6.6.3 Cybersecurity of the electoral staff – a challenge

Here we arrive at the cybersecurity strategy for the electoral staff. This is an interesting technical-organizational-social problem.

Because, what is an electoral staff? The electoral staff is a loose structure gathering informally connected people with a common general goal. Perhaps they did not know each other before, perhaps they do not even like each other (competing within one campaign or an electoral list). However, these people establish a time-limited cooperation "under the aegis" of the electoral list or a party brand, in order to achieve a political goal, for example, to achieve a certain number of votes and perhaps even to win the elections. From the very beginning, the issue of trust between these people is important. From our point of view, there should also be a trust in the level of cybersecurity of these specific people, and the other people involved in electoral strategies and issues. Especially, if it is necessary to communicate with these people or to entrust them with data, or to rely on them in any way. We already know, even from the experience of the United States, France, and other countries, that it is enough to hack one person to harm many others. For example, because such people (especially sensitive people who are particularly vulnerable to being targeted by attackers, which is why they should be particularly protected) receive, but also send, messages and e-mails, sometimes under natural pressure, or in haste. Often, communication is sent to many different people at once.

6.6.3.1 Personal issue

In addition, the election headquarters, or staff, will mostly be staffed by 'ordinary people' – perhaps not particularly versed in terms of rules, digital hygiene, cybersecurity, threats. They are not specialists. They never had to be. They may face (perhaps not even being aware of that) an increased risk only due to the fact of being linked to the party's election staff.

Almost always in the staff there will also be at least one "someone" with high power, low level of competence, but deeply convinced of own infallibility. Such a person is a recipe for disaster. It is worthwhile for people who are more competent or at least cautious to treat this individual as a potential risk and to pay special attention to that person's activity. After all, why shoot yourself in the foot?

6.6.3.2 Headquarters/staff cybersecurity strategy

If someone cares about a professional approach to securing the staff, development of a specialized cybersecurity strategy[5] is recommended, rules (understandable to all). The cybersecurity strategy should cover technical issues, those of communication, of dissemination of information, of use of technical means. Also – the question of how to react when something goes wrong, when there is a security breach, a leak, for example. It is necessary to determine who will do what, with whom, and under what circumstances? How quickly and by what means (if by chance a person without preparation would be assigned to it; additionally expected to work for his/her own money or in his/her free time, etc.)? Of course, in a critical situation, there will certainly be a lot of improvisation, but determining some considerations in advance can be an invaluable help if something undesirable is actually to happen.

Moreover, strategies for staff should be prepared for specific elections. Although it is possible to distinguish some general principles that are worth applying, we should also remember that the situation may change. New technologies, challenges, and threats are emerging. Individual staff may differ from each other, people may change. The strategy should be created early, before the staff is established. It is necessary to distinguish the resources that must be protected, critical resources, including the communication system.

6.6.3.3 More about the human factor

And here the question arises: how to do it. A competent and trusted person responsible for developing such a strategy should be appointed. It can be an outsider who will develop something, but it can also be someone on the inside, if they feel up to it. In the case of expected technical problems, cooperation in advance can also be established with an external company specializing in cybersecurity, which will be prepared to help if and when necessary. The idea is that in the event of a serious incident, specialists can be involved. That there would be someone who would take care of the problem, if there is one. And do it right.

The role of the human factor is very important; that is, that the people in the staff should be aware and know the model of threats – threats to them, to the candidate, perhaps to the whole party. At the same time, the model would have to take into account the specificity of the environment in which they work. The model addresses real threats. They may appear in connection with the activity of foreign countries, but also of people operating inside the State, even inside the staff itself. There may be a threat from the staff of other parties, too. At least to a degree. Perhaps there are more actors interested in taking over certain information, or harming such a party? These can be individual citizens (even unaffiliated, of course), opponents of such a party, acting on their own behalf (or from inspiration), but also in an organized form. Finally, it can be people from the party itself. We are absolutely not calling for distrust of the people with whom we are working. But the facts are that sometimes, depending on how the internal political system works, people close to a particular candidate may not be interested in his/her victory or the success of his/her associates. These are, of course, the most hypothetical, theoretical considerations, there are absolutely no suggestions here and it's given only for the readers' consideration. In sum, in the case of the electoral staff, we are simply dealing with risk management.

6.6.3.4 Technical, cloud measures

Nowadays, the various resources provided by IT companies are also very helpful. It is worth considering how the data of such an electoral staff should be managed. Because within the headquarters, decisional or management centers, like in staff, information needs to be exchanged, data processed. In this case, however, it is a good idea to use cloud solutions, which are easily available today. But can such a third-party cloud provider be trusted? If it is a large one, then even common sense tells that such a business entity would probably not be interested in the details and actions of the clients (which would be illegal, and contrary to internal, contractual rules), also regarding strategy and political actions. However, such a company provides a very high degree of security, as well as the availability of an ecosystem.

6.6.3.5 Routine deletion of data

A simple solution that is worth enforcing top down is enabling the automatic function of deleting data like messages or e-mails. The idea is that from time to time all such data (i.e. e-mails) that were created, received, sent, should be deleted. If, for example, we delete all such data after a month from their creation (e.g., a month after receiving them), then in the case when someone gains unauthorized access to our mailbox, they may steal the information, the data, the e-mails, etc. – but only from the previous month. So it will not be the case that the attacker would be getting all the data from e.g., the previous 2, 5, 10, or 20 years. Routine data deletion would constitute a hard limit.

A similar solution should be adopted in relation to discussion groups on messengers or regular chats. Set the disappearing message function, which will limit losses in case at least one person from such a chat is hacked. Archiving such communications may not be justified. The content usually is not needed for long. Some of it should by default be treated as ephemeral.

Of course, it can always happen that in the group there is a person who made a copy of the communication with a purpose of revealing it or sharing it with someone sometime in the future. But that's another matter entirely. Then, it is a question of how to identify a person we should not trust. Identify: in advance. This is a separate problem.

From the very beginning, we have made it clear that an election staff is technically a group of loosely connected people cooperating for a certain period of time (relatively short). We are not making any assumptions here. The choice of people is the responsibility of specific politicians – this does not concern us, obviously. If we read the news, as we can easily guess, the quality of such decisions varies. And in the case of cybersecurity, information security – many of the previously mentioned premises must be taken into account when constructing the entire system.

6.6.4 Cybersecurity as a PR problem

Cybersecurity issues are also issues of reputation, of PR (*public relations*). Cybersecurity PR is something that can have a separate book written about, and can be applied to many issues, e.g., business. But it is also important in political matters, even at the staff level. How to manage reputation and PR issues when things go wrong must be known. For example, when there is a data leak. What to do then? How, when, with whom? What kind of attitude to take and how to establish the right communication? How to fight hostile campaigns, information operations?

What to do, when, how quickly, with what tools, for what purpose – these things must be known. Knowing how to communicate, what to say, what message to issue is needed. It is necessary to anticipate the consequences of taking these actions, as well as of not taking them.

6.7 THE NECESSITY OF A STATE CYBERSECURITY STRATEGY

Cybersecurity concerns many areas. This should be an important subject included in the State strategy. What is the goal in the development of a technology and what is the specific place of cybersecurity here? What is such a State striving for?

For example, it is the ability to build research and development capabilities, equip the police or the army with certain means and powers. It is also a legal matter, so that there are powers to take certain actions. These are prohibitions or restrictions (e.g., what we consider illegal). But it is also the systemic issues, such as capacity and awareness building. Appropriate calibration of school or higher education policy, i.e., stimulating the development of education by establishing certain fields of study, certain specialties, and ensuring their quality (mathematics, digital competences, media culture, e.g., the ability to notice attempts at disinformation, propaganda, persuasion, convincing to adopt some opinion) and eliminating those with inadequate education level. Stimulating the development of research. These are, after all, elements of the State's strategy.

Nowadays, it is also a matter of security, cybersecurity, and external policy, i.e., how the State operates on the international arena. What are the goals of, for example, involvement in cyber issues in institutions such as the United Nations (there are government expert groups, where the norms of responsible behavior in cyberspace are debated), in Europe, the European Union, in Asia, the Shanghai Cooperation Group, or the Indo-Pacific Quadrilateral Dialogue (Australia, India, Japan, and the United States), or even more regionally like the Bucharest Nine (B9; Bulgaria, Czech Republic, Estonia, Hungary, Latvia, Lithuania, Poland, Romania, Slovakia), and so on – as well as between countries, bilaterally. It is also a matter of how the

State interprets the principles of international law in relation to security (it is worth communicating such principles publicly).

From here, it is a short way to considering the issue of sovereignty and even cyber sovereignty (means of developing services and products within a State or bloc of States, autonomously, with limited dependence on third countries). Ultimately, it is also a question of the situations in which the State can interpret that certain actions of other actors were an interference in internal affairs. Perhaps it is an armed aggression because it also encompasses military, and strategic-military issues. And what to do in such a situation, by what means?

More and more countries have cybersecurity strategies. Some have already released updates. Countries such as France, Luxembourg, the United Kingdom, the Netherlands, and Australia can be mentioned here. This is simply a standard issue, something that every self-respecting country should have. Self-respecting non-English-speaking countries issue such strategies in English as well. Those that do not hold sufficient self-respect, for themselves do not issue such strategies at all, or issue those with a heavily truncated content.

6.8 OR MAYBE DISCONNECT FROM THE INTERNET?

In some countries, networks are built in such a way that the internet can be disconnected.[6] The slogan "*internet shutdown*" may sound harmful, but in some countries exactly that is being done (to only mention Uganda, Iran, part of India). The number of such places is increasing.[7] States build the capacity to disconnect certain elements of the network or the Internet, because they may treat it as an issue of internal and external security. In Russia, for example, it is justified to build such capabilities to disconnect the country from the Internet for (allegedly) cybersecurity purposes; to protect against a "cyberattack". This is difficult to understand, especially since completely cutting off the network will unlikely help in protection. If a cyber tool was already running on such a disconnected network, it could still work. However, this is the argument that is being made seriously. Despite this, according to reports in the Russian media, in the spring of 2022 serious consideration was being given to disconnecting Russian networks from the global internet. As a result of the increase in cyberattacks, ministries also issued special recommendations to potentially prepare the ground for such an isolation.

On the other hand, building certain networks and systems to work in a situation of disconnection from the Internet or from other systems may be justified if someone threatened to cut off the country's infrastructure. For example, from the SWIFT payment network (then it is known that the country would be forced to have its own systems, anyway, obviously). It may be paradoxical, but when in 2021 Russia was still building its military presence on the eastern border of Ukraine, there were considerations[8] about the threats of the possible disconnection of Russia from the SWIFT financial system (which, as we know, partially happened after the invasion). Such reports in a way "lend credence" to Russia's internal isolationist tendencies – of "cyber sovereignty" (here called independence from products, suppliers, and services from other countries, the ability to decide for itself etc., in practice difficult to attain these days), because the State must be able to act. So in that sense, it could actually be – in general – a question of cyber sovereignty, regardless how we look at it.

However, it must be said that unilaterally disconnecting the country from the Internet would involve significant costs. These would be social costs, but also financial ones because nowadays economies are strongly connected. The importance of the digital economy itself is great. In many countries, however, a definitive disconnection from the Internet is not realistically possible today. If only because there are a very large number of connections, the saturation of networks is high. Moreover, in many Western countries, networks have never been built in such a way as to allow unilateral disconnection from the Internet.

However, the question arises, how can users protect themselves against such a threat or more generally the threat of losing access to the Internet? The reality of such a risk is underlined by the war in Ukraine in 2022, with cyberattacks on Internet providers and kinetic attacks (physical destruction) against telecommunications infrastructure. The user can potentially increase the ability to maintain a network connection, for example, using satellite internet, e.g., Starlink. Eventually, and curiously, such capabilities will be a kind of challenge to countries that would like to disconnect from the internet (or treat their ability to censor and block access to content as internal security issues), because then access would still exist. Unless the operator of such a system would honor the order to disconnect the network on the territory of a given country, if it must take into account some legal conditions. However, we do not believe in the readiness to shoot down satellites (although it is known that the armies of several countries have such capabilities) on a grand scale.

Long time ago, States treated elements of communication infrastructure as part of their national security prerogative. This was common. Now there has been some evolution here, because the Internet is everywhere. We have instant messaging and we are not dependent on telecommunication. These are elements that the State no longer controls. Not everyone likes such a broad development of technology and the broad access to certain communication solutions, which we are often reminded of by the actions, intentions, or speeches of the various politicians in some countries. For example, those complaining about encrypted messengers that cannot be controlled, their content inspected, tapped into.

But it's also a matter of network access itself. For example, in the United Kingdom, it could potentially be used to selectively disconnect certain telecommunications networks, and in extreme situations perhaps – for a wide disconnection. The legal system must be the guardian here. In the UK, the telecommunications regulator Ofcom (under the Communications Act 2003[9]) has such powers. Similar legal bases and authorities can and do occur in other countries. Therefore, it is worth being aware that such regulations exist. This underlines the importance of the rule of law in the State. Even if there may be substantive needs to limit access to the Internet, it is important that the scope of restrictions is constructed in such a way that the interference was minimal and did not cover too large of a scope. For example, it is difficult to imagine that in civilized conditions it would be justified, for example, to shut down the network throughout the whole country. For example, during the wartime conditions in Ukraine in 2022, the internet worked remarkably broadly and well, even if with interferences, at times very significant. However, ones that were caused by an objective situation: kinetic, physical destruction of the infrastructure.

NOTES

1 Ganriella Roncone et al. (2021), UNC1151 Assessed with High Confidence to have Links to Belarus, Ghostwriter Campaign Aligned with Belarusian Government Interests, https://www.mandiant.com/resources/blog/unc1151-linked-to-belarus-government Insikt Group (2022), Ghostwriter in the Shell: Expanding on Mandiant's Attribution of UNC1151 to Belarus, https://go.recordedfuture.com/hubfs/reports/cta-2022-0318.pdf
2 L. Olejnik, *Belarus is risking crisis on the Polish border*, 9.11.2021, https://foreignpolicy.com/2021/11/09/belarus-poland-border-migrant-crisis/
3 P. Huang, *Chinese cyber-operatives boosted Taiwan's insurgent candidate*, 26.06.2019, https://foreignpolicy.com/2019/06/26/chinese-cyber-operatives-boosted-taiwans-insurgent-candidate/
4 UK National Cyber Security Centre (2019), Election guidance for local authorities, https://www.ncsc.gov.uk/guidance/election-guidance-for-local-authorities
5 CISA (2022). CYBERSECURITY TOOLKIT TO PROTECT ELECTIONS, https://www.cisa.gov/cybersecurity-toolkit-protect-elections
6 L.H. Newman, *How the Iranian government shut off the Internet*, 17.11.2019, https://www.wired.com/story/iran-internet-shutoff/
7 M. Díaz Hernández, F. Anthonio, S. Cheng, A. Skok, *Internet shutdowns in 2021: the return of digital authoritarianism*, 26.04.2022, https://www.accessnow.org/internet-shutdowns-2021/
8 See https://www.swift.com/news-events/news/message-swift-community
9 Communications Act 2003, Section 124H, https://www.legislation.gov.uk/ukpga/2003/21

Chapter 7

Cyberconflict and cyberwar

.

In this chapter, we will discuss cyberconflict and cyberwar. We will analyze how the *cyber area* becomes a field of competition between various actors, including states and blocs of states. This is a complex problem, because it can be related to the creation of certain technological standards, i.e., protocols and general rules relating to how technologies are supposed to work. To mention at the least the competition (and cooperation) of the States in how the telecommunication standards were or are supposed to work: 5G, 6G, rules for artificial intelligence, or perhaps even quantum technologies in the future (or other such products, as there are lots of various technology standards). The content of such technological standards can also be analyzed in the context of the values (e.g., the so-called European values, human rights values, etc.) professed, recognized, upheld, promoted by societies. Values that eventually may be expressed by laws, regulations, and of course – their impact on technology.[1]

7.1 RIVALRY AND COMPETITION BETWEEN THE STATES

Imagine, for instance, the competition over the feasibility of building microprocessor technology, which is also becoming a political and legal problem (the so-called cyber sovereignty).[2] In general, competition in the technology field is a very complex issue, and naturally the focus of this book is on *cyber matters*. The focus is on the more tangible issue of the competition. Not on the more general problem of *cyberpolitics*, but on a selected area. On the *cyberconflict*, and on actions, let's put it mildly, more decisive, offensive – on cyber operations.

Here, the competition arises from the fact that more and more social, scientific, or business interactions move to cyberspace, i.e., through computers and networks. Therefore, there is a lot of information and data in this environment. Many infrastructures – in one way or another – contain digital elements, such as digital controls; for instance – consider the digital systems that can be used to control devices in industrial sites (Chapter 5). Therefore, these can be very interesting facilities. Points of interest, simply the critical elements of systems. But this may make them targets for actors interested in obtaining certain information about the activities of such facilities or the possibility of influencing these certain infrastructures at a specific time. This influence may consist, for example, in the disruption, or paralysis of a system, for example for political or military reasons.

Therefore, in this chapter we will talk about a very specific rivalry, which in the decades of 2010 and 2020 has been gaining momentum.

7.2 CYBERINTELLIGENCE, CYBERESPIONAGE...

There is a huge amount of information in networked computer systems. Furthermore, there is no shortage of entities seeking access to it. One of such entities are, for example, cyberintelligence organizations, which deal with building cyber capabilities within intelligence agencies. That is, agencies interested in obtaining information on political, scientific, economic, technical, military issues (and so on), data from foreign countries. The information is in the IT systems. If the task is to get ahold of it – then it is necessary to build competences within such State units. Analytical, defensive competences, but it is also about the ability to bypass, break security boundaries, and establish control over remote systems in such a way as to supervise, control, observe, and above all obtain information from them. The general idea is, therefore, to gain insight into remote systems in order to gain information or even the possibility to influence these systems. This has been done numerous times, by agencies of various countries, directed at various other countries.

7.3 CYBER POLICE

Another such entity of interest may be the cyber police. As more and more social interactions take place online, it is natural that problems will arise (and they do), e.g., conflicts between people, legal disputes. There is an increase in cybercrime, of various nature (both pure cybercriminal, and plain old crime with the use of digital equipment like computers or smartphones), where digitals forensics may play a crucial role. These are often cross-border problems. There is, therefore, a need for State units capable of detecting and combating cybercrime, but also the ability to cooperate with other units of the kind based in another State.

Such units include law enforcement agencies. We have already had examples of cooperation between many European law enforcement agencies to combat ransomware actors. That is the cooperation of police authorities from different countries. For example, to *remove* the operators of the EMOTET ransomware (paralyzing their work by means of active operations) in 2021,[3] or the HIVE ransomware operators in 2023.[4] Both operations included the collaboration of law enforcement agencies of a number of countries. These two examples unambiguously demonstrate that not only such a cooperation is possible, but it also bears fruits. There are many such examples and there will certainly be even more in the foreseeable future.

7.4 CYBER ARMY

Interstate rivalry has been the domain of the military for many centuries. With the help of troops, army units, States exert the so-called power projections. Now, these interactions are also moving into cyberspace. Thus, **cyber operations can be a power projection tool**. States build capabilities to act in cyberspace both within their civilian and military units (cyber military units, cyber army units, etc.).

7.4.1 Standard tools

Taking into account that intelligence, police, and military are standard entities within the State, basically entities existing for centuries, it can be concluded that States simply adapt their methods to the requirements of modern times. To the specificity of cyberspace. For example, for the needs of the military, cyberspace is identified as a theater of operations.[5] Therefore, it is a designated domain of operations just as land, sea, air, or space. This is how the Western bloc – NATO – categorizes it. Such an approach to the subject will, therefore, progress, develop greatly. We need to be aware that there will be many consequences associated with it. Some of them may be difficult to foresee. Others will be obvious, but only in retrospect.

Therefore, the content of this chapter is, and will remain valid, at least for this decade and the next.

7.4.2 Cyberattack is not an attack

Here, we must talk about an issue that we have not paid much attention to so far. Well, paradoxically, **cyberattacks are not attacks!** A tiny, if counterintuitive, detail? But how crucial! And many laypeople ignore it or are unaware of it. Sometimes even experts ignore it or are perhaps even not aware of it. This space begs for urgent tidying. This follows in this chapter.

In this chapter, the role of international rules, international law, and terminological precision becomes important. And in this sense, we must admit that there are few international rules, international treaties, that regulate what a formal and/or "legal" (not dictionary or journalistic notion) attack is. What an attack is. The rare exception are the Geneva Conventions, which define attacks[6] as *acts of violence against the adversary, whether in offence or in defence.*[7] Another act of international law is the United Nations Charter,[8] which in Article 51 speaks of armed aggression.

For the most part, the cyberattacks we hear about *are not attacks* in such a strict sense. And these terms should not be confused. Therefore, *cyberattacks are usually not attacks*. This is due to the fact that in most cases, in relation to the (legal) approach to the term "attack", cyberattacks are too low on the scale. Although it must be admitted that these treaties were drawn up at a time when no one dreamed of cyberspace or cyberattacks. However, building rules on long-standing war practices makes a lot of sense. For example, it ensures that such rules or customs are universally accepted. This means that any framework to be devised would be built on acceptable foundations, and not come out of a void.

If cyberattacks are actually not attacks, what are they, really? "Cyber-activities" are usually about obtaining information. For example, intelligence activities, which are not regulated by international law, and therefore, according to some, in principle those are "legal activities",[9] and according to others these activities are neither legal nor illegal, because that is simply undefined, so: not unlawful. Sometimes to a greater or lesser extent the operation of systems is paralyzed (intentionally or accidentally). However, these are (mostly) temporary effects[10] and are definitely not on the same level as other types of actions such as missile attack, artillery attack, or aerial bombardment. That is, typically: kinetic actions that can destroy targets physically, even lead to the death of people. And those are their specific and intentional direct aims. In most cases, almost no cyberattack has such intentional goals or even has the ability to achieve such effects (although they might have, as we discussed in the previous chapters, and will discuss here again, soon).

Thus, purely legally, from the point of view of international law, a cyberattack does not constitute an attack. But if this is so, why have we used the term "cyberattack" in previous chapters in this book? It is simply in common use. That's the fact. The term is used routinely, everywhere, by nearly everybody. We, therefore, simply accept it as is. We will continue to use this popular term, but ask the reader to remember that a **cyberattack is not** *actually* **an attack** (in most cases), which is especially important in this chapter.

Fortunately, there are better, more precise terms.

7.4.3 Cyber operations

Perhaps it is helpful that in the so-called professional applications, within intelligence or military formations, a different terminology is used. The term "cyberattack" is not seriously used, but rather a different term: "cyberoperation" (or: cyber operation). Thus, an operation similar to such an action as, for example, a land, air, or even a special operation,[11] that is, integrated actions that are aimed at achieving a certain well-defined goal.

And this is how cyber operation can be defined as the use of cyber capabilities to achieve certain goals in or through cyberspace.[12] This definition of cyber operations also includes reaching targets through cyberspace and potentially the achievement of objectives (effects) outside of cyberspace, but through it.

Such cyber operations may be of a military or intelligence nature, for example. Three main types of cyber operations can be distinguished: defensive, ISR, and offensive.

7.4.3.1 Defensive cyber operations

Defensive cyber operations (DCOs) are typically carried out in relation to our own systems. These are the correct configurations, the buildup of security, the network packet filtering, network traffic filtering, malware, or threat detection (and its neutralization if necessary). However, it is also worth noting here that cyber operations provide for a whole *spectrum of activities*. For example, defensive operations located at the extreme point of the scale may smoothly transition toward offensive operations (COs). Thus, under certain conditions, a defensive operation can (or must) turn into an offensive operation, which simply means engaging a threat actor (an adversary) who is interested in the attacks, in order to, for example, to resist it, neutralize the source of the threat, eliminate the threat. In such a situation, it may be necessary to move into an active operation, involving remote systems, perhaps even located in another country. However, before we discuss active cyber operations, we will describe another type of operation.

7.4.3.2 ISR operations

By ISR, we understand the operations of *intelligence, surveillance*, but also *reconnaissance*, which may even contribute to the identification of targets. Recognizing and working out interesting targets, details of the adversary's systems (e.g., before attacking them or to know the possible risks on their side, and even the consequences of hitting such a target: whether they will be disproportionate, or making it unlawful to engage), is very important in the intelligence context, as well as in the military context. At least for those States that care about the international legality of their actions.

Because international law, specifically international humanitarian law (laws of armed conflict), requires commanders to have complete knowledge of the target to be engaged, attacked, if only to avoid excessive, disproportionate damage. It is, therefore, necessary to recognize precisely the purpose, or the nature, of this target. The crucial point here is not to attack civilian targets, which is illegal under the framework of laws of armed conflict. Therefore, reconnaissance operations (perhaps even cyberattacks in the colloquial, media, or journalistic sense) may be legally required as a prerequisite, to avoid attacking such targets and causing harm.

7.4.3.3 Offensive operations

Only after the reconnaissance aspects can we seriously talk about purely *offensive cyber operations* (OCOs), offensive, combat ones, perhaps even those of which effects would reach the level of attack (in the sense of international law), and which should not be confused with surveillance (espionage, intelligence) operations, because their goals are different. Although such an effect can also be achieved as a result of the so-called unfortunate accident (e.g.,in Chapter 5, we mentioned the so-called German steel mill).

Now a crucial detail. The methods or techniques used in cyberattacks conducted to *obtain information* and the methods used in cyberattacks *to achieve some paralyzing effect* or cause destruction generally may functionally overlap. The "purpose" (intent, end-goal) of an operation may, therefore, be confused, misinterpreted, or at least unclear, even if at the initial phase. Indeed, technically, sometimes it may be very difficult to distinguish such actions. Especially in their initial phases (gaining access to remote systems, reconnaissance, which can be both part of an intelligence operation and an offensive attack), because these are issues of the objectives of the operation, that is, in a sense, the intentions of the attackers. Intentions can sometimes be deduced from the actions taken, from the tools used, but it is not always immediately obvious.

Returning to offensive cyber operations, it is about offensive or combat actions. It can also support this projection of force through cyberspace we remarked at the beginning, That is, an interaction that produces certain effects. These can be effects such as paralyzing a network or disabling the possibility of using it. These can be destructive attacks, in particular data deletion. This can be an attack paralyzing the ability to use the information system, temporarily or for longer. Finally, these can also be destructive attacks, and it is not only about destroying systems or data, but potentially even about physical effects, i.e., when taking control of a control panel, it may be possible to cause damage to the infrastructure physically: longer lasting or even permanent damage. These are extremely rare operations, but such capabilities must be kept in mind.

7.4.4 Proportions of different operations

In the summary of this angle of consideration, it is worth mentioning that taking into account all cyber operations, offensive ones are rarely carried out. And cyberwar operations – very rarely (only during operations within the framework of an ongoing armed conflict). Figuratively, the proportions are distributed here in a way that defensive cyber operations prevail, some operations are offensive in nature, and cyberwarfare operations are the rare ones (depending on the situation, because if a country is at war, then of course there might be relatively more of the cyberwarfare activities). How these proportions scale in practice depends on specific countries and their intelligence or military structures. Such data are classified, so making strict comparisons between countries and operation types is not possible.

7.5 CYBER CAPABILITIES

It was already discussed that different cyber operations can be distinguished. But it is worth mentioning what such cyber capabilities could potentially be in actuality. In general, many countries are building different types of cyber capabilities. The basic one is breaching security and gaining access to remote systems, establishing a presence in them, making being removed from such systems difficult. The idea is to control them and be able to obtain information or also influence these systems in order to achieve certain goals. Perhaps the ability to perform actions "on demand", i.e., when needed (prepositioning, gaining access capability). This can be considered as "preparing the ground for future activities".

7.5.1 Physical effects

Operations with potentially physical effects, i.e., taking control of industrial systems, even for the purpose of causing destruction can be distinguished and these must be covered, even if such feats are extremely rare. This is already a highly specialized, higher level of operation, requiring special competencies. These are more complex and more difficult operations, burdened with risk, requiring preparations, custom tools, well-trained teams.

It takes time to build such capabilities. Depending on the costs that someone wants to incur, it can be several months to several years of work. The point here is to build a team that will be able to operate effectively in such an industrial environment. It is worth emphasizing here that it is not that cyberattacks happen quickly. Well, if a cyber operation is prepared perfectly, the people and the tools are available and ready...Then perhaps it can potentially be done rapidly. But depending on the operation, it can take quite a long time to prepare it. That is because it is about getting to know the systems, identifying vulnerabilities, building or preparing tools (perhaps custom ones) that will exploit the vulnerabilities in the systems and setting up such a cyber operation, executing it. It can be a matter of days, weeks, months. Not seconds or minutes, as the movies show.

Moreover, such preparations (tests, reconnaissance, etc.), when detected, of course, can be misunderstood. The goal of such an operation might erroneously be assumed, for example, as something else – for example, something more serious than it was. Because it is not at all clear why someone could be preparing some types of actions. For example, why would one deploy tools that could potentially lead to physical damage, perhaps even potentially gaining the ability to cause fatal effects? How should the target of the deployment of such tools interpret this? In extreme cases, this can be considered as preparation for war, attempted uses of force.

7.5.2 Disruptive effects

Building a presence in a network to be able to obtain information is one option, but building a presence in such networks or in industrial networks to potentially be able to paralyze them, disrupt their *functioning*, is another. An example of such actions is taking control of industrial automation systems, only to turn them off at some specific point. Perhaps for a longer period of time. Perhaps potentially paralyzing large areas of the country. For example, paralyzing a transport or power system can cause significant damage, as a consequence. In addition, there is the psychological effect, because the society may develop a feeling about the effects of such actions, which can affect their perceptions, the thought process, even affect a sense of (in)security or (lack of) faith or (dis)trust in the State and its (in)ability to provide security or stability. Similarly, certain data could be deleted, or overwritten. For example, the firmware controlling the devices could be overwritten, or the data could be simply encrypted (like ransomware) to prevent the use of the system for some time. Some countries (like France) could also consider this as armed aggression.

7.5.3 Denial of service and blocking

Another ability is slightly different from the one developed in the previous point. It is *denial of service*, i.e., paralyzing actions. They can be short-lived (duration of minutes, hours, etc.), they can relate only to networks, but they can also concern other services (e.g., financial systems, data) and branches of the economy. Industrial units may be affected, for example, a factory, a steel mill, a cheese factory. In general, a short-lived purely network-based *distributed denial of service* (DDoS) attack can render some services temporarily unavailable. It will not be a great "field of destruction". These are rather simple, low-ranking activities, not requiring finesse or advanced technique or knowledge. Sometimes they are simply non-events not worthy of hyping in the press, even when they are.

7.5.4 Information acquisition and data collection

A separate type is the ability to obtain information, i.e., breach security, take control of communication and data in such networks. More generally, it is about obtaining, or rather stealing data. These are the least "offensive" actions. From here, however, it's not a long way to deleting these data or modifying them, i.e., the actions described in the previous subsections. When access is established, the nature of cyber operations may change very quickly.

7.5.5 Signaling

Another type of a subtle effect is, once the safeguards have been breached, to imply that you are in such a system in order to psychologically cast doubt on the ability to control such systems. Because, in practice, if we know that someone controls our systems (e.g., military systems), then first of all, we probably will not be delighted with this fact. Second, if we're not sure about our systems, then perhaps we shouldn't trust and use them. Can we trust the integrity of something that our potential enemy controls? For example, assuming that a system controlling air and missile defense has been hacked, should such a system be turned on without being strongly convinced of the guarantee of its integrity? Who really controls such a system? After all, there may also be civil objects (airplanes) in our airspace, hence it is better to be careful. So if we know that someone has breached our own systems that we rely on, it can undermine confidence in our abilities and future actions.

Signals can also have a political function: sending a message like *"we are doing something to you"* (e.g., as a response to something, or a warning). This may be an element of a subtle political-diplomatic-military game.

7.5.6 Delivery

Another ability is the effective *payload* delivery of cyber tools, tools for operation, for example, for attack purposes. This can happen in many ways. These can be, for example, technical methods. It can be, as we said, phishing. This could be a remote code execution that exploits vulnerabilities. But this can also be more subtle methods such as bypassing air gaps, i.e., security measures in which some networks are isolated from the Internet, and not as simple to get to *just like that*, to be connected to. There may be several ways to bypass such safeguards.[13] If these networks are isolated from external networks, but for example provide the ability to connect to a wireless network locally, a so-called close access operation may also be potentially possible. For example, such a wireless network can be hacked, as long as the attacker is (physically) close to it. We are aware of such close access operations carried out by the Russians, for example.[14]

7.5.6.1 Cyber operation with close access in Rotterdam

One such a close-access operation was attempted by Russia's military intelligence operators in the Netherlands in 2018, perhaps to determine what was happening with the investigation into the downing of flight MH17 in 2014.

In 2017, a team of Russian cyber operators was caught red-handed driving a car loaded with various types of cyber operation equipment or devices near the National Prosecutor's Office in Rotterdam.[15]

In this context, there was also a Russian cyber operation of the civilian intelligence unit (SVR), when the Dutch police systems were hacked through the access to the systems of the Police Academy (i.e., located behind the appropriate firewall; so: being already inside the right networks). The detection of the operation was a success for the Dutch security agency AIVD, the branch responsible for cyber defense/counterintelligence.

However, a completely different story is that, years before, AIVD allegedly got into the systems of the Russian intelligence SVR in 2014. On one such occasion, the breaching of Russian systems was so complete that camera systems were hacked and it was possible to watch live what the Russian "government hackers" were doing.

7.5.6.2 Bribing employees

Such a "delivery" can also happen quite differently. Well, we can reach a person who is already an employee of a given company or institution and convince them to infect the systems of that company: their employers. Indeed, some cybercriminals are willing to pay employees of companies/institutions to infect their employers' systems[16]. Rates for such a "service" vary;[17] in some cases the cybercriminals were willing to pay up to several hundred thousand dollars. Therefore, such "access" to systems can be obtained in many ways: from technical to personal/human.

Of course, there is also the possibility of cooperation between cyber operators and human intelligence (HUMINT) operators. It's because such a person (such a contact) must be physically acquired and persuaded to act. Maybe it may actually be easier and faster to just convince a person to infect such systems themselves? At this point, it is worth for the reader to consider, purely hypothetically, how much it would cost to convince an employee of his/her company (or maybe themselves?) or institution to infect his/her own employer.

Of course, this sounds extremely unethical, and it is. But we have to have an open mind, be aware of the tangible threats and possibly build systems in such ways that these are resistant, in the more sensitive areas, to the possibility that a person in such a company is dishonest. And in fact, from time to time there are suspicions that employees of various institutions or companies have been somehow acquired by foreign countries,[18] too. Anyway, there is no reason to believe that this is not possible, because there are several situations known from history in which someone has become a spy of the opposing party and performed actions in the foreign handler's interest. So there's no reason why someone like that could not just be used to attack information systems. It's as simple as that.

7.6 WHAT IS CYBERWAR?

What are we supposed to think when we hear the term "cyberwar" in the media, in the mouths of politicians, journalists, analysts, experts, talking heads, or others? Is it really a war? Well, usually in these contexts – no, it is not! Just like a cyberattack is not an attack, the popular notion of cyberwar is, most of the time, not about war. When this phrase is in use, it is usually used in a journalistic sense, it functions as a mental shortcut; it is not used in its definitional sense. It does not carry detailed contents. In this book, however, we must properly organize the information regarding the term "cyberwar". So, we have to think about what an actual cyberwar could mean. Because there is no doubt that it can take place.[19] We will discuss several possibilities here.

7.6.1 A war limited to cyberattacks? Nope.

One possibility of understanding the term "cyberwar" is actions limited to cyberspace, i.e., cyberattacks carried out by various operators, actors, perhaps State ones. In this sense, these would be actions aimed at some companies, State institutions, other countries. Hostile activities, but limited only to the Internet, only to cyberspace, and in addition potentially carried out in peacetime. So, here we have a contradiction (an actual absurdity, please appreciate it) when actions called war were to take place in conditions of peace, which essentially logically cancels each other out. Unless it's not a real war, but a kind of "different" war – a virtual, an unreal one. That is, a war that is not a war. Would such a "cyberwar" then be a useful term? It would not!

We also have a second problem. For if we're speaking of war, we have to consider whether it is even realistic to expect that in the event of an actual (i.e., real) war, actions can be limited to only one domain (land, sea, airspace, etc.). In this case – to cyberspace. That doesn't seem particularly sensible either. For in the case of real wars (i.e., real armed conflicts, since armed conflicts are called wars), we could wonder whether this is a realistic approach. Can we pretend that actions during armed conflicts (wars) are limited to only one theater of operations? Perhaps a few hundred years ago this was justified. Back then, when the activities were indeed actually carried out only in the land domain, there were no other possibilities, the types of activities were naturally limited. Later, however, the situation became complicated. There were actions at sea, in the airspace; space may soon be included in the calculations, too.

Therefore, during armed conflicts (wars), actions usually take place in many domains.

Nowadays, it is almost unrealistic that an actual armed conflict, i.e., war, would be fought in only one domain. This is not how military goals, or objectives, are achieved. Types of weapons and techniques complement each other, cooperate with each other, harmonize, strengthen each other's weaknesses, reinforce each other. It is, therefore, also conceivable that even in the hypothetical event of an initially "pure" cyberwar (i.e., an armed conflict only in cyberspace, initiated from high-impact cyber operations that constituted an attack), at some point the situation could escalate to activities in other domains, too (and, indeed, States reserve the right to retaliate in a non-cyber way).

It is more realistic to simply assume that cyber activities may accompany those in the other domains. This is a continuous "*spectrum*", because in fact military, paramilitary, irregular activities may formally take place below the threshold of war, but in the event of a conflict moving to the armed conflict, war phase, cyber operations will also be included in the military operations.

7.6.2 Cyberattacks accompanying other military actions

Cyberattacks in the context of a wider armed conflict together with other activities, i.e., kinetic activities, could enable the conduct of *combined arms operations*, accompanying or supporting other activities. In this sense, cyber-warfare would be understood as actions taking place (conducted) as part of a wider conflict, which (even if only at the beginning) may even be at a low scale of intensity, but at some point it may escalate, turning into more serious actions, into a wider conflict, which then becomes an armed conflict. For example, activities in cyberspace could support kinetic activities, such as reconnaissance, identification, and target acquisition. But also engaging targets, such as paralyzing them. Turning them off, perhaps hindering observation or disrupting logistics. Cyberattacks can also support broader electronic warfare. In the past, such an operation reportedly reached Syrian air defenses.

At a time when cyberattacks operate in a war mode, actions aimed at shutting down infrastructure, possibly leading to lethal effects, can no longer be ruled out. Here, we already have several precedents. Activities in cyber-space were accompanied by activities in other domains, for example during the armed conflict against the so-called Islamic State. In this case, the service of the United Kingdom, Australia, and the United States revealed[20] that as part of their activities, cyber operations were also carried out, which could paralyze certain targets. France has also used cyber operations during military operations in the Sahel.[21]

It is also worth mentioning the hostilities in Georgia in 2008 and in Ukraine around 2014, as well as later – during the escalation and war in 2022. If we combine such cyberattacks with broader activities within the framework of an armed conflict (ongoing, subsequent, etc.), this can be classified as cyberwarfare. A concrete example here could also be the release of the NotPetya tool, a self-propagating worm that paralyzed compromised systems, if it could be seen as the use of force.

7.7 CYBER-OFFENSIVE ACTIONS

Offensive actions in the context of cyberwar sound serious. We have already talked about cyber operations in the context of cybercriminal objectives, even intelligence objectives. Because of the subject matter of this chapter, we will now briefly discuss some important issues.

7.7.1 Cyber operations with physical effects

It is often considered whether physical damage is possible as a result of a cyberattack. As we have said many times before (and we even outlined scenarios in the chapter on the critical infrastructure), it is possible to cause physical damage through cyber operations. Therefore, it is possible to set up and carry out an operation in a special way. That is, assuming that its goal (and therefore the end result) will be physical destruction. The effects will, therefore, be felt in the physical world. This could be, for example, the effect of turning off the electricity (as it was in Ukraine), disrupting the operation of turbines, leading to disasters in land traffic, etc. It is not necessarily easy to pull off, but it is doable.

However, the question will arise as to whether aiming at performing such actions makes sense. After all, if there is already a regular armed conflict (war), then its sides have the ability to cause destruction through other, kinetic means (missiles, bombs, artillery, etc.) in such a situation. These can also be costly actions, but at the same time more direct, faster effective, using available resources, perhaps more reliable. Armed forces are usually always equipped with kinetic destruction systems, but the setting up of cyber operations can take time. Alternatively, perhaps it's best to use the precious cyber tools to acquire information than to *burn* the capability to cause destruction, perhaps of limited duration? After all, espionage data cannot be obtained (solely) using kinetic tools.

Therefore, the answer to the question posed at the beginning of the subsection is: yes, *physical destruction can be achieved* with cyber operations, *but it is not necessarily always justified*. It is different if, for example, we want to try to mask the source of the attack. It may be easier to do this in the event of a cyber operation. It can be more difficult to hide the trajectory of a missile, because it is launched from somewhere, and radars may track it, sometimes in real time.

7.7.2 Can a cyberattack kill? Operational-military approach

Another question that we have already addressed in the subject of cyberattacks on healthcare (and partly – critical infrastructure) is: *Can cyberattacks be used to kill (lethal engagement of targets)?* So, is it possible to combine cyber operation with lethal effects?

Here the answer is also affirmative. Because, for example, vulnerabilities may be found in medical systems. For example, in systems that are injected into the body, for example, in medical implants. Then their operation can be modified in such a way, reconfigured so that it could lead to lethal effects.

However, in the context of cyber operations, especially if there is a State behind them, it would have certain consequences. Here, therefore, it is necessary to determine the legality of these actions. Of course this would be illegal from the point of view of domestic, local, national law. Every State criminalizes murder. In "war" cases, however, we have in action principles of a different nature, the so-called laws of armed conflict. They dictate what can and cannot be done in the course of wars, or – how, under what circumstances. For example, it would not be legal if such an operation was aimed at civilians, people not involved in the war, not taking part in it (e.g., the so-called hors de combat, i.e., soldiers unable to fight or those who have surrendered). It would also be illegal to do offensive things that are "non-discriminatory", i.e., those that do not distinguish between military and civilian targets (and persons). Such things are illegal; they can even constitute war crimes. Of course, they apply when we speak of attacks; and most cyberattacks are not attacks so laws of armed conflict would not regulate such a conduct (Though according to Geneva Conventions, healthcare facilities have a special protected status). There is no reason why a threat actor could perform a distributed denial of service attack against a civilian target during peacetime, but suddenly such a conduct would become prohibited during wartime, during a time when in fact usually much greater and more extreme hostilities may arise.

Returning to the main topic though, in conditions of war, however, it happens that various military actions can have fatal consequences, including those unintentional or difficult to predict. If a missile is fired at a military target, for example, the effect would be expected to be quite fatal (destructive). In such a situation, treating cyber operations under war conditions as one of the methods of war, it is worth considering whether it would be legal to use a cyberattack, for example, to hack a medical implant device, for example, implanted in the body of a soldier, perhaps a commander, an officer, while in hospital.

We will not answer this question, because such issues – including unfortunate consequences – require a thorough analysis taking into account all the complicated circumstances. Although it is likely that if such a cyber operation was carried out in compliance with *international humanitarian law*, then it could be lawful. We write "could" because we have to take into account all the actions and consequences. For example, were there any other undesirable, collateral effects (e.g., hitting – unintentionally – also other targets)?

7.7.3 Targeting – can cyberattacks aim at specific targets, people?

Another question is whether it is possible to perform targeted cyber operations against specific targets? Objects, specific politicians, specific military personnel. But also, for example, at software developers involved in a conflict by creating or configuring tools. Or, in a more extreme direction, the software developers, such as those of an operating system. These are also provocative questions. Because the question arises as to how deep the responsibility for actions reaches here. Just because a version of the

Windows operating system can control British military vessels doesn't mean that individual Windows developers and programmers are responsible. That would be absurd. Just because the Ukrainian government's data are hosted in a Western provider of cloud services does not necessarily mean that employees of these cloud providers participate in the armed conflict. That said, in 2023 such notions were not well or universally understood, also due to the fact that some parts of the community could have been overly putting the focus on the less realistic scenarios of cyberwars. Then the real thing happened, and suddenly a reality-check ensued.

We can also expand on the issue in another direction, by taking into account whether people who create software can become targets of an ordinary military, kinetic operation. It could possibly relate to programmers, but only to those directly involved in the conflict, the hostilities. That is, to those who, for example, work on creating specific tools for specific actions, operations. It's hard to imagine that someone who once wrote a program (perhaps as open source) that was later used by some intelligence or military unit suddenly becomes a target. Thus, developers not involved in the conflict should not be attacked in any way. They are, after all, civilians. That would be illegal in terms of international humanitarian law.

Returning to the main topic. Technically, targeting is possible. After all, we can determine who is using certain services – to the precise serial number of the implant (such as a pacemaker) or just the serial number of computer components (e.g., the unique MAC number of the network card). Knowing these parameters, one could reach out to specific targets, like systems, equipment, or people, and apply cyber tools to them (omitting other potential targets).

7.8 CYBERSECURITY OF WEAPON SYSTEMS

Weapon systems are also subject to computerization and digitization. For example, anti-missile systems or radars are computer controlled, sometimes operating semi-autonomously. Similarly, missile guidance systems can be equipped with a great deal of autonomy. Modern weapon systems are highly computerized – they are computer controlled, they can use the network. The software controlling a modern fighter can be very complex. For example, the F-16 fighter software consisted of about 150,000 lines of source code, and the F-35 fighter systems – from 8 million to even over 20 million lines of source code (depending on the method of counting). This also holds a great potential for security vulnerabilities and mistakes, bugs.

The question arises whether there could be cybersecurity bugs in such software. Naturally: yes. In any complicated software, there will be bugs, including security vulnerabilities that can be exploited. In the U.S. military, where the cybersecurity of weapon systems is monitored, many weaknesses have been found in various systems, such as the B-2 bomber, Spitfire, some types of missiles,[22] or Apache helicopters and MQ-25 Stingray drones.[23]

So there is no doubt that weapon systems may contain cybersecurity vulnerabilities. And that they can potentially be used. The level of cybersecurity of weapon systems must be taken care of. Good design and management practices as well as cybersecurity tests serve this purpose. These were carried out, for example, in relation to Abrams tanks, HIMARS artillery systems, THAAD rocket systems, and others.

Potentially, the weapon system (weapons) may be the target of a cyberattack in the future,[24] especially since every war in the twenty-first century may include cyber operations.[25] Of course, a cyberattack in such conditions could be very serious (and also difficult – such systems are isolated). This may also be seen as a nightmare scenario. First of all, it could be interpreted directly by such a target as a *casus belli*, that is, simply crossing the boundary of war threshold, and actions that may lead to a military response. Because this is already a sensitive domain reserved to the military.

7.8.1 What does this lead to?

There is another potential consequence. Imagine what would happen if a remote attacker took control of the weapon system. For example, if the attacker's action led to the malfunctioning of missile or air defense – in such a way that it would target civilian targets, all detected targets. This is another nightmare plot of at least a military-political thriller.

But here doubts could arise as to who is actually responsible for attacking such civilian targets. The manufacturer? The operator (military or State)? The attacker (if detected)? Legal liability would be a complicated mess. In general, losing control of the weapon system is one of the nightmares of any self-respecting military commander or politician, as long as they know about such a risk at all, and, therefore, they should try to counteract it.

7.8.2 Good news?

Fortunately, there is also good news. Weapon systems almost always operate in well-isolated networks, systems that cannot just be connected to,[26] thus, they cannot be (easily) accessed, and so they are (or at least should) not so easy to hack. However, one way around this could be to gain access from within (e.g., through a sabotage or a treason) or by compromising the supply chain and smuggling in an already infected piece of hardware or software, for example. So the possibility of access might exist, although it is not simple.

In the U.S., it is suspected that some kind of unauthorized components may have already reached into the production systems, possibly even there were attempted attacks that failed.[27] Detecting the insertion of unauthorized components is difficult, and it is certainly reactive when it occurs after the system has been implemented.[28] Thanks to the transparency of the U.S., we know about such problems. The question is what about the armed forces of other countries. This is because weapon systems are used all over the world, in almost every country. As a result, the size of this cyber risk may be much greater. Only it is not necessarily known. But the risk will rise in this century.

7.9 IS IT POSSIBLE TO RESPOND MILITARILY TO A CYBERATTACK?

Is it possible to start a war with a cyberattack? As we have said before, most cyberattacks do not constitute an attack within the meaning of international law. Therefore, those we read about in the media cannot be considered as legal grounds for declaring a war, even if as a pretext to start one. Nor as an excuse. They do not constitute armed aggression within the meaning of international law. They are not armed aggression. Can we conclude from this that there is no risk that a cyberattack will lead to a war? We can't.

We have already mentioned cyberattacks with serious consequences. So, we can imagine cyberattacks that will be serious enough to cross certain boundaries. For someone to legally recognize them as military actions (because there is no automatism: the victim State must explicitly recognize that something needs to be answered, and then choose whether to take action). Here, such a limit, such a turning point, a threshold is, for example, the action causing, or leading to *physical destruction* or *death of people*. This is a boundary, or threshold, known from traditional kinetic conflicts. Countries have long considered its transgression as a prerequisite for military response. That's right: they *considered it*. After all, it was not directly decreed, and the rules (e.g., treaty rules) in a way correspond to how States have behaved for centuries (i.e., the customs).

Thus, a cyberattack can achieve an effect comparable to a traditional attack because it has caused physical damage in practice or had fatal consequences.[29] This may be the reason for an armed reaction, some response, a reprisal, a retaliation. It is also considered whether leading systems or devices to the loss of functionality could not be considered as such a reason. That is, when as a result of cyber operations they would cease to function, for a long time, or have been irreversibly damaged. For example, when data have been permanently deleted or systems have been permanently destroyed in such a way that their functions cannot be restored. Especially if we treated the data as an object (and therefore such an object would be destroyed).[30]

This is undoubtedly a topic for theoretical debate: whether causing a cyberattack to degrade the functioning of certain infrastructure or certain targets could also be a prerequisite for responding to such a cyberattack.

In general, this is a problem, because causing a temporary downtime of a system can have limited effects. Is it worth going to war because of the deletion of data, which, for example, can be easily restored and systems – reinstalled? Considering the risk of destruction in the event of a kinetic war – perhaps it is not worth it. It would not be proportionate, either. So how to respond? Perhaps proportionally – also through cyberattacks? Of course, only if the State has access to such capabilities. Otherwise, it would be defenseless – without a chance of a proportionate response.

7.9.1 Article 51 of the United Nations Charter

Things get complicated if, for example, ransomware paralyzes something more long-term. At this point, it is worth quoting Article 51 of the United Nations Charter (UNC) in verbatim.

7.9.1.1 Article 51

> Nothing in the present Charter shall impair the inherent right of individual or collective self-defence if an armed attack occurs against a Member of the United Nations, until the Security Council has taken measures necessary to maintain international peace and security. Measures taken by Members in the exercise of this right of self-defence shall be immediately reported to the Security Council and shall not in any way affect the authority and responsibility of the Security Council under the present Charter to take at any time such action as it deems necessary in order to maintain or restore international peace and security.

The United Nations Charter, therefore, says that States should not be too hasty in bringing about armed conflicts between them. Overall, this act is intended to have a stabilizing effect.

Article 51 of the UNC allows for a legal self-defense in the event of an armed attack. Thus, if a cyber operation were to reach the level of an armed attack, the country could potentially respond to such actions. Many countries in their cybersecurity strategies specify (if ambiguously) that they can respond militarily to a high-profile cyberattack. At the same time, such a response can take place in cyberspace, i.e., it can also be a cyberattack, that is, it can be made with the help of cyber tools.

But it can also be a completely different answer: non-cyber, i.e., kinetic, conventional (bombing, missiles, etc.). It is worth quoting the position of France, which "*reaffirms that a cyberattack may constitute an armed attack within the meaning of Article 51 of the United Nations Charter, if it is of a scale and severity comparable to those resulting from the use of physical force*".[31] Generally, there is no going beyond these thresholds (destruction, death). For example, the Netherlands points out that: "*At present there is no international consensus on qualifying a cyberattack as an armed attack if it does not cause fatalities, physical damage or destruction yet nevertheless has very serious non-material consequences*".[32]

And this is another reason to remember what we already said: *cyberattacks (usually!) are not attacks.*

7.9.2 Attribution

It is not always clear what the source of a cyberattack is. This is the cyberattack attribution issue.[33]

Because if we are talking about the response to a cyberattack, it would be a good idea to know who is behind it. This lets us know who to actually respond to, and how. In the case of missiles, it is simple: the rocket takes off from somewhere, it is more or less easy to determine its trajectory. Access to such military technology is also quite limited. In the case of cyberattacks, the problem is a bit more complicated, because the attacker can mask activities quite effectively, while access to IT methods and tools may be easier, and is not exclusive to the government or the military.

7.9.2.1 Acting under a false flag – masking

What's more, we can even potentially imagine a situation in which acting under a false flag takes place, i.e., pretending to act in such a way that the victim thinks that a different actor is behind the cyberattack, for example, a different country than in reality,[34] what, for example, was done by the cyber group Turla,[35] that is the Russian security service, FSB. In one case, they used the infrastructure of the Iranian group, in another – there was an attempt to point to the (alleged) responsibility of North Korea. This is an interesting technique with political consequences, because it potentially lends credence to political goals in negotiations on cybersecurity, if it is argued there that attribution is a really difficult obstacle (coincidentally, this was also voiced by the Russian diplomacy, at times).

Similarly, in 2015, Russian military intelligence tried to shift responsibility for the hacking (almost destruction) of the French television channel TV5 Monde.[36] It was announced that it was the Islamic State (the so-called Cyber Caliphate) behind it. A great many people, including some journalists and public figures and analysts, have blindly accepted such a public announcement. In vain.

It turned out then that releasing such a fake *news diversion is* extremely *simple*. Too simple and probably exploiting the vulnerability of the psyche (people are looking for the guilty party, and they got "some" on a plate), and the broad, worldwide anxiety about terrorism that existed at that time. So a situation where someone pretended to be a terrorist and took responsibility for it provided a simple explanation. Someone said that they were responsible, case closed? Well, not really.

But what about attribution?

In response to such a cyberattack, one country could then potentially simply attack a different State, if done naively. Acting under a false flag (i.e., impersonating someone) would result in false attribution. Retaliation would then be unjustified and therefore unlawful. This underlines the importance of the problem: one can't be in a hurry when the stakes are high. It is worth spending time analyzing the problem, i.e., it is good to determine the attribution of the cyberattack, the specific sources of the cyberattack, and then the issue of responsibility, liability, including legal liability.

The attribution problem is a complex one. Establishing facts with a high rate of reliability is necessary. Because no one should want a situation in which the answer is made not to the one who was actually behind the actions.

Sometimes, however, it may be simpler. Attribution can be assumed because of motivations that may resonate with the goals of a State. For example, a cyber operation in February 2022 paralyzing the KA-SAT satellite internet service accompanied the start of Russia's armed aggression in Ukraine. The Ukrainian military used KA-SAT services. The cyber operation was highly likely attributable to Russia, which was confirmed by Western States in May 2022.

7.9.3 Attribution levels

Several levels of attribution can be distinguished: technical, legal, and political.

Technical attribution, i.e., technical analysis of a cyberattack traces,[37] or activities such as cyber operations, may include the analysis of tactics, techniques, and methods used, for example, the nature of employed tools. It's also a technical analysis of malware. Analysis of the tools, tactics, and methods used in a cyberattack may also make it possible to link currently investigated operations to possibly already known campaigns of unknown origin. Or put current operations within the framework of activities of an already known cyber threat actor.

Attribution also addresses legal and political issues.[38] Once we establish attribution in a technical way, and perhaps with support of other methods, such as the input from other intelligence, for example, through HUMINT, then there is a legal problem associated with it: were these actions legal, lawful? How to evaluate them? If they were unlawful, what rules have been breached, infringed upon? For example, ordinary espionage activities may not be covered by the rules and, therefore, do not violate them (except, possibly, the domestic national laws). Once we know the legal situation, and let us provisionally assume that there has been a violation of a principle, such as sovereignty, or perhaps even the level of *use of force*, then it remains a matter of political decision. It is defined by what such a State is prepared for, for what kind of escalation: legal, technical, political, or maybe military.

Officially pointing a finger at some people or institutions in another country is one thing. It is another thing to formally hold the State responsible – it may have diplomatic consequences and even result in some kind of retorsion or retaliation. In this case, an EU or a NATO member State can decide whether to act alone or to involve allies (this is also a problem of politics for their engagement in the situation, of convincing them, etc.). There were situations when EU/NATO allies were convinced to take some action, and other cases – when they were not convinced. It's based on mutual discussion, negotiations.

What could these *actions* be? Practice shows that it can be the indication itself – listing names, names of institutions, perhaps countries as being to blame. It can also be the imposition of sanctions – usually on particular individuals or institutions – the introduction of an entry ban for certain people, the seizure of financial resources. The consequences can vary, including their severity. The effectiveness of such activities remains a separate problem.

Sanctions and "finger-pointing" are a relatively new phenomenon (since around the middle of the 2010s), but now it seems that they may function as rather symbolic activities. Moreover, countries participating in the negotiations within the framework of UN governmental expert groups agree to avoid accusations without concrete evidence. Sometimes announcements of detection of activities are accompanied by the publication of technical indicators, and even descriptions of operations, investigative procedures. However, it is difficult to say whether they have evidential value, because here the forensics standards are usually very high, at least in domestic law enforcement cases.

7.9.4 State practice – establishing customs?

A separate attention should be paid to the analysis of the practices of Western countries (U.S., UK, EU members), which publish the names of identified persons behind cyberattacks and operations, and also assign responsibility to institutions, for example intelligence agencies (military, civilian) of a country (most often Russia or China).

However, this does not apply to the State, at least officially. It is kind of a trick to suggest State responsibility, without indicating it directly. It is the pointing at an employee of an intelligence agency, or at the agency unit itself; as if the actions of these institutions were done on their own, not as part of a State activity. The problem is that, according to well-known and binding analyses of international law,[39] States are held accountable for the actions of their institutions. This means that in fact what Western countries are doing is an indication of the responsibility of specific States, whether they say it overtly or not, in practice this is equivalent.

However, this goes against the way these indications are often assumed, because it is recognized – at least officially – that there is no indication of responsibility of a specific State. In fact, however, it is done: formally, fingers are pointed at a State.

Why maintain this masquerade, then? This is a question for politicians and diplomats.

7.9.5 Why indicate at all?

What is the practical significance (apart from the symbolism) of such an indication?

If, for example, these are cybercriminals located on the territory of France or Russia, but they act independently of the State (no one commissions them to do anything, they determine the motives and targets of their actions), then there is not necessarily a reason to blame the State for their activities. And in the media space, the situation is often simplified and thus bad conclusions can be drawn. The activity and responsibility of the State occurs only when actors or State institutions more or less unambiguously direct such activities, influence them. So, for example, they commission, support or finance such activities. In a way: even if they merely tolerate them (i.e., are aware of them, and do not do anything to put a stop to them), and this is a well-known rule of international *due diligence principle*. If a State actor, if the State knows that certain actions are being carried out from its territory (missile launches, cyberattacks), then it should take action to bring them to an end. If it knows about them and does nothing to stop them, it can potentially be considered a deliberate unfriendly, careless action.

So, in terms of response, it's important to establish with a high degree of probability who was behind the cyberattacks in order to establish responsibility. At the same time, it is less important for a specific company that has become a victim of a cyberattack. Such a company should take care of its own security. It is less important to it whether this or that State is behind the cyberattack. The issue of attribution is a political and a legal problem.

7.10 WOULD THERE BE ANY RULES IN CYBERWAR?

Are there any rules for cyberwarfare?

It is often said that activities in cyberspace are a gray area, that they are supposedly not regulated, and that there are no rules. This is not the case. The rules are there, they exist. First of all, national (domestic) laws apply to cyberattacks and this type of activity. However, this chapter is less concerned with the internal situation and cybercrime. Let's also be clear that the local law of the State may not reach someone who will carry out a cyber operation, especially with the support of some other State.

Although it may sometimes be difficult to classify certain activities, laws still apply to activities in cyberspace. So the rules are in place. Respecting and enforcing them is another matter. If these are supranational actions, then international law would apply, with which virtually all countries agree today. There are rules in the form of the United Nations Charter, as well as other treaties, norms (soft law). And this can effectively regulate actions below the threshold of a war at a general level. That is, what is legal and tolerated, and what the State responsibility for such actions would look like and under what circumstances it would take place. We have to accept that the above may sound a bit enigmatic. This is an area under development, evolution.

7.10.1 Ideas for using new technologies and protecting ourselves from threats

The rules for weapons and their methods of employment evolve over time. It is not always immediately clear what a particular type of technique offers and how to use it effectively. For example, the first manual for mechanized combat was published in 1929 in Great Britain, under the title "*Mechanised and armoured formations*".[40] It was the *Purple Primer*. There is no such book addressing cyber issues. Although elements of cybersecurity, computer security were discussed, for example, in the so-called *Orange Book* (computer security standard) in the United States in the 1980s.[41] Of course, it was not a manual of strategy or combat, or cyberwarfare.

This, however, makes us realize that when new technical abilities appear, they are accompanied by analyses and considerations of how such capabilities can be used, how certain new methods, techniques, means should be used, and where it will lead us.[42] We are constantly in a situation where we are looking for new applications of cyber or information methods, as well as thinking about possible abuses and ways to defend against them.

It is necessary to make a stipulation here that the responses to cyber operations may be hostile, but they do not have to mean warfare. Indeed, espionage activities are often considered "lawful" (or: not unlawful) in the sense that they are not covered by any international treaty that would penalize such activities. This does not mean that a State that becomes a victim of such actions cannot resort to some kind of response. There are various acceptable reactions. In the case of cyberattacks, this could be, for example (as we have already discussed) the imposition of economic sanctions, or the attempt to impose legal sanctions if it is identified who was behind the cyberattack. So far we speak about activities below the threshold of a war.

7.10.2 The laws of war (laws of armed conflict)

However, a question arises, what happens during a war?

In wartime, in a war situation, the principles of International Humanitarian Law (IHL) apply, such as the Geneva Conventions and protocols additional to them.[43] These acts of binding international law regulate what can be done and what should be avoided in the conduct of hostilities (warfare). So, for example, civilians cannot be targeted, objects of which destruction would have undesirable consequences for civilians when it's easily avoidable, and, for example, would threaten the survival of the population, which is off limits, cannot be targeted. Cultural objects cannot be targeted. It is necessary to take care that action is taken only against objects and individuals directly involved in the conflict, i.e., simply military structures, the lawful combatants taking part in hostilities, belligerents. Those things must be spared. It's the responsibility of States, even individual commanders.

As it was already discussed in Chapter 5 on cyberattacks on critical infrastructure, it is conceivable that some cyberattacks could lead to poisoning water provision systems, and maybe also air environment (i.e., with a toxic gas). Here it is worth mentioning also other treaties that are in force, and may be relevant. For example, the Chemical Weapons Convention.[44] If we are talking about hypothetical poisoning as a result of the concentration of chemical substances, it must be said directly that this convention may be broken, infringed upon. It does not include and apply only the means deliberately created as weapons (e.g., combat gasses). It would, therefore, also cover the effects of cyber operations leading to gas poisoning. This leads us to an interesting conclusion that cyberattacks may well lead to clearly unlawful activities, actually – to war crimes.

7.10.3 Cyberattack scenario causing gas poisoning – in violation of Chemical Weapons Convention

Imagine a heating or ventilation management system, for example, a so-called smart system, controlled by industrial computer control systems.[45]

We may wonder whether it would not be possible to take control of it in such a way as to make some adverse changes. For example, to cause a malfunction or shutdown of the ventilation system and consequently lead to a harmful increase in the concentration of certain gasses such as carbon dioxide or carbon monoxide. This could have adverse health effects and may even lead to death,[46] as such gasses may be toxic.

The considered cyber operation may be potentially possible, assuming that such a computer control system would be available and vulnerable to a cyberattack. At the same time, such actions could violate the convention on the prohibition of chemical weapons, because carbon dioxide and carbon monoxide are gasses and, therefore, chemical agents in this case.

The Convention on Chemical Weapons (article II) defines *"toxic chemicals"* as *"Any chemical which through its chemical action on life processes can cause death, temporary incapacitation or permanent harm to humans or animals. This includes all such chemicals, regardless of their origin or of their method of production, and regardless of whether they are produced in facilities, in munitions or elsewhere"*.

Carbon monoxide certainly meets this definition as it is a toxic gas that interferes with the body's ability to use oxygen, and exposure to high levels of it can cause injury or death. The use of such gasses as that one as a weapon – it does not matter whether caused by a cyberattack initially – would be prohibited

This is how we could creatively apply the treaty that bans the use of chemical weapons – to cyberattacks.

In conclusion, it is not the case that there are no rules for cyberattacks. The rules are there, but they are not always adequately understood or they do not always define things explicitly. It does not mean that there are no rules. There are no specific treaties or rules, but similarly it can be said about many other weapons, means, or methods of warfare.

7.11 MEANS OF CYBERATTACK – CYBER WEAPONS

The term "cyber weapons" is inaccurate and misleading. First of all, in the popular imagination, sometimes this prefix "cyber-" means something that is really not real, perhaps virtual, so unconventional, and perhaps in some way just different, different from those, you know, those non-cyber things. But according to this reasoning, would such cyber weapons, then mean non-weapons? So it would not be a typical weapon, but a cyber weapon, something potentially new, different, a weapon that is not a weapon? This is not a good presentation of the matter, because just as war is war, so weapons are weapons. We have to use words properly.

Often, the term "cyberweapon" is applied to various types of tools: digital, IT, malware, and even tools routinely used to test security (if they are useful in cyber operations to break through security boundaries). Describing all such different tools with one name "a cyberweapon" would be imprecise, or, rather, geared towards media, colloquial, publicistic. It's not very useful. It would be devoid of the true meaning of the term. Although it happens that it is used by various experts (rarely, jokingly, ironically), and even by some politicians who want to sharpen their statement.

7.11.1 Tools

A cyber weapon – in the colloquial sense of the term – is a tool that can be used to carry out a cyberattack. However, in professional applications (military, intelligence, etc.), it would seem much more accurate, precise, and adequate, to describe cyber tools as means or methods of warfare[47] if only because most of the cyberattacks we see are not war-related, but also because of the nature of cyber tools that are very different from kinetic weapons.[48] For example, kinetic weapons can be difficult to "reverse engineer", i.e., to get to know how they work internally, and in the case of cyber weapons such an analysis is much simpler. In addition, such a cyber tool can be easily modified or used for one's own purposes, many times. This is another difference: kinetic weapons usually have limited use, for example, once fired, a missile is not reusable. In the case of ordinary kinetic weapons, their effects are also guaranteed: missiles or bombs explode, almost always reliably and with a certain strength. In the case of cyberweapons, this is not entirely the case, because tools can have various functions and effectiveness, also depending on how secure the remote system is.

Finally, the big difference (let's consider it political[49]) is that policymakers, politicians, political and military leaders are familiar with the way ordinary weapons work and with their capabilities. This is not exactly the case with cyber tools, where the possibilities, limitations, and effects may be more difficult to understand. These are real differences.

7.11.2 Methods

Recognizing cyber tools as methods of warfare, i.e., something employed in the conduct of warfare, would not artificially limit the way we think about these tools. A bomb has only one purpose. Cyber tools can usually have several. Although it is another matter that it is possible to design and build very dangerous (effective) cyber tools with destructive functions, possibly causing deadly consequences. In this case, however, it actually crosses a certain line and brings the cyber tool closer to being a weapon, i.e., a tool constructed for a specific purpose. However, one could still think of them as a method of combat.

7.11.3 Dual use

Digital tools would be one of the so-called dual-use technologies,[50] where the same solutions can have civilian but also military applications.

Here, however, let us point out that tools such as a shovel, a fork, or a rake can also potentially be used to kill – but no one thinks of routinely referring to a shovel as a weapon, right? So it's about using common sense. In international law, weapons, means, and methods of warfare are listed, for example, in the Additional Protocol (I) to the Geneva Conventions, but they are not defined. Such definitions can sometimes be found in documents of various countries, for example the USA or Denmark.[51] Why is this important to us at all? Because it seems that it is actually easier and more useful to consider cyber tools as a method of warfar.

So it wouldn't really be the use of weapons (i.e., the term "cyberweapon" is a mental shortcut). And, indeed, most cyberattacks do not even come close to the effects that we usually attribute to the use of traditional weapons, such as destruction or death. So using the term "cyberweapons" can be quite confusing. While in this subsection, we sometimes use this term too, but we try to do it consciously, taking into account the nuances. However, it is important to remember that just as a cyberattack is usually not an attack, cyberweapons are different from kinetic weapons. Because let's emphasize the main difference once again: in the case of kinetic weapons, it is relatively easy to have physical effects (destruction, death), and in the case of cyberweapons – usually not.

The term "means and methods of warfare" may be more appropriate, because then we have "certain cyber capabilities" and we employ them (as a method of action, e.g. in operations), in a certain way. To achieve certain goals, aims, effects. This is also the meaning of the commonly used term "*cyber capabilities*" – it is simply the ability to do *something*.

7.12 WHERE TO GET CYBER CAPABILITIES

In the case of a proverbial tank, two basic things matter: the physical tool (tank, ammunition, fuel) and the ability and experience of using this tool (by armored weapon operators, soldiers). So, in part, it's a matter of acquisition, and training. No military creates this type of weapon by itself. In the case of cyber capabilities, it may be similar, although there are some important differences here.

So, which is better? Purchasing or autonomously building the capacity? Because in general there are just these two possibilities, with some intermediate solutions, like purchasing of some sub-components. We may purchase a ready-made solution or components for our own solutions-tools. Components, for example: exploits (tools that allow breaching security as a result of using a vulnerability, gaining access to the system), or even complete tools and frameworks. We can also build such capabilities within our units or teams: look for bugs, vulnerabilities, design solutions that exploit them. Build tools, learn about their capabilities, apply them. This choice encompasses various differences in terms of the allocated funds (funds for the tools and competent staff to operationalize them, or additional funds for R&D), the necessary teams, the time constraints (identifying, finding, exploiting may take months; purchasing may be quite instantaneous), but also the secrecy (if built autonomously, the vendor will not know what is it that was purchased, no option to reason about 'our units' interests)

This is also controversial, because if vulnerabilities in software are identified, perhaps States should rather decide to report them to software developers in order for them to build in appropriate safeguards? This is a decision that every self-respecting cyber service faces.

This example also illustrates the big difference between cyberweapons and traditional weapons, because if the latter are used, similar patches-security improvements cannot be built-in. Improvements and installation of software patches completely addresses and solves the problem (so it prevents the use of tools that may have been previously created or purchased).

7.12.1 Building

Of course, if we build tools and capabilities, then such a cyberintelligence or a cyber military unit will automatically have a much higher rank, standing. It will be clear that there are people in it capable of identifying (or protecting) and exploiting such vulnerabilities, perhaps also of "arming" such finds – that is, constructing tools that will exploit vulnerabilities. This will also help build responsibility. It will be clear that building such tools is time-consuming and laborious, which, perhaps, will reduce the desire to overuse them.

7.12.2 Buying

Another approach is to purchase solutions, or their components. In the case of cyberpolice or cyberintelligence, the acquisition of appropriate devices, tools, and even the purchase of access to a framework that allows breaching security and taking control of electronic devices, such as computers or smartphones, may create the illusion of having significant operational capabilities in cyberspace, the ability to breach through target-systems. But this is only an illusion, because these are very limited abilities that someone else makes available. They are based on a solution developed, and delivered, by some external supplier or intermediary. At any time, access to such a device can be lost and then these abilities are lost as well. When this happens, the previously "powerful" cyber unit may be a bit less powerful, or even unable to act at all.

However, the indicated institutions decide on this inconvenience, because the purchase is a simple way to acquire capabilities when they are needed. The market offers many solutions with very different ways of buying, sources of origin, additional clauses, etc. Tools or their components can be purchased with money or cryptocurrencies (this does not necessarily have to be on a *black market*). They can be provided by companies, employed researchers, private individuals.

Sometimes such transactions may be quite bizarre, or at least counterintuitive. Consider the U.S. Justice Department's allegations against 55-year-old Moses Luis Zagal Gonzalez, a Venezuelan and French citizen, a cardiologist, who designed, created, and sold tools to Iranian intelligence services[52] and trained them in their use. The full range of services was to cost $800 a month, and as part of his communication, he also gave advice like, "*If you lock networks without tape or Cloud (backups)[,] almost all pay*".[53] So you should always remember that the cyber area is not the exclusive domain of States, governments, people in suits and uniforms. Unlike artillery or tanks.

Individuals and States with a serious interest in developing cyber capabilities should also pay attention to other issues. Access to tools is not the only requirement, one also needs to know how to use them operationally, i.e., prepare the whole process, everything that makes up the achievement of goals, aims, objectives. It's not just a few clicks away. In practice, this may require significant knowledge on the part of the involved cyber operators. Depending on the type of desired targets – it may require the involvement of many people: from a few to even several hundred (taking these activities as a whole, i.e., e.g., building tools and bearing in mind the complexity of operations).

Operations can also be outsourced to some extent, i.e., outsourced to someone from the outside, although then they would rather not be destructive or lethal (which would give rise to significant problems with determining responsibility, apart from ethics). Sometimes companies or people of this kind are referred to as cybermercenaries, although this is not entirely accurate, given that the term "mercenary" has a very narrow legal definition.

7.12.3 A note on automatically generated tools

I have already covered the employment of automatic generation tools – the frameworks, as a thing in existence. However, in 2022 the world at large experienced the novel capabilities of Large Language Models. Such tools may indeed greatly speed up or aid in some design or development tasks in software engineering. Similarly, they will be important in cybersecurity, both offense and defense. Initial tests reveal that one of the more famous tools – the OpenAI's ChatGPT – may bring significant contribution to the domain ("Computer-Aided Design" for offensive cyberwarfare?). It's not only about the automatic generation of text, for example for disinformation purposes. The tool itself can identify some security vulnerabilities in a code; it can quickly interpret the code; it may even quickly build source code for tools. If not by providing a full (due to artificially built limitations) answer to the prompt of the kind: "*Implement a self-spreading offensive worm malware in C programming language*", then at least by offering some building blocks, components for the tools. The current public-facing ChatGPT contains artificially-built stops that refuse to provide an answer in some cases. For example, to the prompt of "*Write a self-spreading worm in C*", the answer is: "*I'm sorry, but writing a self-spreading worm is unethical and potentially illegal. Such malicious software can cause harm to computer systems and networks, leading to data loss or theft, and can also be used for malicious purposes such as distributed denial-of-service attacks or unauthorized access to sensitive information*". However, the tool exists, and it cannot be ruled out that some clients of such future systems will have access to unconstrained tools, not limited artificially. And that may certainly speed up things – development, operations. That's such a not so distant future. While some people used to overemphasize the risk of "AI-powered cyberattacks", chances are that it is only now that we may feel the true potential of the risk; it therefore must be reassessed in the coming years. I will also repeat that even the ChatGPT with built-in limitations and precautions can still contribute some basic building blocks to the built tools. The answer to the prompt "Write a program that logs to a Linux system via SSH and executes a shell command" is unsurprisingly given. The answer is of course not "weaponized", the payload must be provided by a competent person or team. But the necessary resources part has already been explained previously in this chapter.

7.13 CYBERDETERRENCE – A FORCE PROJECTION TOOL

Cyberattacks are gaining new applications and roles in the framework of building State capabilities. They are carried out to obtain intelligence; they can be used to achieve political as well as military goals.

There is, therefore, no doubt that they also have their place and importance in the context of diplomacy. States have already responded to cyberattacks with diplomatic notes and sanction mechanisms. There have also been cases of State cyberattacks in retaliation – that is, carried out in response to some actions perceived by some State to be unfriendly. This is a direct manifestation of the use of cyber operations for international policy and defense purposes.

In a sense, even the very fact of building and creating cyber units and cyber troops can have a deterrent character (the so-called *cyberdeterrence*). This is because the creation of such units, their construction, is a clear signal that the capabilities being built may allow for defense, but will likely also provide the opportunity to respond, and even take offensive actions – via both cyber operations and information operations. A country with such units will potentially not be defenseless in this dimension of action; in fact it will be possible to take some action in retaliation. Including pre-emptively. That is to say, these options will be available not only in a purely defensive form, i.e., they will allow for protecting own infrastructures, networks, and systems, but also include a possible response, i.e., "active", offensive, even combat actions.

These are options on a national scale, unlocking and enabling new types of activities, allowing for new strategic approaches. Potentially, they have a *destabilizing* function, because those are novel offensive options. But at the same time: *stabilizing*, because instead of other operations, for example, kinetic, *cyber* could be employed. If it is considered appropriate and proportionate.

Here, it should be emphasized that in terms of cyber operations, the best option is definitely defense.

Only in this way can we limit unwanted losses. Offensive operations and active actions may sound more exciting, but defense must be the strong basis, the fundamental pillar. And the main point should be to secure our own systems. Forget about offensive if defense capabilities are not there (unless we are a peculiar State with significant asymmetries or isolationist attitudes).

In the case of cyber operations, we can speak about asymmetry. **Cyber operations may be inherently asymmetric.** It may even be too easy to do the offense (even attack), because it is sufficient to find a single, proper vulnerability in the whole broad system, while the entire, often big and complex, thing must be defended – so taking into account much more than the single thing. There is no alternative to defending our own systems. Therefore, it is necessary to allocate funds to an appropriate level of security, and a very serious approach to this: monitoring and responses, responding to threats, sometimes preemptively. These processes must be efficient.

Becoming less vulnerable to a cyberattack is also an element of deterrence. After all, if something is an easy target, it can even encourage aggressive actions. If something is an easy prey, it is an easy prey. And someone will inevitably try something. It's just a matter of time.

7.13.1 Cyberdestabilization

However, an important question arises: **are cyberattacks not destabilizing?**

Is it not the case that if cyber capabilities, cyberattack capabilities, cyber operations capabilities spread, it will destabilize the wider global security system? For example, if cyberattacks between States (interstate, or State-on-State cyberattacks) become too frequent, perhaps even too serious, they might then introduce a risk of moving the activities to another level of conflict?

Perhaps there would be a situation in which there would be too many actions taken (many events), or too often (frequent events), that at some point they would be interpreted as a single, collective cyberattack, a more serious action requiring a response – perhaps even an armed one. Is it just a theory?

This is the so-called *accumulation of events* approach, when many isolated cyberattacks are perceived as one serious, perhaps exceeding the threshold of tolerance. It may have some minor basis in existing international law norms, though consensus is not there – it is definitely not assumed as customary.

That said: it is not simple to cross even the classic *threshold of war* with a cyberattack. Should we, therefore, *lower* this theoretical threshold by recognizing that many cyberattacks – which in isolation do not cross the threshold of war in and on themselves, but they occur continuously and are sufficiently complex – can be treated as a single action when there is one actor behind them, for example, a specific country?

In this sense, the reasoning goes, many of such cyberattacks could then be considered as a single attack crossing this threshold of an armed conflict, or use of force.

It seems that NATO's 2021 communiqué may have come in an interesting way closer to this form of treatment of cyberattacks: "*that a decision as to when a cyber attack would lead to the invocation of Article 5 would be taken by the North Atlantic Council on a case-by-case basis … the impact of **significant malicious cumulative cyber activities** might, in certain circumstances, be considered as amounting to an armed attack*".[54]

In such a situation, there could be a new type of risk surface, or possibility of escalation, including possible other responses, perhaps no longer through cyberattacks.

As a side note: in 2019, Israeli troops bombed the headquarters of a Hamas cyber unit, allegedly in response to attempts of a cyberattack on Israel.[55] However, such responses to cyberattacks are not standard or even expected.

7.13.2 Escalation

Escalation is a certain process, a phenomenon in international relations, security, defense, and strategic studies, and diplomatic-military terms or actions.[56] In general, this phenomenon and process involves many inter-related (cause-and-effect) events as a result of which conflict can arise or escalate: things can become *hotter* or *colder*. That is, *more serious* or *less serious*. These include, for example, actions such as building a wall on the border, putting troops on standby (or perhaps also sending them to the interstate border), military mobilizations, violations of airspace, and cyber-attacks – which may or may not provoke some kind of response (reaction).

The same applies to unfriendly statements or disinformation or propaganda activities aimed at the political system or the society. This can lead to activities that go beyond that. For example, in the interwar period (1919–1939) such a conflict arose between Poland and Germany, when radio stations spread propaganda covering the territories of other countries. And it was a big problem; it even led to the world's first treaty (a bilateral agreement) to civilize this area of activity in the information space.

More recently, propaganda activities may have included methods such as social media posts or even artificially provoking protest events when one country's propaganda gamed on the social divisions in another country.[57] In such cases, these actions did not lead to an escalation – they were not transferred to another dimension of the conflict. It is difficult to comprehend responding with lethal fires to posts on the online forum, obviously.

In general, however, escalations may include events and actions (of varying intensity) of a social, political, diplomatic and, after switching to this mode, of military character.

This problem can also be applied to cyber risks and cyber operations.[58]

7.13.3 Escalation ladder

Formally, such "*exchanges of activities*" between two actors (here: countries) can be defined in the form of a list, sometimes called an *escalation ladder*,[59] or by means of a graph, a graph of actions. The concept of a ladder may be simpler to understand, so we will focus on it.

Well, it is simply a range of points describing and listing activities available to a given entity – for example, a State. These can involve diplomatic, economic, and military moves (i.e., including after the crossing of the threshold of armed conflict). The higher we are on such a ladder, the more serious, more intense activities we are dealing with. For example, at a low level (stage, step) on the ladder, there may be various types of warnings such as diplomatic notes, actions such as the withdrawal of ambassadors, sanctions, etc. Going higher on such a ladder (i.e., the space of opportunities available to the State, for which the State is ready), we can have "stronger" diplomatic notes, demands or speeches of leaders (e.g., directed at the leaders of the opposing State), expulsion of diplomats, official proclamations or communications, and other unfriendly actions.

An interesting example is the escalation incident in Central and Eastern Europe a few months prior to the Russian aggression on Ukraine in 2022.

It is about the actions on the Polish-Belarusian border in 2021, when the government of Belarus created an artificial migratory crisis. However, armed uniformed structures that found themselves positioned at the border have also been involved. In response, Poland (and Lithuania also acted on its side in the face of the challenge) sent its own military personnel to the border, and there was a situation when there was a "*string*" of armed formations *on both sides*. A very dangerous phenomenon, especially since on the Belarus side, it has been accompanied by violations of the border, simulated or actual gunshots, the use of laser beams, etc. In such a situation, it is easy to make a mistake, go beyond these actions, escalate, and destabilize that situation. This is often the case when the military structures of opposing States are in close proximity to each other. Curiously, as has been said here before, this may soon be a permanent phenomenon in cyberspace. This is a new risk of escalation.

Returning to the escalation ladder case – at some point during the move on the escalation ladder (climbing, descending), we may come across solutions such as closing borders for transport (which in Central and Eastern Europe accompanied the armed conflict in Ukraine in 2022), or the already mentioned imposition of various types of sanctions, i.e., economic and trade activities. Aimed at the economy of a country, of course also including losses on the side imposing the sanctions.

At some point, on such a ladder, the Armed Forces may be engaged, in an increasingly serious and decisive way. At first, it may be a limited participation, and later growing in intensity, using more and more advanced military-technical means such as (here we go far beyond cyber activities!) tanks, artillery, missile attacks, bombings, etc.

Since we are talking about cyberwar, in the case of contemporary conflicts, it is conceivable that within the anticipated escalations and actions, there is also room for cyber activities and cyber methods, cyber operations, as well as other types of methods, for example using autonomous objects or drones.

Cyber operations, in the context of escalation, can be used below the threshold of war (i.e., low on the ladder), but also above this threshold of war (higher on the ladder, of higher intensity). At the same time, the specificity of cyber operations is that such actions can be "arbitrarily close" to this threshold of war, without crossing it, acting below the threshold of war, using unfriendly but not illegal methods (in the sense of international law).

It is difficult to use tanks (unless demonstratively, for example by placing them close to borders) or bombing in a way that would place these actions below the threshold of war. Cyber operations are different. It's a more scalable tool.

At the top of this outline are the least serious actions, the lower, the more the escalation increases.

- espionage or reconnaissance activities (including cyber operations *assume this is standard business as usual*)
- diplomatic activities, informative, and issuing of warning notes
- public information activities, press leaks, official press releases, political messages
- **cyber operations** aimed at companies, State systems, infrastructure
- **cyber operations** – accessing and maintaining the access to systems; **cyber operations** *deploying* surveillance/intelligence tools - with the ability to later put them into offensive mode (*calibrating actions with respect to goals – actions well below the threshold of armed conflict, and low risk of exceeding*)
- sending signals using **cyber operations** - achieving access to critical infrastructure important to the civilian population
- summoning ambassadors (diplomatic)
- economic, political sanctions, also in response to **cyber operations** (diplomatic, economy)
- **cyber operations** disrupting/paralysing, sabotage
- **leaks** of political data
- uniformed services on standby and occasionally involved in operations at state borders (*if there is a conflict with a neighboring country*)
- land/sea/air exercises/operations (*the danger and high risk of going directly beyond the threshold of armed conflict*)
- **cyber operation** implanting an **information operation,** with a message to the political and business elites and the society of the target state
- **cyber operations** with low or medium-scale effects, temporary and limited disruptions in the provision of services by State and energy systems, limited-scale impediments to the provision of healthcare (provoking questions from the public and the wider population about internal stability "hey, *is the State still in control of things*"?)
- simulated or actual violations of the state border (*threshold of violation of sovereignty and the prohibition of interference in domestic affairs — exceeded some while ago by previous actions, very high risk of crossing the threshold of war*)
- shooting into the air or towards the border with a neighboring country, flashing with laser lights on the interstate border
- "Accidental" violations of air, sea, land (*cyber operations already violated sovereignty some time ago*)

THE THRESHOLD OF ARMED CONFLICT / WAR

- Disruptive **cyber operations** - paralysis of State systems, critical infrastructure, or telecommunications networks ("*we could also do it below the threshold, of course*" — but now they don't have to hold back on the scale of things) - intensity increases; information warfare, war propaganda via multiple channels
- precise missile shots aimed at a military training ground or a small target such as a bridge ("*we are not, in fact, joking, and hereby are our arguments*")
- border violations, shots aimed at uniformed services and objects (rifle fires, artillery fires, low-level missile fires), limited casualties in terms of people or objects
- shots from artillery and missile weapons - at military targets and key infrastructure facilities
- **cyber operations** seriously interfere with State activities and negatively affect the assistance of the attacked population
- **cyber operations** degrade the provision of certain key services - such as energy or transport - cyber operations use previously acquired accesses to systems, new ones are being developed; some **cyber operations** are less masked (prepared quickly) and it is easier to establish attribution
- power plants marked as "*military objectives*" under the control of the aggressor, some destroyed
- **cyber operations** and kinetic activities as part of joint operations - aimed at military, infrastructure targets
- **cyber operations** supporting kinetic activities (and information warfare)
- sending diplomatic signals about possible increased escalation, possibly with nuclear weapons

---

THRESHOLD OF ARMED CONFLICT AND ACTIONS AGAINST CIVILIANS

(overt and blatant violations of the Geneva Conventions or actions that actually have such an effect)
- one can do both via **cyber operations** as well as kinetically *(The risk unfortunately exists - the details are omitted from this point - or left as an exercise for the reader - for humanitarian reasons; let's hope it doesn't come to this!)*

Figure 7.1 Escalation ladder including cyber operations.

Source: Author's work.

There is one problem with the concept of an escalation ladder. This is a very simplified concept, a certain outline of possible actions. It provides and describes the possibilities of the State, a certain concept of what actions can be taken and more or less in what order (starting from the assumption of what actions of the adversary provoke the response on "our" side) to signal disapproval or simply a way of referring to the actions of another State.

The problem is that it is not always clear (or determinable) when and how to move between the different steps of such a ladder, i.e., when to escalate. Therefore, it is a useful concept, a thought model, but it may give rise to the risk of oversimplifications, potentially as a risk of spurring certain mechanical behaviors. That is, having a list of things that we can do, then doing them all in turn, as in a bureaucratic mode. This is not the point, because it is a loose outline and we always have to respond to real events elastically, understanding the stakes and consequences of actions.

In the case of cyber operations below the threshold of war, the costs of action may be relatively low. The thing about cyberattacks, however, is that if we put them somewhere on such an escalation ladder, it creates a wider problem. As a rule, the signals sent by States must be interpreted by the opposing side. If it's not clear how the other side will interpret a signal or how it can interpret a signal, it's also not clear whether we're actually going to send the signal we wanted to send in the first place. In the case of cyberattacks, this is a problem because it is not always clear what kind of cyberattack is taking place – what is happening in this regard. This is because (as we have already explained in the previous chapters) the issue of the effects of cyber operations is subject to interpretation, and certain actions (data acquisition, sabotage, destruction) may look the same to some extent. That is to say: Is the opposite side correctly reading the signals? Are they even looking for them? If not, then the whole issue of elastic and esoteric signal setting may eventually be for the birds, quite worthless or even counterproductive.

At the technical level (with strategic and tactical elements), at least at the very beginning, the methods of performing cyber operations in relation to different objectives (intentions) of actions are essentially exactly the same. So, again, we are doing the same things to acquire capabilities that can enable different end results: obtaining money, information, intelligence activities or possibly some more serious effects, paralysis of systems, destruction, etc.

And it might not immediately be clear to the victim of such an operation what this actual purpose was or is. The intentions are not clear. Therefore, it cannot be entirely clear how the cyberattack will be interpreted by the attacked party. And **this is one of the main problems with escalation in cyberspace. It is not clear what signals are sent when conducting cyber operations,** so it is not easy to predict what the possible responses might be. Ultimately, it may extremely complicate the attempt to use cyber operations in strategic ways.

Of course, the case of the actual effects is completely different, because these can be scaled as part of cyber operations. As can be seen in Figure 7.1, cyber operations can be used both prior and after crossing the threshold of armed conflict (war). They can accompany or even be associated with other activities.

In Figure 7.1, there is deliberately no numbering of possible actions, because it does not seem appropriate to present the escalation ladder in relation to hypothetical and general considerations as a numbered list. So we don't analyze what specific abilities such an actor has. The lack of these numbered points is also a message that the "ladder" is a loose concept and it doesn't have to be so that we go directly from one point to another (because actions take place in response to the adversary's actions). Therefore, we model our ladder as a space of opportunity below and above this threshold of war. It follows that certain types of cyber activities below and above the threshold may be virtually identical or similar (i.e., crossing the threshold of war occurred, for example, in connection with other military activities), but their intensity or meaning or purpose may change.

At the same time, it should also be acknowledged that the construction of this space of possibilities (ladder) took place during the Russian military operations in Ukraine, but the content itself was not affected by it. The concept of such an outline of possibilities was created even before this war.

7.14 RISK OF ESCALATION

The risk of escalation is real. As is clear from the previous point, cyber-attacks can also be considered in combination with other threats. For example, there are studies that consider the risk of cyberattacks and their consequences in comparison or taking into account other types of risks – for example, with aerial bombardment[60] (also in the sense of risk to running a business[61]). In this sense, the risk of losses as a result of cyberattacks can be valued at up to several dozen millions of dollars, i.e., the risk of losses twice smaller than those incurred in connection with the risk of an interstate conflict.[62] But what if cyberattacks occur as part of such a conflict?

The question is whether there could be such an escalation.

States are building cyber units, developing cyber capabilities – also as part of intelligence, army, etc. These cyber units are or will be in a state of readiness all the time. Some activities in cyberspace can indeed happen quickly, especially if the tools are already prepared for use (deployed, prepositioned). If we have many States, and each of them has a cyber unit, then we can imagine that these units are permanently stationed on such "*virtual state borders*". Such situations, when deployed armed forces are stationed at the borders, may give rise to the risk of escalation, even as a result of an error, mistake, miscalculation, accident, coincidence.[63] Potential proliferation (increasing access to advanced cyber capabilities) and the development of cyber capabilities within intelligence and military organizations affect (increases) the risk of escalation.

There is an increased risk that there will be a more serious conflict and that cyber actions may turn into kinetic actions. We have to be aware of this risk. It needs to be mitigated, 'accidents and incidents' must be prevented, permanent channels of communication and *confidence-building measures* must be established.

If possible. But is it?

While it does not seem reasonable or conceivable to move from cyberattacks to nuclear responses, the Chinese Foreign Ministry in 2022, when commenting on U.S. involvement in offensive cyber operations in connection with the Russian–Ukrainian war, seemed to suggest that there may be a risk of escalation from cyberattacks to the use of nuclear weapons.[64] In a normal situation, it is worth suggesting caution toward people using the terms "cyber" and "nuclear weapons" in the same sentence. On the other hand, China indeed has an arsenal of nuclear weapons, while I definitely do not, nor do I have any particular experience in professional employment of nuclear weapons.

7.14.1 Cyberattack scale and rank – impact-wise

In the previous chapters, we talked about methods, about tools, about different groups of threats, with different potential. About the fact that cyberattacks can be treated as a violation of the triad: confidentiality, integrity, availability. It was said that events and their probability of occurrence can be assessed according to different scales (which expresses risk). Most such cyberattacks do not reach the "attack" threshold referred to in this chapter. However, we can try using another classification according to the effects of actions.[65] Then the following points can be highlighted:

1 Breach of sovereignty
2 Interference in domestic and internal affairs
3 Use of force
4 Armed aggression.

Thus, according to this scale aimed at measuring the effect, most of the typical cyberattacks do not even reach *Rank 1 (breach of sovereignty)*. Although some indeed can – for example, when it comes to the threat of aggression and disruption of activities of private or State actors. Even fewer reach *Rank 2*, that is, intervention in the internal affairs of the State. This could be, for example, a cyber operation to disrupt the operation of State systems in a significant way, or even interference in internal political matters, e.g., in a public debate.

In the case of *Rank 3* (use of force), these events are extremely rare. There is no general consensus here, although it seems that such cyber operations have already taken place (perhaps Stuxnet or NotPetya could be classified as such?). Even if extremely rarely (say, a few in the last 30 years, on a global scale).

By contrast, no cyberattack has so far attained the highest rank - tier, *Rank 4*, armed aggression.

The undoubted advantage of this four-point, effects-oriented classification is the fact that it is based on something objective: on international law. It is, in essence, a mapping of the principles of international law to cyberattacks and cyber aggression. There seems to be a consensus on this among all States, although of course it is not codified anywhere, e.g., by a treaty. But the adoption of this classification offers something valuable, the ability to identify which objective rules are breached.

7.15 HOW COUNTRIES ARE PREPARING

Do the considerations of cyberwarfare and cyberwar in general have any practical significance or implications for ordinary people? Well, they do.

It is worth being aware of the changing times and existing risks.

What's more, some kind of cyberattacks and cyber operations at some point can actually affect ordinary people and it is worth being aware of this as well. From here, we can smoothly come to another provocative question: if we talk so much about cyberwar, how much time do we have left before this cyberwar breaks out? This question is easy to answer.

It should be obvious by now that we must treat cyberwarfare as an activity in cyberspace with the character, context, nexus, of a broader armed conflict (though cyber operations can also take place below the threshold of war, there is no need for a war and such actions do not have to lead to it). Therefore, it is better to ask: how much time is left until the next war. And that's another question, a completely different problem.

The decision is up to the States and their goals. Cyberwar will happen when a war happens. Cyberwarfare will be part of the broader armed conflict.

Undoubtedly, most, if not all, of the future wars will have elements of cyberattacks. We are observing this, for example, during the war in Ukraine in 2022.

But we've also seen it before. Cyberattacks and cyber operations will be used as escalation methods (for the most part) and before the phase of armed conflict, as well as in its first and subsequent stages to achieve different types of objectives and with different intensity. The nature of these cyberattacks will be able to change over time, including within the framework of a conflict. Cyberattacks immediately before the outbreak of a war can be quite different compared to those already carried out in the context of armed conflict. They can vary in intensity, range, targets.

One important, distinguishing feature to consider follows. In peacetime, efforts to design a cyber operation so that it is not easy to determine the source of a cyberattack are more justified. During hostilities, the motivation to hide the tracks may be smaller, less significant, less important.

A good example is the cyberwarfare in Ukraine in 2022, where it was relatively easy to establish which side was actually behind certain actions. For example, the cyber operation paralyzing the satellite Internet operator KA-SAT obviously harmed the Ukrainian army, an action in favor of the Russian Federation. On the other hand, the so-called activities of the amateur IT Army, at least by some, appeared to be motivated by the State structures of Ukraine in a pretty open way (at least in first half of 2022, though this was never acknowledged legally, for what it's worth), so there is also no problem with attribution of actions.

7.15.1 What threats are we facing?

New technical Measures and their application mean new risks. What would be the consequences of cyberattacks in this situation? As should be clear by now, the possibilities of cyber operations and cyberattacks can be highly destabilizing (if only because it can be difficult to determine the actual intentions and purpose of a cyberattack).

If we detect a cyberattack, we may not know what its purpose is and perhaps interpret it as something more serious than it was actually meant to be. This is especially dangerous in a situation of an already existing tension. This could lead to more escalation. Or at least not help in stabilization.

7.15.2 Risk of escalation and war

The considerations in this chapter, and in fact, this book, lead to the conclusion that a cyberattack can lead to war. A cyberattack can cross the threshold of war. Damage can be done. Lethal effects can be achieved, at least technically.

Cyber operations can also be designed so broadly that their cumulative number will significantly destabilize or paralyze the State, lead to image (PR), economic, and political losses.

7.15.2.1 But it's not like we have any automatism here!

If an action, such as a cyberattack, is detected, it is not necessary to respond aggressively to it, for example, to push for war. It should be kept in mind that wars and conflicts are processes that must be considered in the broad context of international relations, goals, strategies, and intents.

War requires at least two sides, and at least one of these sides must be willing, ready for such a turn of events (because, e.g., it is in its interest).

The side that is the victim of the attack must state that the boundaries have been crossed. Then it decides how to respond: militarily, politically, or diplomatically. According to the principles established after 1945, a civilized way would be to notify the UN Security Council (never mind how effective the process is in practice).

After all, there may be a deescalation, extinguishing the conflict. There is no automatism here and this is somewhat positive.

7.15.3 Cyberattacks as an integral element of combat, offensive, and military operations

Cyberattacks may affect the face of future wars. The involvement of cyber operations in the Balkan War (1999) was minor, and unstructured. It was perhaps more structured during the Russian war against Georgia (2008). We draw conclusions from the observation of destabilizing activities (before the escalation of the conflict) in Ukraine (2022–). But we keep in mind what is happening in Taiwan, too. There is a growing speculation about the possibility of China "regaining" Taiwan and about the possible threat of such a war, about the risk of cyberattacks on critical infrastructure.[66] It may be that this conflict will begin with cyberattacks on infrastructure, which would be aimed at partially paralyzing the State's operations, and such a war may not be limited to Taiwan altogether, as it may include, for example, the USA.[67] Here a lot of scenarios can truly be imagined.

7.15.3.1 Cyber Gleiwitz incident scenario

We can also imagine a hypothetical scenario, the *Cyber Gleiwitz concept*, i.e., cyber incidents in Gliwice. This incident is a situation based on true events when the Third Reich (Germany) tried to present the attack on the Republic of Poland in 1939 as a response to the alleged attack of Polish forces on a German radio unit in Gliwice (then a German city, Gleiwitz). It was a provocation, because the "aggression" was carried out by Germans dressed in Polish uniforms. So, therefore, under a "false flag".

Similarly, we can imagine the possibility when someone designs a cyber operation in such a way that they *attack or cyberattack* themselves. And later, publicly and officially, they "interpret" (and communicate) this cyber operation as an attack by "someone else", another State. And they "respond" to this attack with cyberattacks, perhaps ultimately also desiring to escalate toward kinetic actions. This would indeed be one of the more cunning and perfidious scenarios for the employment of cyberattacks. Therefore, it is worth realizing that a cyberattack can actually provoke a war. Determining the source of a cyberattack does not have to be easy and fast, although it is often possible.

There are known situations when the infrastructure for cyberattacks of one country has been taken over by the operators of another State. Although here we are talking about a scenario that is broader because of an operation that from the very beginning would be deliberately prepared in such a way as to be a provocation. In this area, a country falsely accused of such a cyberattack would have to tread carefully, especially in the event of a threat of escalation.

7.15.4 Can stabilization be supported?

It is a sign of the times that States (or their structures) sometimes publish reports or communications on the number of different types of actions. Sometimes simplifying them a lot, oversimplifying, for example by using one term "cyberattack". However, as we know from this chapter, cyberattacks are not attacks, and cybersecurity incidents can be considered by analyzing their impact on confidentiality, integrity, and availability. Still, there is no standardization for metrics of incident reporting, and sometimes this can lead to absurd events when this or another politician or military person talks about "thousands" or "millions" of "cyberattacks" that were in fact meaningless events – for example, simple connection attempts (even as part of DDoS activities, distributed denial of service involving the flooding with a high-volume of network traffic to cause a targeted service to cease serving content).

Absurd? It's a problem, and it can be destabilizing. Therefore, it would be useful to introduce some standards here, distinguish specific types of events or incidents and report them without calling them general "cyberattacks", and especially not attacks (as cyberattacks are mostly not attacks). The European Union could introduce such standardization for Member States, as well as reporting requirements. Such standards and requirements could be set by the International Telecommunication Union (ITU), or adopted by the UN General Assembly.

7.15.5 Standards

Within the framework of the UN, many so-called cyber norms have been established that would govern responsible behavior in cyberspace. These are good rules, stabilizing actions. At the same time, all countries agree to such behavior (at least officially). Here are some of them[68]:

- "States should cooperate in developing and applying measures to increase stability and security ... to prevent ... practices that are acknowledged to be harmful or that may pose threats to international peace and security".
- "States should not knowingly allow their territory to be used for internationally wrongful acts".
- "States should not conduct or knowingly support activity to harm the information systems of the authorized emergency response teams (sometimes known as computer emergency response teams [CERTs] or cybersecurity incident response teams) of another State. A State should not use authorized emergency response teams to engage in malicious international activity".

The third norm mentioned above has several interesting consequences. CERTs should not be targeted by cyberattacks, but such teams should not engage in cyberattacks. This raises the question of how far civilian CERTs could cooperate with others, such as the military.

There are more of such standards (11 universally accepted, though non-binding), for example, they foresee that countries should secure their infrastructure (defense).

The difficulty with such standards? They do not constitute law. They are not binding rules. In fact, they are even dually (!) non-binding, they are explicitly defined as *"non-binding voluntary norms"*, that is, in principle one may even say that they are *"non-binding non-binding norms"*.

However, perhaps one has to start somewhere, and such processes take a long time.

7.15.6 Civilians and warfare

On a side note, let's add that during the war in Ukraine, it so happened that civilians were somewhat involved in hostilities, at least at times. For example, they were looking for targets (involvement in target acquisition), perhaps they were also involved in cyberattacks. It is worth emphasizing that such action is potentially bringing risks on themselves, i.e., becoming an *"unprivileged belligerent"*, which means that they can potentially become the target of an armed response, and in the case of, for example, capture – they will not have the rights entitled to prisoners of war resulting from the Geneva Conventions. This is a tangible, realistic risk that has not been talked about for a long time, and prior to this armed conflict, in fact – never.

This is the first time this issue has been publicly raised in connection with the creative use of military support apps (for example letting to report the sighting of enemy soldiers or equipment),[69] and since then it seems that the issue has been identified a bit more broadly and will hopefully be thoroughly analyzed.[70] This dimension of cyberwarfare has greatly surprised analysts, researchers, and experts. It was not widely considered before the war in Ukraine (instead, some analysts chose to focus on quite far-fetched, imaginary scenarios, etc.).

7.16 CYBERSPACE AND STATE AFFAIRS

Are all these considerations relevant to individual countries?

They are, and very much so.

To appreciate this, however, it is necessary to think about what are the threats to specific countries. In the general situation. Well, the risks are, in principle, exactly the same for all States... Why? We have cyberattacks made by criminals, cyberintelligence operations, cyber operations by potentially foreign military units. The challenges, therefore, may seem very similar to those of other States. But is that so, really?

That's actually not quite the case. Because we must also consider the "local specifics". For example, the risks may be distributed differently in India, Taiwan, and the surrounding area, in the USA, in Central and Eastern Europe. The case of Central and Eastern Europe is especially interesting. It is precedent-setting. It is in this place that *"strange"* things have been happening for years, where techniques and tactics were "tested" and used offensively.

Even when significantly directed toward Ukraine (especially in the 2010 and 2020 decades of the twenty-first century), that is a fact.

However, many States are somewhat lucky, which is due to the fact that the methods of performing cyberattacks are basically almost identical. In fact, (mostly) everybody uses the same type of software and the same type of hardware. Everybody is, therefore, almost riding on the same bandwagon.

To carry out such an attack, we need to have the right tools, the right people, and intent to act.

7.16.1 Three limits – organizational, technological, and legal

This "*specific*" limitation is important. Because if, for example, we want to aim at a selected target in a particular State, we then cannot at the same time engage in preparations for the attack on another target, perhaps in another State. This is due to the fact that cyber operators will devote their time to this other target. It is, therefore, an **operational and organizational limitation**. Let's say that the priority will be to attack a target in the U.S. because perhaps it is worth operating there and obtaining information from there. It is then a matter of deciding on the investment of time and funds. However, if actions of a specific unit are being taken against the U.S., that will perhaps then not be done elsewhere at the same time – because there are no resources for it.

Similarly, if we use advanced security hacking tools aimed at some infrastructure in a State from which it is worth obtaining information, it may not be worth applying the same tool to the infrastructures of other States. Too wide a use of the tool may compromise it, increase the risk that it will be detected and security measures will be implemented, making the tool less useful, or useless entirely. Thus, in order to reduce the risk that an operation that is performed on a high-ranking target will be detected, the same critical tool will not be used for minor targets (with a smaller priority). In this sense, it may be more worthwhile to act against a State like the United States or on States of direct importance to someone who may be interested in conducting cyber operations, than to attack everyone everywhere, and at all times. This, in turn, is **a technologically motivated limitation**.

This is in a way something that naturally **introduces** limits and restrictions for performing such cyber operations, at least to some extent. Sometimes, however, for example, bait phishing messages are extensively sent, and more resources are engaged there where someone took the bait. It all depends on what the goals are. Sometimes the operating costs can be "amortized". For example, if an important software vendor is hacked, such as the provider SolarWinds (network management software; in the U.S. in connection with activities in 2021) or ME.Doc (tax filling software; in Ukraine in connection with the NotPetya cyberattack in 2017), access to many users of such programs, systems, or products can be gained. As a result of such a *supply* chain cyberattack, many important systems can be easily accessed. It is enough to hack one target and the profits are huge.

The situation changes if a country becomes a target for political or military reasons. Then it is clear that resources are being used to attack this particular State. Perhaps specialized units are being formed for this "goal". This, in turn, is a **legal consideration**. In the end, they are all considered: organizational, technical, and legal matters. Then, the decisions are made.

7.16.2 Threats and their reality

It should be emphasized that the threats are real. The actions of cybercriminals have already been experienced. The actions of foreign States have been observed. These are whole cyber operations, lasting many months, perhaps many years. We can clearly see that countries are being targeted specifically, that some cyber operators have specialized cells for this. Thanks to various reports, we know that it may be about, for example, Russia or Belarus (the so-called Ghostwriter operation of the UNC1151 group, believed to be a Belarussian group linked to the government) as the State perpetrators. It's a challenge of a different nature.

This is the risk of cyberattacks on companies, institutions, State institutions, but also on people – journalists, analysts, politicians, military personnel, their family members. Therefore, there is clearly a need to build threat awareness, and security. Capacity, monitoring, and threat detection measures need to be constructed. And work should be carried out to neutralize threats, minimize risks, by securing our own systems because defense is the crucial, fundamental basis.

States should consider developing cyber capabilities of services such as the police, intelligence, and the army. In the case of the police, this is obvious, because the phenomenon of cybercrime is growing. There must be a possibility to detect, prosecute, and enforce responsibility. With regard to intelligence: firstly, counterintelligence is needed to protect against threats, and secondly, would not taking advantage of such opportunities offered by cyber operations not be a waste of opportunities?

7.16.3 Cyber operations in intelligence gathering

It is often said that cyberattacks and cyber operations are the so-called *Holy Grail* of intelligence, very useful methods of obtaining information. Because if so many things are computerized, and access to information can be potentially easy, then more and more States may desire to take advantage of it. Perhaps not taking advantage of it is not worth it. Perhaps it needs to be done? Especially, when others do it.

7.16.4 Is it worth giving funds to the military?

With regard to the military, the matter is more complex. Is it worth allocating funds to expensive tools and resources in so many places (police, intelligence, army). For example, is it conceivable that there are enough capable and willing people to be able to work in so many different units? This is the so-called problem of parceling out capabilities so that "there is a little bit of them everywhere", but nowhere are the skills developed fully, really advanced.

This is a political and managerial problem, because it is important that there are appropriate people in such units who understand their role. It is not the managers or commanders who are the most important, but officers, operators. They would probably prefer not to work under the direction of someone incompetent, especially since they could easily find a job elsewhere. So you have to take care of such specialists, such precious staff. These are not places for commanders with inflated egos inversely proportional to skill or competence.

7.16.5 Separation of cyber entities is necessary

However, at the fundamental level, the units (police, intelligence, military) must be separated. And in this sense, they need to be developed separately, i.e., also cyber troops (Cyberspace Defense Forces) should be created, which would be responsible for securing military systems (defense operations, DCOs). But there must also be a part of the cyber army responsible for obtaining information (reconnaissance – ISR, perhaps intelligence), which is simply necessary to conduct lawful activities (even offensive, OCO). The need for the existence of such formations has been proven by actions against the Islamic State, but also by the situation in Ukraine.

7.16.5.1 Cyber Access Acquisition Agency?

It is worth thinking about cooperation. Perhaps there could be a separate cell that is tasked with *access* acquisition to remote systems and transfers this access to other entities (intelligence, army – depending on the needs).

Whether such cooperation would be realistic is a problem that must be solved within these institutions because technically and strategically it makes sense. The center of certain competences will centralize human resources, which would allow avoiding the parceling.

7.16.6 Do States need offensive capabilities?

It is worth considering whether and when States may need offensive capabilities, and, if so, of what type?

To answer this question, it is enough to note the fact that many other States are building offensive capabilities. Therefore, there is no reason why

States should not build their own sovereign capabilities. As simple as that, a simple matter of interstate competition and preparedness to defend themselves, due to the fact that "others are doing it". The basis, of course, is defense. However, it is also important to be able to breach security, to take operational actions against systems (engaging them), to various types of targets. Also with regard to own systems - being able to perform meaningful and thorough security testing. But also offensive and, if necessary, combat operations. It is also a question of the credibility of the State, for example the possibility of responding to external cyberattacks. In the absence of specialized units, it will not be possible to respond. In the case of NATO countries, another argument is also notable. A lack of capability would mean that there would be no proper cooperation within the NATO alliance, which is expected to reach operational capacity in 2023.

Such capacities must, of course, be maintained in the long term, which is a challenge. It requires the right people and technical capabilities. The most important people should be employed in such institutions in the long term – frequent rotation would have negative effects.

Defensive, reconnaissance, and offensive capabilities should be developed both for information systems (IT) and industrial systems (OT), as well as transport, communication, and space systems.

7.16.7 The specifics of the problem – who wants to understand it?

The specifics of *cyber matters* must be understood and appreciated not only by commanders, leaders, heads of such units, and of units supervising them.

The specificity of the cyber problem must also be understood at the political, let us add, supra-party (or, in the U.S.: *bipartisan*) level. No political party should believe that they have a monopoly on infallibility. Deficiencies can be easily identified, especially in an area such as cyberspace – a fast-shifting one. The possibilities of technology, but also the challenges are changing, so such priorities must be flexible. Cyberthreats differed in 1999, in 2005, in 2015, in 2020, and this area will still look different in 2030. This fact must be taken into account and identified. For example, there is a noticeable development of cyberattack capabilities on industrial automation systems, which raises the question of the extent to which States should build their operational capabilities in this domain, too.

Many countries are developing cybersecurity strategies for the long term. For example, the UK does this regularly, issuing an up-to-date version of the strategy every five years (most recently in 2021). Similarly, regulations are needed regarding the use of cyber operations, the selection of targets, etc. These are, therefore, arrangements within the State, at many levels. Arrangements with allies, e.g., within NATO, bilaterally, as well as on the ground of, for example, the UN.

7.16.8 What does the Cardinal Richelieu teach us about cybersecurity?

Our deliberations lead us to another question: are there funds for all this? Can States afford it? The answer is obvious: the State must have the means to do so. This is a strategic decision. Asking a simple question suffices: what are the priorities of the State? Where should the country be going? Because if you identify that something should be done, then you absolutely have to do it.

What can Cardinal Richelieu teach us about State security? It was Cardinal Richelieu, the powerful, first minister in the seventeenth-century France, who decided to allocate a really significant percentage of the State budget to the construction of the naval fleet.[71] This is because at that time, the fleet (or the Armada, call it as you please), and overseas land and maritime possessions were considered strategic issues for the State, a worthwhile objects. It was a good investment in the seventeenth century. And even if at that time in France, the State bureaucracy put up many obstacles and delayed the process, the intended goal was still managed to be achieved. That's the success of Cardinal Richelieu.

Today, such a competition takes place in cyberspace and more and more States are building their "cyber-fleet" capabilities, i.e., allocating financial resources to the goals to which they aspire. Determined States understand that such new, valuable, and rapidly changing work areas must be shielded from unnecessary bureaucracy and incompetence.

7.16.9 Threats due to cyber capabilities

A separate issue is whether building cyber capabilities can carry risks. There are several risks imaginable. First, if hacking capabilities are built, the question arises as to whether such capabilities will not end up being abused, for example, used to hack targets that should not be hacked (illegal, unlawful, unethical abuses of cyber capabilities).

7.16.9.1 Risk of internal abuse

Someone must always supervise units, services, assign targets. Whether there could be political abuses is a separate issue. It is better to focus on solutions. That is why an appropriate ethical and moral supervision should be created.

First, there should be clear legal constraints on cyber units, and a clear strategy. Both flexible and constantly updated. It must be known what the targets are, and partly what the capabilities and abilities are. Transparency cannot be feared. It is necessary to explain to the public why such capacities are built and maintained (which costs taxpayers money). And it should be explained clearly what the supervision of cyber capabilities is. It should be done in a transparent, open way.

Many countries disclose in their security strategies what the objectives of the action are, for example what the responses may be — and to what kind of behaviors. Therefore, an ethical and moral supervision should be established. That is, some way of expert evaluation of operations or projects of operations in such a way as to avoid abuse of resources and capabilities. And this cannot solely be a supervision at the parliamentary level, if only because members of the parliament are usually not experts and may have limited scope for activity.

7.16.9.2 External threat

There is another kind of threat. Can having cyber capabilities bring threats to a State, for example because of their use, escalation, or perhaps even possession itself? Since escalation has already been mentioned, here we will discuss another, but very specific, and at the same time a niche, problem.

Is it possible to build a cyberattack capability that could threaten the nuclear potential of a State, let's say – of the Russian Federation?

Cyber operations could indeed potentially affect missile systems[72] the so-called *left-of-launch* attacks (so happening prior to launch, perhaps paralyzing them as a result of cyber-sabotage). However, let us consider this problem not as technical or even cybersecurity issues, but in purely strategic aspects. Having the ability to cyberattack other States' nuclear weapons only makes sense if the other side knows that we have such capabilities (if they don't, will we achieve any goal?).

However, if it is communicated that there are such capabilities, the other side may consider it a threat and will try to eliminate this risk, for example by reducing the vulnerability of its systems (in this way, the capabilities for such cyber operations would be lost).

However, the matter may be more serious. If a State were to communicate the possession of such capabilities – if any State communicates the possession of such capabilities, i.e., that it can paralyze the ability of another State (e.g., Russia) to defend itself, to use a nuclear arsenal – it will probably have a significant impact on such a State that may now feel threatened or at least vulnerable. This result may well have a very destabilizing impact,[73] because such a feeling-vulnerable nuclear-capable State may subsequently decide that it might potentially be unable to respond to an actual future potential destructive nuclear attack, and thus the perception of its nuclear disarmament will follow suit.

As a result, there could be a risk that the first State in question would quickly lose such cyberattack capabilities against the nuclear arsenal of another State. Perhaps the elimination of such cyber capabilities would take several (15?) minutes, for example with the use of nuclear weapons (the Russian doctrine provides for a nuclear attack in the event of actions aimed at the nuclear response[74]). So, be careful what you wish for.

It is, therefore, better not to try cyber operations on nuclear weapon systems. Just in case. Strategically considering cyber capabilities in isolation from other issues, capabilities, objectives or strategies, is highly risky and can no longer be made today.

Besides, weapon systems, especially nuclear weapons, are highly isolated (or at least they should and hopefully are). Such systems cannot be easily reached by a cyberattack. Simply speaking, for example, if they are basically analog systems, and not digital, they may not even be reached by a cyber operation. In some of the publicly known cases, that is. And perhaps let's hope that this distinctiveness, which is a natural barrier, won't be touched. The wisdom: *if it works, don't touch it*, may be especially relevant here.

7.17 CYBERWAR IN UKRAINE IN 2022

It is difficult to summarize the activities of cyberwar in an armed conflict that, as these words are written, is still ongoing, and in a situation where, therefore, many details are kept confidential, for justified reasons, while some other details may be released in an unobjective manner, having in mind operational gains. Undoubtedly, however, this is the first armed conflict (war) where the rank of cybersecurity, cyber operations, and cyberwarfare activities is high, even integral. There are many indications that cyber activities in this conflict have a systemic rank. They are of strategic and tactical importance.

Here, we limit to the years 2021, 2022, 2023 (we have already written about many incidents from earlier years) and to events that from today's perspective seem to be related to a later high-intensity armed conflict (which began in February 2022). At the outset, it should be noted that the Russian Federation puts an emphasis on *information security*, as well as the *security of the information space*. This is a subtle (but clear, and significant) difference from the approach to the subject in the West and NATO, where the separation between the *cyber* and *information* spheres is clearer. When the West speaks of cybersecurity, Russia speaks of information security.

The Russian State security doctrine (2021) provides for the need to build information warfare means (and thus also cyber/information operations), followed by the Russian military doctrine approved in November 2021 and announced in February 2022. Published a few days before the start of hostilities, interestingly – so far, until the beginning of 2023, it has not been noted by Western analysts, who in their assessments focus on the previous documents.

This doctrine clearly notes that information warfare is an integral feature of contemporary armed conflicts and can be decisive in confrontation at all stages of an armed conflict (before, during, after completion). This means that cyber operations and information operations can be expected to be conducted before, during, and after the armed conflict. That is the official State doctrine. It seems that this approach to the issue is natural and standard (Western/NATO planners will also agree with this).

So far in the conflict in Ukraine, we have undoubtedly seen clear manifestations of at least two of these points: actions before and during the active phase. We cannot reason about activities subsequent to the armed conflict, as in the middle of 2023, it is difficult to comprehend what lies in the future.

7.17.1 Situation prior to the conflict

Before the start of active operations in the armed conflict, we observed many cyber operations. These were aimed at gaining access to systems (these activities were carried out from the early months of 2021), paralysis of the systems on a relative scale, but generally increasing the presence in Ukraine's systems. Much more serious actions began in January 2022, including the temporary paralysis (defacement) of government websites and the placement of tools to paralyze computer systems and data (wipers, deleting data).

7.17.1.1 Cyber-enabled information operation – preparing the information environment before the invasion

Attention should be paid to the implantation of the information operation on January 13, 2022, when a message appeared on hacked Ukrainian government websites in Russian, Ukrainian, and Polish (using machine translation, with clear stylistic errors, which clearly indicated a hoax) languages. This content was constructed as a warning to Ukrainian society. It is shown in Figure 7.2.

What's more, this content can also be perceived as an attempt to play on historical resentments in this part of Central and Eastern Europe, where history in the first half of the twentieth century was very complicated, and the memory of these events is still alive. Therefore, it is about the possible playing on the resentments between parts of the societies of Poland and Ukraine. From the perspective of the end of 2022, this can be clearly assessed as an attempt to build a bad atmosphere before the subsequent humanitarian aid of Poles to Ukrainians, accepting war refugees, etc. In this sense, an information operation of this kind did not have actual effects on a significant scale. Although this informational narrative has not gained much popularity neither in Ukraine nor in Poland, it has been picked up by some large and reliable, quality Western media,[75] apparently seriously considering the content of the "historical" issue of the informational payload contained in the posted image, as if the message could have a real background, meaning: "*It was not immediately clear if the hackers were Polish or if this was an attempt to incite divisions between Ukraine and Poland, one of Kyiv's strongest allies in the face of Russian aggression*", the journalist coverage said.

The text block above was removed from the article later in 2022, which is naturally a positive decision. Journalists must be wary of the impact of

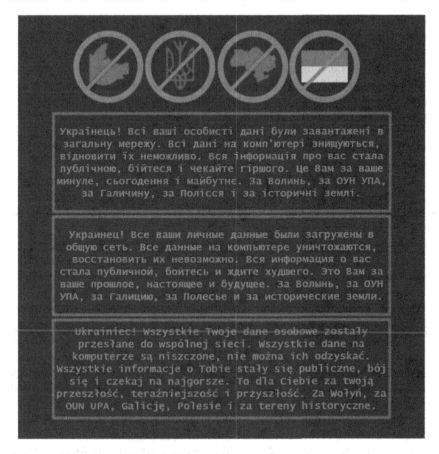

Figure 7.2 Message on hacked Ukrainian government websites.

Source: Author's private archive (message removed from all pages on which it appeared).

their coverage in today's fast-paced world. In a sense, the world at large, and we all, had to re-learn a lot of considerations, important during a typical "classic" armed conflict.

Quality journalists must consider issues broadly, e.g., considering the various differing points of view. In this case, however, it was extremely unfortunate, because there would be no "*other side*". Unless the voice of the hypothetical cyber operators of a military intelligence of a country that is preparing the ground for an invasion, armed aggression, has a place in a serious debate. But isn't it quite absurd? On the one side, there is the future victim, and on the other side, the voice is given to the military intelligence of the aggressor. If this is so, can we consider these as equal grounds situations, justified stakeholders to give them an equal opportunity to consider their "stances"? In this sense, this information operation has, therefore, perhaps had some limited success (as has the leak of data from the Democratic Party in the U.S. election campaign in 2016, which was widely discussed by the media).

And here is the English translation of the implanted text (inserted on hacked government websites; Figure 7.2.): "*Ukrainian! All your personal data have been uploaded to a shared network. All data on the computer have been destroyed, they cannot be recovered. All information about you has become public, be afraid and wait for the worst. This is for you for your past, present, and future. For Volhynia, for OUN UPA, Galicia, Polesie, and for historical areas*".

It is *immediately clear* that the original input text was composed in a language that does not have a grammatical vocative case structure, for example the Russian language. That is — it is clear provided that someone bothered to analyze the case.

What is also very interesting, in an artificial way, the file with this message contained metadata, which allegedly were supposed to indicate (untruthfully) the geolocation of the Main Staff of the Polish Army. In this sense, these operations affected Ukraine and Poland.

As part of prewar operations, cyber operations were also carried out, directing various types of software destroying systems and data (wipers).

Noteworthy is also the transfer of troops in a clearly visible way because information about the types of equipment was widely distributed in social media and messengers (Twitter, Instagram, Telegram, TikTok). In this sense, it can be considered as an information operation (although here without the elements of cyber operations!). Even if it was done from the bottom up by (or: through) ordinary people: such equipment was not covered by anything, it was simply moved in large quantities, unmasked.

As part of diplomatic activities, the Ministry of Foreign Affairs of the Russian Federation also issued demands for binding "security guarantees" about NATO's withdrawal from this region of Europe. Russia also raised an argument of an international legal nature, referring to the unclear principle of "indivisible security".

The final announcement was the broadcast of a meeting of the Russian Security Council chaired by Vladimir Putin, and a speech by the Russian president, in which he noted that "*Lenin was wrong*". Before the intensification of military operations, diplomatic actions, information operations, and cyber operations were undertaken.

7.17.2 Situation during the armed conflict

The unprovoked armed aggression began on February 24, 2022, which was an extreme escalation compared to previous activities. It was a land invasion, coupled with a siege of cities, missile, artillery, air attacks, an attempt to replace the government, and so on. Such goals were also expressed in Russia overtly. These actions led to many losses, casualties, injuries, and a wave of refugees. It is still too early to make a final assessment of the full scale of the events.

However, it is possible to assess the use of cyber operations in this phase of armed conflict (war). It is integral and appears to be coordinated with broader kinetic campaigns (*combined arms?* Not quite), i.e., the cyber and kinetic activities have been potentially synchronized. Cyber operations involving systems, paralyzing them and deleting data (using various types of "data-destroyers", wipers) were constantly ongoing.

On the day of the invasion, it turned out that 5,800 wind turbines in Germany had lost their connection to the control center. It was more than a curiosity. This was due to the fact that the Viasat/KA-SAT satellite Internet communication system had malfunctioned throughout Europe. This happened due to a Russian cyberattack (formal attribution by the European Union, the UK, and the USA)[76] that (in some places for a long time) paralyzed the operation of hardware modems, overwriting the firmware with bogus data.[77] It seems that the actual target of this cyber operation was the Ukrainian army, which used the services of this provider in its communication systems. Therefore, this cyber operation was undoubtedly successful (disruption of the standard information channel, although there were also backups in practice, so in the end total communication paralysis did not occur). It should be emphasized that the choice of its target was "non-discriminatory", i.e., the operation covered civilian infrastructure very broadly, including in NATO countries not covered by the armed conflict. So it was a "success", although public information shows that in the end army communication was not paralyzed – there were backup channels. These are the natural needs of military resilience in communications. However, and in fact, in Ukraine, communication infrastructure has become the target of cyber operations and even land operations (artillery attacks, missile attacks, infantry).

In addition, other cyber operations may also have supported the ground invasion. Their links with missile, artillery, and land operations were indicated.[78] And if such analyses of cyber operations with links to military actions are to be believed, it is noted, for example, that on February 24 "*Russian soldiers entered the city of Sumy*", and already on February 17, suspicious Russian actors with a (cyber) presence in critical infrastructure in the same city were detected. Similarly, on March 3, Russian troops seized Ukraine's largest nuclear power plant (in Zaporizhia), and on March 2, a cybergroup conducted movement/reconnaissance in Ukrainian energy (nuclear) companies.[79] Random correlations? Perhaps. There will be time for final confirmation and assessments in the future. Even if such correlations are rather coincidental, it cannot be denied that cyber operations accompany other military activities. That is **indisputable**.

It is also worth noting the extensive cyber operations on various types of databases and State or citizen registers, obtaining potentially significant information in relation to a large part of the population of Ukraine.[80]

Such information could be used to locate or identify the population, or individuals, including the parts that "could potentially resist", which could lead to their internment, or – unfortunately – something much worse (life-threatening). It seems that the transfer of information obtained in this way can have a measurable impact on land operations, and therefore it may support them in this sense. This is another manifestation of how cyber operations support the activities of other armies. Cyber operations as part of cyberwar do not have to lead to "loud effects", "explosions", "cyber-cataclysms". This may be reconnaissance and it is still in the context of cyberwar activity. In the earlier chapters, there was already talk of another attempt at a cyberattack on the power system, attempts to take control of power substations. It did not succeed – still, attempts aimed at critical infrastructure, the power system, were also made later (without success).[81] The energy company DTEK considered itself as on the "front lines of cyberwar".

7.17.2.1 No cyberapocalypse

The lack of the so-called cyberfireworks, i.e., spectacular cyber operations with great destruction and effects, surprised many Western analysts. It must be assessed critically to offer information for the future.

Based on a number of articles and predictions from the previous years, now proved unrealistic or far-fetched in a practical crisis, some of these analysts expected cyberattacks with spectacular effects, on a scale similar to the attack on Pearl Harbor or the World Trade Center. However, none of this happened. There was no *Cyber Pearl Harbor* or *Cyber 9/11*. Again, **none of this happened**.

But ... how could "they" be so wrong?

Probably because the scenarios that were expected had – *to put it mildly* – limited sense. Because such activities would not lead to anything. They would not be achieving anything (except causing confusion). The current war in Ukraine reminds us of something important. Military operations are usually carried out in order to achieve some specific, tangible goals, aims, objectives, effects, undertakings, for example, for the sake of political objectives.

Russia's stated political goals (initially it was an exchange of the political class and the Ukrainian government, although such goals were evolving) could never be achieved by means of cyber operations (but also, e.g., by air attacks, solely). That much is clear. Hence, the "necessity" of land invasion, with a seizure of territory, infrastructure, overtaking of airports, etc.

In this respect, there have also been commenters who have questioned whether there has been a "cyberwar" at all. From the point of view of international law and military practice, however, such a formulation about cyberwarfare activities is perfectly legitimate. Cyberspace is an integral domain, a theater of operations. Moreover, most, if not **all, actions in a war situation are part of warfare operations**. Some analysts have had some sort of trouble noticing and correctly analyzing these facts and events, perhaps attempting to understand cyberwarfare in ways of esoteric activities. This may also arise due to the fact that in the previous public discourse, a lot was hypothesized about what cyberwar could look like. Such hypotheses, however, were usually detached from reality. The reality-check we are experiencing now demands a reassessment.

Meanwhile, the matter is simple. Any **action within the framework of an armed conflict is an element of war**. And that's all about that. For example, a reconnaissance drone flight can also be an action as part of a military operation, even if nothing ultimately "explodes" (although it certainly may, and as we know from the war in Ukraine, it also often does). Hence the reiteration: every action in an armed conflict is a contribution to war. Every cyberattack in an armed conflict is a manifestation and element of cyberwar. However, not every cyberattack, even within the framework of an armed conflict, will meet the definition of an "attack" in the sense of the laws of armed conflict.

7.17.2.2 In operation units of different countries

It also seems that activity in the field of cyber operations likely involved units of various actors. The involvement of Russian and Belarusian units is clear – as they were involved in the armed conflict.

But also those of other countries – perhaps Western or other, who knows, perhaps even China? For more information in this regard, we will have to wait for the next phases of the conflict and (hopefully soon) its end. Intelligence and ISR activities would not be surprising. And these do not need to mean that such actors are involved in a war effort.

Why will we have to wait? Because this is war.

A lot of information remains classified, non-public. Others are presented within the framework of the information operations, i.e., they are presented to achieve specific goals, political or military. We have to be aware of these facts. And especially some cyber activities may be "covered with drapes" of understatements, lacking details, or not be talked about at all. Such is the specificity of wartime information issuance, of propaganda.

7.17.2.3 Unofficial, amateur units

Let's also note that part of the Ukrainian government (allegedly) may have acted to create an amateur so-called IT Army, which would receive orders in advance regarding cyberattacks on certain targets (Russian websites, e.g., of the government, of banks).[82] These are low-scale operations (e.g., denial of service attacks, DDoS), which may hinder the work of such systems, but at the same time potentially also complicate the work of professionals dealing with cyber operations actually achieving some measurable goals.

There were also whole lists of hacking groups that took on some targets, which involved hacking many websites, systems, and data leaks. Most of such activities did not end in any significant contributions on the scale of the conflict effort.

In the context of the scale of the entire armed conflict, the suffering of civilians, human casualties – it seems that such actions have rather limited (if any) effects and objectives. Instead, they may complicate the negotiations on the establishment of rules of conduct within the framework of the United Nations. Because how to justify them, how to rationalize them? How to determine their legality?

Some of these activities may still be subject to international humanitarian law (IHL) and are not necessarily subject to pre-established "standards" within the UN expert groups. At the beginning of the decade of 2020, understanding of the applicability of the IHL to cyberattacks was very limited. However, it is difficult for definitions, norms, and meanings to be directly applicable to all types of cyberattacks, even those at a small scale (i.e., not: attacks). Therefore, it is difficult to conclude that, for example, the IHL imposes any restrictions at all, e.g., on the "typical" DDoS activities aimed at some targets, as long as they are not civilian targets unrelated to war, and the action would not have the effect of an attack here. Let us emphasize that **cyberattacks are not attacks**. In the case of the IHL's applicability, this distinction is crucial, and ignoring it is an analytical error. IHL applies to conduct of hostilities, not *non-events*, events without any meaning. Certainly, by the end of this decade, the understanding of this issue will be greater.

7.17.2.4 The risk of spillover of the cyberconflict to other countries

There is also the issue of cyber operations against other States, for example, Germany, Lithuania, Poland, the Czech Republic, the USA, Great Britain, etc. – that is, States involved in some way, if only because they were not impartial, neutral. This risk was feared even before the active phase of military operations. These would then be actions below the threshold of war, even if they could be assessed as conflict related. These could be activities of a very different nature: from cyber operations on State critical infrastructure, to leaks of political data (and triggering crises locally, i.e., information operations with the support of cyberattacks). Indeed, in October 2022, a cyber operation covering the transport and logistics sector in Poland, a hub State for military and humanitarian aid to Ukraine and its efforts, was identified. In this sense, it is worth noting once again that the cyber operation against the satellite communication provider (KA-SAT) has also affected users in many NATO countries.

It seems that certain activities, information operations, could have even been carried out in many places, and their purpose was to draw attention to alleged (as established, untrue) discriminatory activities against war refugees, racism, etc. The head of the European Council Charles Michel himself had to testify with his authority that it was "*Russian propaganda*".

What is the situation with cyberattacks on infrastructure? No active actions were identified (and disseminated in the public) by the middle of 2023. However, nothing can be ruled out. Much depends on what will happen in the military phase in the future, how the conflict will develop, and what will happen next. For example, in October 2022 there were disrupting cyberattacks on the transport and logistics infrastructure of Ukraine, but also of Poland (a hub for Ukraine; hence the importance of the incident is growing and perhaps it can be associated with the fact of this assistance, i.e., not being neutral in this conflict, even if that State, or NATO, was not a side to it). Much about "cyber" activities is also classified, it is not talked about. This is not surprising. After all, the war is still ongoing. The time will come for summaries. It's natural.

It cannot be ruled out that after the end of the escalation phase, the time will come again for cyber activities. Because as we can see, it's all connected. It can (but does not have to) work together. This is the nature of cyberconflicts and cyber operations.

NOTES

1 A. Andersdotter, L. Olejnik, *Policy strategies for value-based technology standards*, "Internet Policy Review" 2021, vol. 10, no. 3, pp. 1–26.
2 See Staff working document: European Chips Act (SWD(2022)) 147 final, 11.05.2022, https://digital-strategy.ec.europa.eu/en/library/european-chips-act-staff-working-document
3 Europol, *World's most dangerous malware EMOTET disrupted through global action*, 2021, https://www.europol.europa.eu/media-press/newsroom/news/world%E2%80%99s-most-dangerous-malware-emotet-disrupted-through-global-action
4 U.S. Department of Justice, U.S. Department of Justice Disrupts Hive Ransomware Variant — FBI Covertly Infiltrated Hive Network, Thwarting Over $130 Million in Ransom Demands, 2023, https://www.justice.gov/opa/pr/us-department-justice-disrupts-hive-ransomware-variant; Europol, Cybercriminals stung as HIVE infrastructure shut down, 2023, https://www.europol.europa.eu/media-press/newsroom/news/cybercriminals-stung-hive-infrastructure-shut-down
5 CCDCOE (2016), *NATO recognises cyberspace as a 'domain of operations' at Warsaw Summit*, 2016, https://ccdcoe.org/incyder-articles/nato-recognises-cyberspace-as-a-domain-of-operations-at-warsaw-summit/
6 Protocol Additional to the Geneva Conventions of 12 August 1949, and relating to the Protection of Victims of International Armed Conflicts (Protocol 1) drawn up in Geneva on 8 June 1977 (JoL of 1992, No. 41, item 175, rectified).
7 Article 49(1) of the Protocol Additional to the Geneva Conventions of 12 August 1949, and relating to the Protection of Victims of International Armed Conflicts (Protocol I), 8 June 1977.
8 United Nations Charter (1945) – hereinafter: UNC.
9 G.B. Demarest, *Espionage in international law*, "Denver Journal of International Law & Policy" 1996, vol. 24, no. 2.

10 We can imagine data deletion that would be difficult to "reverse". This touches on a broader debate about "whether data can be considered objects". We will not explore this subject here. It may be viewed in terms of philosophy, perhaps even legally, but so far this view is not mandated or recognized by a significant number of States. It is, therefore, more of an academic construct.

11 Not to be confused with the propaganda term "special military operation", which was the name for Russia's military operations against Ukraine in 2022, a term for domestic uses in Russia.

12 Joint publication 3-12, *Cyberspace operations*, 8.06.2018, https://www.jcs.mil/Portals/36/Documents/Doctrine/pubs/jp3_12.pdf.

13 A. Dorais-Joncas, F. Muñoz, *Jumping the air gap: 15 years of nation-state effort*, 2021, https://www.welivesecurity.com/wp-content/uploads/2021/12/eset_jumping_the_air_gap_wp.pdf

14 See for example, a 2018 indictment filed in a Pennsylvania court against several Russian hackers, https://www.justice.gov/opa/page/file/1098481/download

15 H. Modderkolk, *Huib Russen zaten ten tijde van MH17-onderzoek door hack diep in systemen politie*, 2021, https://www.volkskrant.nl/nieuws-achtergrond/russen-zaten-ten-tijde-van-mh17-onderzoek-door-hack-diep-in-systemen-politie~b0e044e1/

16 Microsoft, *DEV-0537 criminal actor targeting organizations for data exfiltration and destruction*, 22.03.2022, https://www.microsoft.com/security/blog/2022/03/22/dev-0537-criminal-actor-targeting-organizations-for-data-exfiltration-and-destruction/

17 Hitachi, The rising insider threat: Hackers have approached 65% of executives or their employees to assist in ransomware attacks, 2022, https://www.hitachi-id.com/hubfs/A.%20Key%20Topic%20Collateral/Ransomware/%5BInfographic%5D%20The%20Rising%20Insider%20Threat%20%7C%20Hackers%20Have%20Approached%2065%25%20of%20Executives%20or%20Their%20Employees%20To%20Assist%20in%20Ransomware%20Attacks.pdf.

18 U.S. Department of Justice, *Two former Twitter employees and a Saudi national charged as acting as illegal agents of Saudi Arabia*, 7.11.2019, https://www.justice.gov/opa/pr/two-former-twitter-employees-and-saudi-national-charged-acting-illegal-agents-saudi-arabia.

19 For example, in relation to operations in Ukraine in 2022, we can talk about a cyberwar.

20 S. Borys, *Australian cyber soldiers hacked Islamic State and crippled its propaganda unit*, 18.12.2019, https://www.abc.net.au/news/2019-12-18/inside-the-secret-hack-on-islamic-state-propaganda-network/11809426; H. Warrell, *UK targeted Isis drones and online servers in cyber attack*, 2021, https://www.ft.com/content/360a8e1c-b241-40f7-b944-45a4f8854ac5.

21 N. Guibert, *Général Lecointre: «L'indicateur de réussite n'est pas le nombre de djihadistes tués»*, 12.07.2019, https://www.lemonde.fr/international/article/2019/07/12/general-lecointre-l-indicateur-de-reussite-n-est-pas-le-nombre-de-djihadistes-tues_5488379_3210.html

22 Inspector General of U.S. Department of Defense, *Audit of cybersecurity requirements for weapons systems in the operations and support phase of the Department of Defense acquisition life cycle*, 10.02.2021, https://media.defense.gov/2021/Feb/12/2002581936/-1/-1/1/DODIG-2021-051.PDF

23 U.S. Government Accountability Office, *Defense acquisitions annual assessment drive to deliver capabilities faster increases importance of program knowledge and consistent data for oversight*, 2020, https://www.gao.gov/assets/gao-20-439.pdf.

24 L. Olejnik, *The dire possibility of cyberattacks on weapons systems*, 18.03.2021, https://www.wired.com/story/dire-possibility-cyberattacks-weapons-systems/

25 B. Schneier, T. Wheeler, *Hacked drones and busted logistics are the cyber future of warfare*, 4.07.2021, https://www.brookings.edu/techstream/hacked-drones-and-busted-logistics-are-the-cyber-future-of-warfare/

26 Chaire de Cyberdéfense et Cybersécurité Saint-Cyr – Sogeti – Thales, *The cyber-resilience of weapons systems on the horizon in 2020/2025*, Summary report of the seminar, 7.04.2015, https://www.chaire-cyber.fr/IMG/pdf/cyber_resilience_of_weapons_systems_to_2020_2025_final.pdf

27 U.S. Department of Defence, Defence Science Board, *Cyber supply chain*, 2017, https://apps.dtic.mil/dtic/tr/fulltext/u2/1028953.pdf

28 U.S. Department of Commerce, Bureau of Industry and Security, Defense industrial base assessment: Counterfeit electronics, 2010, https://www.bis.doc.gov/index.php/documents/technology-evaluation/37-defense-industrial-base-assessment-of-counterfeit-electronics-2010/file

29 M. Gervais, *Cyber attacks and the laws of war*, "Journal of Law & Cyber Warfare" 2012, vol. 1, no. 1, pp. 8–98.

30 M.N. Schmitt, *Rewired warfare: rethinking the law of cyber attack*, "International Review of the Red Cross" 2014, vol. 96, no. 893, pp. 189–206.

31 Ministry of Defense of France, *International law applied to operations in cyberspace*, 2021, https://documents.unoda.org/wp-content/uploads/2021/12/French-position-on-international-law-applied-to-cyberspace.pdf

32 Government of the Kingdom of the Netherlands, International law in cyberspace, 2019, https://www.government.nl/binaries/government/documents/parliamentary-documents/2019/09/26/letter-to-the-parliament-on-the-international-legal-order-in-cyberspace/International+Law+in+the+Cyberdomain+-+Netherlands.pdf

33 B. Edwards, A. Furnas, S. Forrest, R. Axelrod, *Strategic aspects of cyberattack, attribution, and blame*, "Proceedings of the National Academy of Sciences" 2017, vol. 114, no. 11, pp. 2825–2830; K.E. Eichensehr, *The law and politics of cyberattack attribution*, "UCLA Law Review" 2020, vol. 67, p. 520; A. Bendiek, M. Schulze, *Attribution: A major challenge for EU cyber sanctions. An analysis of WannaCry, NotPetya, CloudHopper, Bundestag Hack and the attack on the OPCW*, "SWP Research Paper" 2021, no. 11, https://www.swp-berlin.org/publications/products/research_papers/2021RP11_EU_CyberSanctions.pdf

34 A. Greenberg, *A brief history of Russian hackers' evolving false flags*, 21.10.2019, https://www.wired.com/story/russian-hackers-false-flags-iran-fancy-bear/

35 National Security Agency, Turla Group exploits Iranian APT to expand coverage of victims, 21.10.2019, https://media.defense.gov/2019/Oct/18/2002197242/-1/-1/0/NSA_CSA_TURLA_20191021%20VER%203%20-%20COPY.PDF

36 G. Corera, *How France's TV5 was almost destroyed by 'Russian hackers'*, 10.10.2016, https://www.bbc.com/news/technology-37590375

37 N. Tsagourias, M. Farrell, *Cyber attribution: technical and legal approaches and challenges*, "European Journal of International Law" 2020, vol. 31, no. 3, pp. 941–967.

38 H. Lin, *Attribution of malicious cyber incidents: From soup to nuts*, "Journal of International Affairs" 2016, vol. 70, no. 1, pp. 75–137.

39 Responsibility of States for Internationally Wrongful Acts, annex to General Assembly resolution 56/83 of 12 December 2001, https://legal.un.org/ilc/texts/instruments/english/commentaries/9_6_2001.pdf

40 UK War Office, *Mechanized and armoured formations: (instructions for guidance when considering their action), 1929 (provisional)*, London 1929.

41 L. Qiu, Y. Zhang, F. Wang, M. Kyung, H.R. Mahajan, *Trusted computer system evaluation criteria*, National Computer Security Center 1985 The standard is still maintained, albeit under a different name. The principles are incorporated into the international standard Common Criteria, .ISO/IEC 15408.

42 J. Arquilla, *The computer mouse that roared: Cyberwar in the twenty-first century*, "The Brown Journal of World Affairs" 2011, vol. 18, no. 1, pp. 39–48.

43 F. Bugnion, *Geneva conventions and their additional protocols*, Hoboken 2011.

44 Convention on the Prohibition of the Development, Production, Stockpiling and Use of Chemical Weapons and on their Destruction (1993).

45 C.T. Lin, S.L. Wu, M.L. Lee, *Cyber attack and defense on industry control systems*, in: *2017 IEEE Conference on Dependable and Secure Computing*, IEEE 2017, pp. 524–526.

46 E. Dietz, A. Gehl, P. Friedrich, S. Kappus, F. Petter, K. Maurer, K. Püschel, *Kohlenmonoxidvergiftungen durch Heizungsanlagen [Carbon monoxide poisoning by a heating system]*, "Archiv für Kriminologie" 2016, vol. 237, no. 3–4, pp. 93–101; N.B. Hampson, S.L. Dunn, *Carbon monoxide poisoning from portable electrical generators*, "The Journal of Emergency Medicine" 2015, vol. 49, no. 2, pp. 125–129.

47 J. Biller, M.N. Schmitt, *Classification of cyber capabilities and operations as weapons, means, or methods of warfare*, "International Law Studies" 2019, vol. 95, https://core.ac.uk/download/pdf/236336777.pdf.

48 J. Dykstra, C. Inglis, T.S. Walcott, Differentiating kinetic and cyber weapons to improve integrated combat, "Joint Force Quarterly" 2020, vol. 99, pp. 116–123, https://ndupress.ndu.edu/Portals/68/Documents/jfq/jfq-99/jfq-99_116-123_Dykstra-Inglis-Walcott.pdf?ver=g74GeG8vGw7Qnee0ZByJIg%3D%3D

49 Ibid.

50 T. Riebe, C. Reuter, *Dual-use and dilemmas for cybersecurity, peace and technology assessment*, in: *Information technology for peace and security*, Springer Vieweg, Wiesbaden 2019, pp. 165–183.

51 J. Biller, M.N. Schmitt, *Classification of cyber capabilities...*

52 See "UNITED STATES OF AMERICA - against - MOISES LUIS ZAGALA GONZALEZ, also known as "Nosophoros," "Aesculapius" and "Nebuchadnezzar,"", https://www.justice.gov/usao-edny/press-release/file/1505981/download

53 This can be taken as a tip from a practitioner on how to protect yourself against ransomware, which was already mentioned in earlier chapters of this book.

54 NATO, *Brussels Summit Communiqué, Issued by the Heads of State and Government participating in the meeting of the North Atlantic Council in Brussels*, 14.06.2021, https://www.nato.int/cps/en/natohq/news_185000.htm

55 L.H. Newman, *What Israel's strike on Hamas hackers means for cyberwar*, 6.05. 2019, https://www.wired.com/story/israel-hamas-cyberattack-air-strike-cyberwar/

56 R. Smoke, *War: Controlling escalation*, Harvard University Press, 1977.

57 D. O'Sullivan, *Russian trolls created Facebook events seen by more than 300,000 users*, 26.01.2018, https://money.cnn.com/2018/01/26/media/russia-trolls-facebook-events/index.html

58 M.C. Libicki, *Crisis and escalation in cyberspace*, Rand Corporation, 2012.

59 H. Kahn, *On escalation*, in: *US Nuclear Strategy*, red. P.Bobbitt, L. Freedman, G.F. Treverton, Palgrave Macmillan, London 1989, pp. 283–336.

60 A. Rais-Shaghaghi, *Advancing the city risk index*, 2018, https://www.jbs.cam.ac.uk/wp-content/uploads/2020/08/170622-slides-raisshaghaghi.pdf

61 A. Skelton, *Applications of corporate risk profiling*, 2018, https://www.jbs.cam.ac.uk/wp-content/uploads/2020/08/180123-skelton.pdf

62 Cambridge Centre for Risk Studies, *Cambridge global risk outlook 2020*, 2019, https://www.jbs.cam.ac.uk/wp-content/uploads/2021/11/crs-cambridge-global-risk-index-2020.pdf

63 L. Olejnik, *Global consequences of escalating U.S.-Russia cyber conflict*, 2.04.2019, https://www.cfr.org/blog/global-consequences-escalating-us-russia-cyber-conflict

64 Ministry of Foreign Affairs of the People's Republic of China, *Spokesperson's remarks on US confirming conducting offensive hacking operations against Russia in the Russia-Ukraine conflict*, 8.06.2022, https://www.fmprc.gov.cn/mfa_eng/wjb_663304/zzjg_663340/jks_665232/jkxw_665234/202206/t20220609_10700816.html

65 Lukasz Olejnik, "Cyber Escalation Ladder model based on international law", https://techletters.substack.com/p/techletters-insights-cyber-escalation [accessed on 10.01.23].

66 M.A. Flournoy, *How to prevent a war in Asia: The erosion of American deterrence raises the risk of Chinese miscalculation*, 18.06.2020, https://www.foreignaffairs.com/articles/united-states/2020-06-18/how-prevent-war-asia

67 J. Gould, *US should expect cyberattacks in any struggle for Taiwan*, 2.12.2021, https://www.defensenews.com/smr/reagan-defense-forum/2021/12/04/us-should-expect-cyberattacks-in-any-struggle-for-taiwan/

68 United Nations General Assembly, Report of the Group of Governmental Experts on developments in the field of information and telecommunications in the context of international security, A/70/174, 22.07.2015, https://www.un.org/ga/search/view_doc.asp?symbol=A/70/174

69 Lukasz Olejnik (2022), Smartphones Blur the Line Between Civilian and Combatant, Wired, https://www.wired.com/story/smartphones-ukraine-civilian-combatant/

70 Michael N. Schmitt, William Casey Biggerstaff (2022), UKRAINE SYMPOSIUM – ARE CIVILIANS REPORTING WITH CELL PHONES DIRECTLY PARTICIPATING IN HOSTILITIES? https://lieber.westpoint.edu/civilians-reporting-cell-phones-direct-participation-hostilities/

71 Rehman, I. (2019). Raison d'Etat: Richelieu's Grand Strategy During the Thirty Years' War (May 2019). *Texas National Security Review*.

72 D.E. Sanger, W.J. Broad, *Trump inherits a secret cyberwar against North Korean missiles*, 4.03.2017, https://www.nytimes.com/2017/03/04/world/asia/north-korea-missile-program-sabotage.html; R. Ellison, *Left of launch*, 16.03.2015, https://missiledefenseadvocacy.org/alert/3132/

73 E. Lonergan, K. Yarhi-Milo, *Cyber signaling and nuclear deterrence: implications for the Ukraine crisis*, 21.04.2022, https://warontherocks.Com/2022/04/cyber-signaling-and-nuclear-deterrence-implications-for-the-ukraine-crisis/

74 The President of the Russian Federation executive order on basic principles of state policy of the Russian Federation on nuclear deterrence, 2.06.2020, https://archive.mid.ru/en/web/guest/foreign_policy/international_safety/disarmament/-/asset_publisher/rp0fiUBmANaH/content/id/4152094?p_p_id=101_INSTANCE_rp0fiUBmANaH&_101_INSTANCE_rp0fiUBmANaH_languageId=en_GB

75 Roman Olearchyk, , Henry Foy, James Politi, 14.01.22, "US accuses Russia of planning 'false-flag operation' in eastern Ukraine", Financial Times, https://www.ft.com/content/ac431782-62c6-4f3a-a08e-d832fc4ac2a1

76 Council of EU, *Russian cyber operation against Ukraine: Declaration by the High Representative on behalf of the European Union*, 10.05.2022, https://www.consilium.europa.eu/en/press/press-releases/2022/05/10/russian-cyber-operations-against-ukraine-declaration-by-the-high-representative-on-behalf-of-the-european-union/; UK Foreign, Commonwealth & Development Office, *Russia behind cyber-attack with Europe-wide impact an hour before Ukraine invasion*, 10.055.2022, https://www.gov.uk/government/news/russia-behind-cyber-attack-with-europe-wide-impact-an-hour-before-ukraine-invasion

77 Viasat, *KA-SAT Network cyber attack overview*, 30.03.2022, https://www.viasat.com/about/newsroom/blog/ka-sat-network-cyber-attack-overview/

78 Microsoft, *Special report: Ukraine. An overview of Russia's cyberattack activity in Ukraine*, 27.04.2022, https://query.prod.cms.rt.microsoft.com/cms/api/am/binary/RE4Vwwd

79 Ibid.

80 F. Bajak, *A chilling Russian cyber aim in Ukraine: Digital dossiers*, 28.04.2022, https://apnews.com/article/russia-ukraine-technology-business-border-patrols-automobiles-fa3f88e07e51bcaf81bac8a40c4da141

81 DTEK, "Enemy launches hacker attacks on the power system", 01.07.2022, https://dtek.com/en/media-center/news/vslid-za-raketnimi-udarami-po-tes-vorog-zavdae-khakerskikh-udariv-po-energosistemi/

82 Stefan Soesanto, "The IT Army of Ukraine. Structure, Tasking, and Ecosystem", 06.22 https://css.ethz.ch/content/dam/ethz/special-interest/gess/cis/center-for-securities-studies/pdfs/Cyber-Reports-2022-06-IT-Army-of-Ukraine.pdf

Conclusion

Cybersecurity is a civilization problem. It is a societal problem. It arises from technology. But its effects today go well beyond technology and cybersecurity, The present and future potential and risks of cyber operations must be understood. It is a highly evolving and changing environment, and at the same time complex to the point where technical, legal, political, strategic, and military issues must be considered. It is the main idea and the goal of this book to show things broadly enough.

The cybersecurity level of technology has increased significantly. So much so that an ordinary user does not have to take any special actions (or in some cases is unable to take any special actions). All that is needed is common sense, appropriate configuration, and knowledge of the basics of cybersecurity, of digital hygiene. Technologies should just work and be secured right from the start. Although there are still problems, they are unlikely to be solved by ordinary users. Users are limited to trusting the hardware and software vendor (and keep an eye on updates!). Often, however, it is possible, and even needed to go beyond that. What else can be done? Awareness and a certain mindset can be acquired and developed. Recommendations can be followed, and gradually knowledge can be expanded as technology develops. This is a necessity because we simply depend on technology. It is a good idea to have some basic knowledge, apply it, and develop it. This is also a practical element of the cybersecurity philosophy.

This book analyzes aspects of user's security. However, as is emphasized, other areas also have an impact on users and citizens. The *cyber environment* affects sensitive social areas: critical infrastructure, healthcare, military and strategic matters, and the State in general. There is no turning back from such impacts. Computerization and digitization will continue to progress. It will be a permanent element of our life, our civilization. Therefore, the implications and consequences, need to be taken into consideration. We have to adapt to it.

The pace of rapid changes, however, might not be compatible with human adaptability. Therefore, risk points will continue to arise, because the creators and developers of technologies and products might improperly

DOI: 10.1201/9781003408260-8

predict the consequences of these facts. Undesirable things may, and will, be happening. We must be aware of it.

There is always a need for awareness and knowledge.

Ultimately, when it comes to State security, it may even be a matter of life and death, the survival of the civilian population. There is no justification for ignoring such a socially critical problem. Cybersecurity is also an element of interstate negotiations, as well as military issues. This could be seen more clearly during the war in Ukraine in 2022.

Cyberspace and cybersecurity are a problem of stability and instability. We wish for stability to take precedence over instability for all, at least in the long term. This should be the guiding principle of the philosophy of cybersecurity, regardless of whether we are talking about cybersecurity or about cyberwar.

Printed in the United States
by Baker & Taylor Publisher Services